MYSTICISM IN RELIGION

MYSTICISM IN RELIGION

By

THE VERY REV. W. R. INGE

K.C.V.O., F.B.A., D.D.

Formerly Dean of St. Paul's

STX

ST. JOSEPH'S UNIVERSITY

BL625.I5 1976 Mysticism in religion /

3 9353 00019 6152

BL
625
.I5
1976

181266

GREENWOOD PRESS, PUBLISHERS
WESTPORT, CONNECTICUT

Library of Congress Cataloging in Publication Data

Inge, William Ralph, 1860-1954.
   Mysticism in religion.

   Reprint of the ed. published by University of Chicago
Press, Chicago.
   Bibliography: p.
   Includes index.
   1. Mysticism.   I.   Title.
BL625.I5   1976   248'.22   76-15407
ISBN 0-8371-8953-5

Copyright 1948 by The University of Chicago
All rights reserved.

Originally published in 1948 by the University of Chicago
Press, Chicago, Ill.

Reprinted with the permission of Hutchinson Publishing
Group.

Reprinted in 1976 by Greenwood Press,
a division of Congressional Information Service, Inc.
51 Riverside Avenue, Westport, Connecticut 06880

Library of Congress catalog card number 76-15407
ISBN 0-8371-8953-5

Printed in the United States of America

10 9 8 7 6 5 4 3 2

CONTENTS

PREFACE

IT may be doubted whether a very old man ought to write a book, even if he is asked to do so. I cannot expect that the critics will be very kind to this my latest piece of authorship. "He has said all this before, and said it better. He has no sympathy with the hopes and aspirations of the young. When he looks towards the future he sees only the approach of another Dark Age."

Well, it is true that in my last chapter I have predicted a change in what is called the climate of opinion in this country. A man need not be senile to see that our period of expansion is over, and that we must adjust ourselves to new conditions, which, he hopes, may not be unfavourable to a revival of personal religion in our people. I have never thought that the Britannia who in George Meredith's words 'thumps her distended middle as Mammon's wife' is a type of the real England. Nor do I think that the town labourer, blackmailing the community with continual strikes, represents our national character at its best. The quintessential Englishman used to be John Bull, a farmer, and the squire, now extinct, was not a courtier like the French aristocrats of the old regime, but a glorified yeoman. I do not think it is pessimistic to hope that we may some day return to the pre-industrial England, with simpler and healthier habits.

For the rest, I have not said it quite all before. I have been studying Russian theology and philosophy, now available in English. These writers, exiled from their country, have been brought into contact with Western thought. The two branches of Catholic or Orthodox Christianity have hitherto been almost strangers to each other. In comparing Eastern and Western modes of Christian thought, the Russians find that the West has not given enough weight to the office and work of the Holy Spirit, in other words to the presence of the Spirit of the glorified Christ in the hearts of men. I am inclined to think that this is true of the official Western Churches, though not of some of the sects, nor of course of the mystics. Perhaps one cause is the jealous suppression of independent thinking in the Roman Church, and the undue emphasis on the juridical Atonement and bibliolatry among Protestants. Spiritual religion must never be petrified. 'Where the Spirit of the Lord is, there is liberty.'

Further, following many of the leaders of thought in our day, I have been deeply interested in the 'wisdom of the East.' I have quoted a saying of Whitehead, that if Christianity and the Asiatic religions both

7

show signs of weakness, one reason may be that they have remained too much aloof from each other. It is a reproach to us that with our unique opportunities of entering into sympathetic relations with Indian thought, we have made very few attempts to do so. The Germans have done more work upon Indian philosophy than we have. I am not suggesting that we should become Buddhists or Hindus, but I believe that we have almost as much to learn from them as they from us.

My treatment of my subject will disappoint some of my readers, but here I can make no apology. My subject is Mysticism in Religion, not the psychology or pathology of the mystics. Mysticism means communion with God, that is to say with a Being conceived as the supreme and ultimate reality. If what the mystics say of their experience is true, if they have really been in communion with the Holy Spirit of God, that is a fact of overwhelming importance, which must be taken into account when we attempt to understand God, the world, and ourselves. It is quite inadequate to treat mysticism as a branch of psychology, which is really a natural science not concerned with ultimate truth. The psychological approach is now the most popular; it is part of the disintegrating relativism of modern thought, which, by ignoring, really denies the faith which for all mystics is the sole justification for the choice which they have made. Our opponents accuse us of 'erecting into postulates our moral prejudices.' Prejudices is an ugly word. They are not prejudices; they are the necessary presuppositions of any religious philosophy. Accordingly, most books on mysticism consist of testimonies collected from visionaries in various degrees of *schwärmerei*. We are invited to decide how far these states are purely pathological, and how far they are practically useful in deepening personal conviction and influencing moral conduct. Those who treat mysticism in this way must remain in what the mystics call the psychical as opposed to the spiritual level of consciousness.

It is almost equally unsatisfactory to treat mysticism as emotional religion at its highest pitch. Mrs. Herman says, severely, but not without justification, 'Many of our most popular mystical volumes present the distressing appearance of entirely sophisticated and reflective persons cudgelling themselves into an attitude of lisping childishness.' The love of God, which is one legitimate definition of mysticism, is certainly an emotion, and in some of the mystics it is almost entirely emotional; but we might claim that the basis of mysticism is reason above rationalism, reason (*nous* or *intellectus*) being used for the affirmations of the whole personality acting under the guidance of its highest faculty. The seven gifts of the Holy Spirit, we may remember, are primarily intellectual—wisdom, understanding, and the rest. 'I will sing and give praise with the best member that I have,' and our best member is reverent thought, not unrestrained feeling.

McTaggart says truly, 'A mysticism which ignored the claims of the understanding would be doomed. None ever went about to break logic, but in the end logic broke him.'

I will quote some wise words from the Oxford philosopher, Professor William Wallace. 'In the Kingdom of God are many mansions; and while some are content to live on tradition and authority, to believe on trust, to repose on the common strength, it is necessary that there should be a few, a select number, who resolve, or rather are compelled by a necessity laid upon them, to see for themselves. Theirs also is faith; but it is the faith of insight and of knowledge, the faith which is gnosis. Hard things have been said of gnosis, and harder things of gnosticism; but it cannot be too clearly seen that gnosis is the very life of the Church, the blood of religion. It is the faith which is not merely hearsay and dependence but which really envisages the unseen for itself. It does not believe *on* a Person; it believes in and into him: it becomes, by an act at once voluntary and impelled from without (as all human action that is really entitled to that name) participant with him and through him of a force of life and conduct.'

Mysticism is bound to distrust and repudiate the current anti-intellectualism which rests on despair of reaching ultimate truth. Ultimate truth, we believe with Plato, is fully knowable though not fully known, and the mystical quest leads to what St. Paul calls an earnest of the vision of God which may be ours when we see Him face to face and know even as we are known. My studies have led me to agree with Troeltsch, that 'the sharper stress of the scientific and philosophical spirit in modern times has made the blend of Neoplatonism and New Testament Christianity the only possible solution of the problem of the present day, and I do not doubt that this synthesis will once more be dominant in modern thought.'

But belief in an absolute reality obliges us to consider the relation to ultimate truth of our 'amphibious' human personality, to form some idea of the relation of time to eternity, and to examine the various symbols in which the invisible things of God are imperfectly represented under the forms of space and time. These philosophical problems cannot be avoided if we take mysticism seriously, for it is not merely a way of escape from the worries of this unintelligible world. I have tried to be as untechnical as possible.

There are, I think, four questions which we must ask if we believe that the inspiration of the individual is real. The first is how far the inner light can supplement or even supersede those external authorities which have so long buttressed religious belief—an infallible Church, an infallible book, and human reasoning, whether this is based on scholastic logic or on natural science.

Secondly, since mysticism rests on belief in what St. Paul calls the putting off of the old man and the putting on of the new, we must ask, What is the real self? 'Be not conformed to this world, but be ye transformed by the renewing of your mind.' To this question mysticism has an answer, and I have said that the answer may be found in the Epistles of St. Paul, the real founder of Christian mysticism.

Thirdly, since mysticism bids us to look not at the things that are seen, which are temporal, but on the things that are not seen, which are eternal, we must try to form some idea of the meaning and the status in reality of the world that we know, the world of space and time. It is a problem which has baffled the acutest thinkers, and I cannot hope to have written anything to solve it; but we cannot simply put it on one side, for it deeply concerns us during our earthly pilgrimage.

Fourthly, we must consider the meaning and value of symbols, another vast and difficult problem. Here we come to a divergence among the mystics, who for the most part agree so well together. There are mystics who bid us to discard all images as unworthy of our spiritual quest. This is the famous negative way, which is often severely judged. Others, like the mystical poets, would have us rise through and by means of the visible to the invisible. The Platonists are, on the whole, on this side; the Indian mystics and some of the contemplatives of the cloister on the other.

I cannot see how these difficult problems can be dispensed with, if, as I say, we take the mystical experience quite seriously as a revelation of ultimate truth. Those who prefer another way of approach will understand why I cannot follow them.

My chapters on Greek mysticism, and on Plotinus—the latter a reprint of a 'Master Mind' lecture to the British Academy—are, I think, a necessary part of the book, for there is happily no break between the spiritual religion of classical antiquity and Christianity as understood by the European nations. The primacy of love is Christian; there is not much else that is not at least adumbrated in Plato and Plotinus.

The chapter on English mystics is intended to direct my readers to some of the most attractive and beautiful mystical books in our language. We lose a great deal by not reading old books. The French, I believe, make much more use of their noble literature. I have chosen in particular two whom I have not dealt with in my other books, namely the unknown author of *The Cloud of Unknowing,* and Thomas Traherne, the recent discovery of whose works by Mr. Bertram Dobell is one of the most extraordinary literary finds of our time. I have not troubled my readers with Margery Kempe, unearthed in 1934, though Rufus Jones considers the discovery of her manuscript as 'an event of first importance for the history of English literature.' This hysterical young woman calls herself a poor creature, and a poor creature I am afraid she was. She is obviously proud of the 'boisterous' roarings and sobbings which made her a nuisance to her neighbours. She never quite rings true. I have also given several pages to the Society of Friends, for whom, as I have shown, I have a very great respect. Their rejection of symbolic usages is, I suppose, one variety of the negative road; it will prevent them from ever becoming popular. But they have the root of the matter in them.

The book is complete without the last chapter, which is also rather controversial. But we are not in a mood to live in a timeless world. We are all asking anxiously whether Christianity can help us to live through the hard times which are coming. I am quite sure that Christianity is indestructible, and I do not think that our country is sick unto death, but I have no great confidence in the Churches. We must go back to the 'light which lighteth every man that cometh into the world,' which for Christians is the presence of the Spirit of Jesus Christ, 'the same yesterday, to-day and for ever.' We are to 'grow up into him in all things,' not to grow out of Him into something which we may think more up-to-date. Christian mysticism is communion with the glorified and indwelling Christ.

The lecture on the Philosophy of Mysticism is of the nature of a supplement. It covers much of the same ground as parts of the book itself, but it may perhaps help to make my position clearer.

He that believeth in the Son of God hath the witness in himself.

1 JOHN V, 10.

Thoas. Es spricht kein Gott; es spricht dein eignes Herz.
Iphigénie. Sie reden nur durch unser Herz zu uns.—GOETHE.

Wird Christus tausendmal zu Bethlehem geboren
Und nicht in dir, du bleibst noch ewiglich verloren.

ANGELUS SILESIUS.

I will not make a religion for God, nor suffer any to make a religion for me.—WHICHCOTE.

The longest sword, the strongest lungs, the most voices, are false measures of truth.—WHICHCOTE.

One thing I know, that whereas I was blind now I see.—JOHN IX, 25.

Now it may be asked, what is the state of a man who followeth the true light to the utmost of his power? I answer truly, it will never be declared aright, for he who is not such a man can neither understand it nor know it, and he who is knoweth it indeed, but he cannot utter it, for it is unspeakable. Therefore let him who would know it give his whole diligence that he may enter therein; then will he see and find what hath never been uttered by man's lips.—THEOLOGIA GERMANICA.

Whoso hath felt the Spirit of the Highest
Cannot confound nor doubt Him nor deny:
Yea, with one voice, O world, though thou deniest,
Stand thou on that side, for on this am I.

F. W. H. MYERS.

CHAPTER I

AUTHORITY AND THE INNER LIGHT

W H A T is the province of authority in religion, and what, for a Christian, is the seat of authority? These are the first questions which anyone who discusses the place of mysticism in religion must try to answer. For this kind of religion stands or falls by what we believe about the trustworthiness of what is called the inner light or the testimony of the Holy Spirit, which sometimes comes into conflict with other voices claiming to speak with final authority. This is the treatment of the subject which will be followed in this book; it is the only one which does justice to the supreme importance of the problem. There are some who connect the word mysticism with what the older Catholic writers call mystical phenomena or supernatural favours—mysterious sights, sounds and smells, 'boisterous' fits of weeping, cataleptic trances, stigmata, apparitions and the like.[1] These results of unrestrained emotionalism belong rather to psychology and psychopathy than to religion. The best mystics do not encourage those who expect and value them. They are not often experienced in our time, and descriptions of them are likely to prejudice the reader against the contemplative life, which has no necessary connection with abnormal psychical states. This branch of the subject will be neglected in this book. As for the 'phenomena,' I know that psychical research has rehabilitated, in some minds, beliefs about the 'borderland' which in the last century were generally discredited. Sensible men have been found to profess belief not only in telepathy but in second sight and foreknowledge of future events, and even in the flying exploits of Home the medium and Christina Mirabilis. My tendency is to be very sceptical of these alleged discoveries; and if some of them are true, they belong to what St. Paul calls the psychical, not the spiritual, level of reality, and give no confirmation to the intuitions of spiritual religion. The vision of God is the culminating point of our whole nature, not of any single 'faculty.' There are many paths up the hill of the Lord, though all meet at the top. The prize is no monopoly of the contemplative or of the philosopher or of the poet or of the man of action. 'All these worketh one and the selfsame Spirit, dividing to every man severally as he will.' The life of devotion has its mystical state; but so also has the intellectual life, as when Spinoza's intellectual love of God enables the thinker to envisage for a while the unity which underlies all diversity, the harmony which reconciles all contradictions. The poet, a Spenser or a Wordsworth, mounts up through visible beauties to a vision of eternal beauty. The scientific worker has a sense of the sublime, the majesty of the boundless

[1] Dom Butler bids us to go back from the later mystics to Augustine, Gregory and Bernard, who give us 'the personal experiences of their soul, with no philosophizing about contemplation,' and no 'records of divine favours.' The advice is good, but Augustine was a Platonic philosopher. Butler adds that 'nearly always it has been women who have had pictorial visions.'

13

universe, the infinitely great and the infinitely small, which is genuinely religious. Among men of action, there have been genuine mystics like Charles Gordon. Every path leads up to God; but while we live here every path ends in unfathomable mystery; we see through a glass darkly.

The silence of God has at all times been a trial to mankind. Men have sought in all sorts of ways for an infallible, unmistakable, authoritative answer to their questions, which shall save them from the responsibility of judging, and once for all lift the 'burden and the weight of this unintelligible world' from their shoulders. They would gladly consent to be led blindfold, if only they could be quite sure of being led right. They shrink from the right and duty of private judgment; they will even put on manacles to keep their hands from trembling, and take refuge in a shelter to which no winds of doubt are allowed to penetrate.

This sense of weakness and insecurity is the source of the demand for an infallible authority in religion. Authority, within the religious sphere, is essentially a guidance which is conceived of as external to ourselves and infallible. It is an assistance which we crave for because we are not at home in the world in which we live. To accept authority is to submit voluntarily to the dictation of a will or wisdom which is not our own. We are sometimes reminded that all our beliefs are founded on authority, because the greater part of our information has been acquired at second hand and not tested personally. But here there is no confession of defeat, no surrender of individual judgment. When we accept authority in religion, we accept it as revelation, that is to say, as knowledge imparted to us by a higher Power. Its correlative on our part is humble and grateful submission. Auguste Sabatier in his well-known work contrasts the religions of authority with the religion of the Spirit. It has been reasonably objected that to classify Catholic saints as unspiritual is not only unfair but ridiculous. Sabatier would probably have answered that authority in the former case is external, in the latter internal; the former enters a man from without, the latter wells up in him. But 'without' and 'within' are crude spatial images. It is possible, as the early Quakers sometimes did, to make the inner light itself external, as being wholly other than ourselves. This is a danger of which we must beware, for it gives a spurious infallibility to what may be very fallible operations of our own minds. St. Augustine said that he could not believe the Bible if it were not guaranteed by the Catholic Church. Chillingworth said that the Bible is the religion of Protestants. An old Quaker woman said, "Jerusalem? It has not yet been revealed to me that there is such a place." These vain appeals are all of the same kind.

The dualism of natural and revealed religion is hardly tenable. All religion is natural, and all religion is revealed. That is to say, we cannot separate natural and supernatural events as Roman Catholic theologians do. Some Catholic writers distinguish between supernatural and miraculous. I cannot see that this removes an intractable dualism. The conception of God as first cause may explain everything; it cannot explain some things and not others. But if we say that infallibility is a category which man cannot use, though it is broadly true, we may still accept Plato's brave act of faith that the fully real is fully knowable—not fully known to us here, but fully knowable. The spiritual man, says St. Paul, judgeth all things, and in spiritual matters, not in worldly affairs, he may, as the reward of a life of earnest seeking, come near to the direct 'seeing' which he claims. Besides the communion with God in prayer, God has revealed Himself to man as perfect Love, perfect Truth, and perfect Beauty. These ultimate values must be accepted as given, not to be judged by anything outside themselves. But for the application of these values to our practical life we have no infallible guidance. We may ask, more respectfully than Pilate, 'What is truth?' We may debate about our duty, and differ about aesthetics. But when we know what we ought to do we must do it; when we know what is true, we must accept it; when we know what is beautiful we must love it. So far as this, we must believe that there has been a direct revelation.

There has never been a time when there has been such a widespread disbelief in any external authority as there is now. Or it might be truer to say that in place of religious beliefs, held with unquestioning assurance, we have now racial, national, and political fanaticisms giving rise to wars, revolutions, and tyrannies of a kind which in the eighteenth century would have been considered an incredible reversion to barbarism. These evil weeds have sprung up on a soil left bare by the disappearance of traditional beliefs. It may therefore be worth while to consider what were the foundations of authority which have now crumbled, and what we may put in their place.

There seem to be four possible types, three of which are in manifest decay. The fourth is the belief in the inspiration of the individual, which is known as mystical religion. The other three are belief in an infallible Church, in an infallible book, and in the human reason, rationalistic humanism.

The prestige of an authoritative Church, of which the Church of Rome is the most prominent example, is still able to evoke the devoted and sometimes fanatical loyalty which even in secular affairs an exclusive and militant society can often command. It rests on a tradition which has been moulded by many centuries of study of human nature. It has not only enlisted the devotion of an unrivalled corps of janissaries in the Catholic priesthood; it has sheltered cloistered saints who are among the most famous examples of contemplative piety; and it has preserved a philosophy of religion which is once more full of life among independent thinkers and in the studies of the Neo-Thomists. Nevertheless, except to those who have made their submission, and therewith have accepted the doctrine of the Catholic Church that to criticize tradition and harbour doubts is a sin, it is almost impossible to believe that divine grace has been canalized in a single political institution. Such a claim reminds us of a familiar and not too creditable trick of trade. The only apostolical succession that we can recognize is in the lives of the saints. Church history is not pleasant reading. Institutional Churches are really secular corporations, moulded to attract average humanity. Powerful Churches have gained the upper hand by methods utterly opposed to the Spirit of Christ. As Berdyaeff says, men have set themselves to hate in the cause of love, to use compulsion in the name of freedom, and to become practising materialists for the inculcation of spiritual principles. Another Russian writer, S. L. Frank, calls it an indisputable fact that the idea of man's freedom and dignity, and in particular the idea of the freedom of conscience and of the blasphemous folly of compulsion in matters of faith, became generally recognized only some two hundred years ago. And yet inward religious freedom is an elementary expression of the spirit of Christianity. We do not make a divine truth our own by 'swallowing it without chewing,' as Hobbes said. We must seriously ask ourselves whether the 'good churchman' would or would not have been found shouting with the mob on a celebrated occasion at Jerusalem. 'Have any of our rulers believed on him?' *Melius est ut unus pereat quam unitas.* I have actually seen this horrible saying quoted with apparent approval by an Anglican bishop.

That the religion of authority is 'totalitarian' is obvious. Radhakrishnan says: 'Even as modern man when overcome by a sense of fear and insecurity resorts to the principles of force, authority and suppression of freedom in the political sphere, so also in the religious sphere when he gets tired of himself and disillusioned about life, he tends to throw himself on a transcendental superhuman power or social collectivity. When he cannot bear to be his own individual self, and longs to feel security by getting rid of his burden, he takes shelter in a person or an institution.'

A curious variety of the exclusive Catholic claim was popular among Anglican high churchmen when I was young, and may still be found in these circles. It is that ecumenical Councils are supernaturally protected against error, so that creeds sanctioned by these assembles must never be altered. Since the political disruption of the Church no ecumenical Council can be held. The infallible guidance of the Holy Spirit has gone into abeyance, like an old English peerage when a nobleman leaves two or more daughters and no son. Practically, it is as if no Act of Parliament were valid unless it was passed at a joint session of the British Parliament and the American Congress. When we read an impartial account of the proceedings at these great Councils, we shall not be tempted to treat their decisions as supernaturally exempt from human infirmity.

Extreme institutionalism is not a lost cause, any more than totalitarianism in politics. Josiah Royce held that 'membership in a community is necessary to the salvation of man. Such a community exists, and is an indispensable means of salvation for the individual man.' This view, which would satisfy the most rigorous of Ultramontanes, and would justify the policy of 'Compel them to come in,' is not a little strange in a thinker who not only belonged to no Church, but who admits that 'the beloved Community' is not to be identified with any existing Church. Aubrey Moore, one of the ablest of the *Lux Mundi* group, connects the distrust of institutionalism with individualism in politics and atomism in natural science. There is 'a brotherhood in which men become members of an organic whole by sharing in a common life.' A Christian mystic would gladly subscribe to this, but he is willing to find the sharers of a common life in unexpected places, even 'among the tents of Kedar.' Troeltsch, who was a Protestant, emphasizes that 'the essence of religion is not dogma and idea, but cultus and communion, the living inter- course with the Deity.' This is certainly true, but why confine 'inter- course with the Deity' to 'cultus'? Community worship is very helpful, as the Quakers, the mystical sect *par excellence,* know. But do we not have 'intercourse with the Deity' when we 'enter into our closet, and when we have shut the door pray to our Father who is in secret'? This, rather than standing and praying in the Temple courts, seems to have been what our Lord had in His mind when He spoke about prayer.

The main argument for institutionalism is that it works. It cannot be denied that Christ never contemplated the foundation of a semi- political international society, such as the Catholic Church has been. But if He had known that the Messianic expectation of an 'end of the age' was illusory, would He not have approved those developments which were necessary for the survival of His revelation? If we want to assure ourselves of the identity of a grown man with the same person in his infancy, we do not try to squeeze him into his cradle. So Loisy argued, when he still hoped that this modernist apologetic might be accepted by his Church. It could not be accepted; it exposed the *arcana imperii* too baldly. The argument is not valid as a defence of a divine institution. Every organization when it seizes political power strangles the ideas which gave it birth. The first object of a successful revolution is to prevent any further activity of the revolutionary spirit. There is nothing in the political history of Catholicism which suggests in the slightest degree that the Spirit of Christ has been the guiding principle in its councils. If our Lord had returned to earth in the so-called ages of faith, He would probably have been burnt alive for denying the dogmas about His own person. The rigorous staticism of Catholic theology has obliged the Church to oppose and quench all independent thinking, and to reject, as long as possible, the most irrefutable discoveries of science and scholarship. It was not till 1835 that the teaching of Copernicus and Galileo was removed from the Index. Politically, the inner logic of the system has ended in making the Bishop of Rome an infallible potentate, just as the principate of Augustus ended in the sultanate of Diocletian and his successors. The liberalizing movement in the Roman Church has been stamped out; its future, so far as we can guess, is with the Ultramontanes, who represent the logical evolution of a political Church. Many of the most beautiful characters in the roll of Christian mystics have been loyal Catholics; but the stronger minds among them have never been comfortable under the authority of the Church. Origen, Eckhart, and Erasmus have been formally condemned; the Jesuits, I think, have tried to forbid the study of Ruysbroek and

Tauler. Institutionalism and mysticism have always been uneasy bedfellows.

The Church of England has characteristically refrained from acknow-ledging any single seat of authority. Hooker, a very typical Anglican divine, says: 'What Scripture doth plainly deliver, to that the first place both of credit and obedience is due; the next whereunto is whatsoever any man may necessarily conclude by force of reason; after these the voice of the Church succeedeth.' The honourable place here given to 'reason' has hardly been admitted by our Church authorities as a rule, though it was energetically defended by Benjamin Whichcote and the other Cambridge Platonists. What they meant by 'reason'—an ambiguous word representing the very different functions of what the Greeks called *Nous* and *Dianoia*—must be considered later. What concerns us here is the primary homage paid to Scripture, from which, it is assumed, all the doctrines of our religion have their source and justification. 'The Bible is the religion of Protestants.' This, of course, has not been the view of all Anglicans. Tyndale regarded the Roman Church as hostile to the authority of the Bible. Laud regarded Puritanism as hostile to the authority of the Church. Butler regarded the Methodists as yielding an authority to the emotions which was hostile to that of reason. The Cambridge Platonists held that the authority of reason (*Nous*) was prior to that of the Bible or of the Church.[1]

It is easy to see how bibliolatry arose. In times of war controversy is rough and crude. The Reformers needed a rival oracle to match the infallible Church of the Catholics, and they could only find it in the Scriptures, which were acknowledged by their opponents. They redis-covered the New Testament: that was well; but they also rediscovered the Old, and raised it almost to the same level as the New. In the early Church the Marcionites wished to get rid of the Old Testament. The God of the Hebrews, they said, is not the Father of our Lord Jesus Christ. But the Church could not make this concession.

The breach with Judaism was not complete till near the end of the first century. In preaching to the Jews the main argument was to show that in Christ the prophecies in the Old Testament were fulfilled. In several places the Gospel narrative seems to have been adapted to this line of defence. But on the whole the uncritical acceptance of the Jewish Scriptures has been a very doubtful boon to the Church. Origen says boldly that if the Old Testament is taken literally, God was guilty of actions which would disgrace a ferocious tyrant. Such texts as 'Cursed be Canaan; a servant of servants shall he be'; 'thou shalt not suffer a witch to live'; 'the Lord is a man of war,' have done terrible mischief. The book is full of stories which are as incredible as they are unedifying. Many of the Psalms, the later chapters of Isaiah, and the Book of Job, are of priceless value; but they do not justify us in regarding the whole collection of books as the treasury of plenary inspiration. In any case, this seat of authority is hopelessly discredited, except in low intellectual strata.

[1] Canon R. D. Richardson. *Conflict of Ideals in the Church*, p. 4.

But does the New Testament remain intact as an 'impregnable rock'? St. Paul's Epistles are a first-hand document of inexhaustible truth; I hope to deal with them rather fully when we come to the discussion of Christian mysticism. But criticism has not spared the Gospels. There is no unanimity among scholars as to the historical trustworthiness of the three Synoptics. Matthew and Luke were not compiled till fifty years had passed since the events which they describe, and in the growth of a religion fifty years is an ample time for legends to grow, for facts to be forgotten or distorted, and for the faithful to use the Founder, as Samuel Butler says, as a peg on which to hang their own best thoughts. Professor Lightfoot[1] says: 'It seems that the form of the earthly no less than that of the heavenly Christ is for the most part hidden from us. The Gospels yield us little more than a whisper of His voice; we trace in them but the outskirts of His ways.' Personally, I think this doubt goes too far. I think that a very clear picture of the unique personality of our Lord emerges from the artless narrative of the Synoptic evangelists, whose very limitations forbade them to construct an ideal or imaginative portrait of the Saviour. But we cannot forget that some able critics are less confident; and we certainly cannot be sure that all the words to which we should like to appeal in confirmation of our own convictions were actually spoken by Christ. It is still not uncommon to see the words attributed to our Lord in the Fourth Gospel quoted as if they were on the same footing historically as the Synoptics. But nearly all scholars are now agreed that this Gospel is a mystical treatise, the work of an unknown Christian in Asia Minor, or as some think in Egypt,[2] between A.D. 100 and 120. The son of Zebedee was probably martyred by the Jews, as we are told that our Lord predicted. In any case, he cannot have been the author of the Gospel. Clement and Origen call it a spiritual Gospel, as opposed to a mere record of events. It is a very wonderful book, an inspired exposition of the permanent meaning and value of the Incarnation. But both events and discourses are the free composition of the evangelist.

There is another point, of great importance, which it would be cowardly to shirk, though it may give offence in some quarters. We believe that the incarnate Christ was 'perfect man,' that He was 'in all points tempted as we are,' and that He 'increased in wisdom' as well as 'in stature.' No one supposes that He was omniscient as a child. St. Paul speaks of His *kenosis*, 'self-emptying.' If He was thus subject to human limitations, does it not follow that He knew no more about the future, including what we call the future life, than we do? The parables of the sheep and goats, and of Dives and Lazarus, are often taken as descriptions of things that must come hereafter. They were not so intended. It may be that, like many Jewish apocalyptists, He thought that the 'days of the Messiah,' to be followed by the last judgment, were approaching.

[1] R. H. Lightfoot, *History and Interpretation of the Gospels*, p. 225.
[2] A possible confirmation of this theory may be found in the 'palms' which, according to this evangelist, the disciples carried into Jerusalem. There are no palms in Judea—they will not grow at this elevation; and there are no palms at Ephesus; but there are in Egypt. But I think the 'palms' have a symbolic meaning.

But He frankly admitted that 'of that day and that hour knoweth no man.' When He was questioned by the Sadducees, who disbelieved in a resurrection, His only answer was that 'God is not the God of the dead but of the living, for all live unto Him.' St. Augustine restates this argument very beautifully: '*Quod Deo non perit sibi non perit.*' All the rest, Hades and Gehenna, the worm and the unquenchable fire, the twelve thrones and the restored Kingdom of David, is not revealed truth but the current symbolic faith of his countrymen. Nothing has been revealed except that 'as God lives, so shall we live also.' It is probable that we could know nothing more, for we can form no clear idea of a state when 'there shall be time no longer.' If this is accepted, we may surely dismiss, as hardly compatible with what our Saviour has told us about God, the grisly pictures of future torment and the rather crude pictures of future bliss, which all the Churches have offered to reinforce the sanctions of morality. We may remember that in none of the old catalogues of the deadly sins does cruelty find a place.

I do not for a moment mean to suggest that in the absence of direct revelation about the future we must face the possibility or probability that death is the final extinction of our personality. The 'perennial philosophy' which is the traditional and orthodox philosophy of the Church asserts positively that, as Browning says, 'what is at all lasts ever past recall.' As Thomas Aquinas says, '*Non est potentia ad non esse.*' When we think of the eternal world, we are obliged to figure it under the forms of time and place. We cannot help it, and I do not think we need resist this inevitable limitation of our minds, if we will only remember that all eschatology must be symbolic. 'We do not yet know what we shall be'; and those traditional pictures of future bliss and torment which we have inherited from pre-Christian ages, if they seem to conflict with the character of our heavenly Father which Christ came to reveal to us, need not, in my opinion, trouble our faith. Several of the mystics have wished that they might forget these promises and threats, 'in order that we may love God for himself alone'; and I think that this feeling is now very common.

We are considering the claims of these traditional seats of authority, not to an important place in building up belief, but as the final court of appeal by which all opinions must be judged. It seems plain that the infallible Church can be believed in only by those who have enlisted as members of a militant institution, and that the infallible book is no more than a broken reed. It remains, before coming to the claim of mystical religion to give us certainty, to consider the third of the authorities to which Hooker says that credit and obedience are due, namely human reason. By rationalism we mean reliance on the evidence of our senses, on the discoveries of natural science, and on logical reasoning such as we find in the Schoolmen. In the nineteenth century naturalism rather than rationalism describes the dominant trend of thought outside the Churches. It was based on what philosophers call naive realism, and sometimes took the form of dogmatic materialism, which orthodoxy countered with materialistic dogmatism. The dreary conflicts between religion and science in the Victorian age now seem to us out of date. It was often assumed that if certain events in the past and in the future are true—that is to say that they actually happened or will happen in the world as known by science—Christianity is true; if they did not so happen it is false. Those scientists who aspired to have a philosophy assumed that ponderable things in the world of time and space are the only solid facts; the whole world of values floated ineffectually above them. 'Epiphenomena' the world of values was called, but sometimes its affirmations were called dreams as opposed to realities. The real world consisted ultimately of hard little billiard balls called atoms. They were indestructible, impenetrable, and mutually exclusive, inert in relation to one another. Such atomism recalls the windowless monads of Leibniz's theory of personality. Both combatants have had to haul down their flags. There are still a few hard-boiled biologists who adhere to the old materialism. But physicists and astronomers have often been religious men, and now they are ready to admit that natural science is an abstract study, which necessarily neglects what Bismarck called the imponderables, the whole world of values. Science itself is the faithful servant of one of the ultimate values, truth; but there is no philosophy to be made out of a universe of stars and atoms regarded as the only real things. Philosophy must take into account all kinds of evidence, and the affirmations of thought, conscience, the mystical vision, and the sense of beauty are as much entitled to respect as our sensations. As Bradley says, 'There is nothing more real than what comes in religion. To compare facts such as these with what is given to us in outward existence would be to trifle with the subject. The man who demands a reality more solid than that of the religious consciousness seeks he does not know what.'[1] Now that science has disposed of the hard little billiard balls, and has 'defecated matter to a transparency,' it has been more and more controlled by mathematics, the clearest and emptiest of its branches. Physicists are impatient at the interference of brute facts with their calculations. They are willing to call the concrete realities of the materialists 'pointer readings.' Jeans and Eddington coquet with Berkeleyan idealism. There are, I believe, other unsolved difficulties. For instance, the quantum theory does not seem to agree well with Einstein's relativity. This breakdown of scientific dogmatism has given heart of grace to every kind of barbarous superstition, including even astrology; and in philosophy we have the American school of pragmatism, which holds that since there is no such thing as truth, we may and should believe whatever suits us. In this field, no less than in the two courts of appeal already considered, authority has been deposed. It is no longer believed in.

The collapse of materialistic dogmatism has been as complete as that of dogmatic materialism. There can be no revelation either of past or of future events. The future is entirely hidden from us; the past is preserved only by the treacherous records of history, much of which, as Napoleon said, is only 'une fable convenue.' We are amphibious creatures, living partly in a world of ponderable things and partly in a world of

---

[1] Bradley, *Appearance and Reality*, p. 449.

imponderable values. And since we must somehow bring them together, traditional theology intercalates acts of God in the physical order, rather than believe that God is a 'roi fainéant.' That historical dogmas are unconscious symbols is plain from one consideration. If I say that I believe the queer fancy of the Anglo-Israelites, or that Bacon wrote Shakespeare, or that Napoleon is a solar myth, my friends will have a poor opinion of my intelligence, but they will not think that I am necessarily damned. Yet this is the reaction of the traditionalist when he hears any of his historical dogmas questioned. He seldom asks, if these 'fact-like stories,' as von Hügel calls them, are literally events in the external world, what do they prove that is of interest to religion? They are plainly a bridge between fact and value, between the seen and the unseen, between the temporal and the eternal, between appearance and reality, put it how we will. Miracle, says Goethe, is faith's dearest child. It is the child, not the parent of faith, and the child was born in a pre-scientific age. Nevertheless, most of us need a bridge, and the traditional bridge still bears well enough for simple faith.

We are considering the claim of rationalism to be the final court of appeal, the basis of a religion or the substitute for it. It has failed to substantiate this claim, because it neglects or ignores some of the data which a comprehensive philosophy must take into account. It practically denies the validity of spiritual intuition. It may sanction religious feeling, but only as a feeling. It may allow religion to exist as an emotional state fenced off from the activity of the intellect. Psychology, which belongs to natural science, though in its backward state it can hardly claim to be itself a science, may be content to regard religion in this way; and notoriously some of the recent books on mysticism take this view. Spiritual intuition, for them, may be a normal though not a common condition, or it may be pathological; ontologically, that is to say as belonging to ultimate reality, it has no validity. This is a view which all genuine mystics must emphatically reject. They are not interested in states of consciousness as such; rightly or wrongly they are convinced that they have *seen*. Rightly or wrongly they are convinced that they are or have been in contact with objective reality, with the supreme spiritual Power behind the world of our surface consciousness. If they are right, this intuition must be a factor in what we believe about reality; it means that reality is spiritual. This is the fourth of the seats of authority which we have undertaken to examine. The failure of the other three, not to fill a place, and an important place, in our scheme of life, but to provide us with an infallible appeal which can override our doubts and give us the firm basis which we need for building up our lives, makes it a supremely important question whether our faith in God and in an eternal spiritual world can stand after the traditional supports on which it has so long been buttressed have proved inadequate. Is the inward light, or, as mystics believe, the testimony of the Holy Spirit, a sufficient guide for men and women during their earthly probation, their pilgrimage through a country which is not their real home? Has God, who has partially revealed Himself, not 'clearly,' as our versions mistranslate a verse in the Epistle to the Romans,[1] but 'darkly, as in a mirror,' through 'the things that are made,' revealed Himself also, and more clearly, in the purified hearts of those who have sought Him earnestly? Have those who have sold all that they have to win the pearl of great price really found it, or have they deceived themselves?

That the life of Christianity depends on the answer to this question seems to be admitted by most of those who understand the present climate of opinion. A few typical pronouncements have been selected. They are all from the writings of laymen; but this is characteristic of our time. Our prophets are not ministers of religion; I do not think that this is a fact to be regretted.

'Personal inner experience is the only source from which religion in these days of naturalism and agnosticism, of indifference and hostility, can draw its life.' (J. B. Pratt).

'The religion of first-hand experience is not a substitute for Christianity; it is Christianity alive and vocal in personal experience and in individual love.' (Rufus Jones).

'Spiritual religion is based on a firm belief in absolute and eternal values as the most real things in the universe, a confidence that these values are knowable by man by a wholehearted consecration of the intellect, will and affections to the great quest, a complete indifference to the current valuations of tribes, races and nations, and a devotion to the ideal of a world community. They are the common possession of the great religions.' (Radhakrishnan).

'The technique of mysticism, properly practised, may result in the direct intuition of, and union with, an ultimate spiritual reality that is perceived as simultaneously beyond the self and in some way within it.' (Aldous Huxley).

'In an age when custom is dissolved and authority is broken the religion of the spirit is not merely a possible way of life. In principle it is the only way which transcends the difficulties.' (Lippmann).

'That which is immediately given us in the religious experience is a reality which we apprehend on the one hand as something primary, as the deepest source and the absolute foundation of our being, and on the other as something absolutely valuable, giving us the supreme perfect joy and delight.' (S. L. Frank).

'Every idealistic theory of the world has as its ultimate premise a logically unsupported judgment of value—a judgment which affirms an end of intrinsic worth and accepts thereby a standard of unconditional obligation.' (Pringle Pattison).

If we believe in the gift of the Holy Spirit, the indwelling Christ who is 'with us always, even to the end of the world,' we shall find no difficulty in accepting this testimony.

---

[1] Romans I, 20. The Greek is τὰ ἀόρατα αὐτοῦ ἀπὸ κτίσεως κόσμου νοούμενα καθορᾶται. The organ that sees the invisible, symbolized in the visible creation, is the νοῦς, which in St. Paul is almost the same as πνεῦμα. St. Paul would never have said 'clearly'; cf. I Cor. xiii, 12.

This is life eternal, that they might know thee, the only true God, and Jesus Christ whom thou hast sent.—JOHN XVII, 3.

Of all things good and fair and holy there is a spiritual cognisance which precedes and is independent of that knowledge which the understanding conveys.—JOHN CAIRD.

I would fain be to the Eternal Goodness what a man's hand is to a man.
THEOLOGIA GERMANICA.

The mystic insight begins with the sense of a mystery unveiled, of a hidden wisdom now suddenly become certain beyond the possibility of a doubt. The sense of certainty and revelation comes earlier than any definite belief. The definite beliefs at which mystics arrive are the result of reflection upon the inarticulate experience gained in the moment of insight.—BERTRAND RUSSELL.

CHAPTER II

THE MEANING OF MYSTICISM

I N my Bampton lectures on Christian Mysticism (1899), a book which I venture to think had some influence in turning the attention of the religious public to the subject, I gave in an appendix twenty-six definitions of mysticism. The word was then used very loosely, and more often than not in a disparaging or even contemptuous manner. The Germans have two words, *Mystik* and *Mysticismus,* by which they can distinguish between mysticism as a genuine type of religion and the perversions of it. It is a pity that we cannot do the same. But the meaning of the word is now better understood than it was half a century ago, and there is so little difference between the way in which it is used by competent authors that it will be enough to select a very few of the definitions quoted by me in 1899, and to add two or three from more recent authors.

'Mysticism is the immediate feeling of the unity of the self with God; it is nothing, therefore, but the fundamental feeling of religion, the religious life at its very heart and centre. But what makes the mystical a special tendency inside religion is the endeavour to fix the immediateness of the life in God as such, as abstracted from all intervening helps and channels whatever, and find a permanent abode in the abstract inwardness of a life of pious feeling.' (Pfleiderer).

'Mysticism appears in connection with the endeavour of the human mind to grasp the divine essence or the ultimate reality of things, and to enjoy the blessedness of actual communion with the highest. The first is the philosophic side of mysticism, the second its religious side. God ceases to be an object and becomes an experience.' (Pringle Pattison).

'True mysticism is the consciousness that everything that we experience is an element and only an element in fact; i.e., that in being what it is, it is symbolic of something more.' (R. L. Nettleship).

'Mysticism is religion in its most concentrated and exclusive form. It is that attitude of the mind in which all other relations are swallowed up in the relation of the soul to God.' (E. Caird).

'If I may speak no longer as a psychologist but as a man, the experience of life confirms my belief that the possibility of some communion between God and the individual is not an illusion.' (Dr. William Brown).

'Christian mysticism is the doctrine, or rather the experience, of the Holy Spirit—the realization of human personality as characterized by and consummated in the indwelling reality of the Spirit of Christ, which is God.' (R. C. Moberly).

'Spiritual and mystical apprehension within Christianity is truer and more real than the objective and psychical apprehension which is given symbolic expression on the natural and historical plane. The inner depths of Christianity and the mysteries of the spiritual life are revealed within Christian mysticism. Christianity is the revelation of the mystery of the spiritual life.' (Berdyaeff).

These definitions make it quite clear what mysticism means. They agree together. We shall find that this harmony is found, to a very remarkable extent, among mystics of all times, of all countries, and of all religions. The only point on which they speak with an uncertain or divergent voice is on the value of sensible objects, and of our knowledge of the world of time and space, as symbols of ultimate reality. There have been two schools of mystics, one of which distrusts and rejects the affirmations of ordinary consciousness, while the other welcomes the visible as a partial manifestation of the spiritual. This must be dealt with later.

Having shown what mysticism means, we may note briefly the unfriendly attitude of some theologians and philosophers, and answer those of their objections which seem unreasonable. Protestant theologians on the Continent have generally been cold or unfriendly. Calvin was unfavourable: the Lutherans more opposed than Luther himself. The Ritschlian school is frankly hostile, and with them we must include the great Harnack, who makes the strange statement—a condemnation from his point of view—that mysticism is Catholic piety. He disparages the German mystics, and will 'give no extracts from their writings, because I do not wish even to countenance the error that they expressed anything that one cannot read in Origen, Plotinus, the Areopagite, Augustine, Erigena, Bernard and Thomas, or that they represented religious progress.' The assumption that Luther represents progress over Augustine and Thomas Aquinas may provoke a smile. 'A mystic,' he concludes, 'who does not become a Catholic is a dilettante.' We may object that dilettante is about the last word that could be applied to Böhme, George Fox, or William Law. But it is equally thoughtless to suggest that the mystics have been most at home in the Catholic Church. It would be strange if they had been. To believe that the vision of God may be attained without priestly intervention, that the sacraments are not essential, and that spiritual experience is a surer basis of faith than ecclesiastical authority, is to strike at the root of Roman Catholic churchmanship. Some of the independent mystics in Catholic countries have been imprisoned and pronounced heretics; a large number have been tortured, massacred, or burnt alive. Protestants must not forget the fate of Servetus, and of the four Quaker martyrs at Philadelphia. Böhme and George Fox had much to suffer. That many of the most beautiful characters among the contemplatives have been loyal Catholics we have already said, and no one would wish to deny it; but mysticism is certainly not 'Catholic piety.' Herrmann, a declared Ritschlian, goes beyond Harnack and professes the crudest antagonism. 'The mystic's experience of God is a delusion.' According to him 'we are confined to the fact of the human Jesus.' The main reason of this prejudice seems to be the admitted fact that mysticism values the Incarnation more than the Atonement. Aubrey Moore notes that this is one of the characteristics of the Catholicizing movement in the Church of England. Some have tried to soften this difference by saying that Atonement only means At-one-ment, which is very far from the meaning of the word as used by Continental Protestants. For most of them the Atonement is a juridical transaction by which the merits acquired by the Passion of Christ are transferred by 'imputation' to the believer. This strange doctrine was fathered upon St. Paul. It is certainly true that it plays a very small part in the faith of the mystic. The reactionary theology of Barth, which has rather unexpectedly taken hold of many in Germany and some in this country, is essentially anti-mystical. A God who is 'wholly other' can enter into no relations with man, for we cannot apprehend what is entirely alien to ourselves. Among our own theologians, Forsyth, Oman and Mackintosh have written against mysticism, but there is no widespread hostility.

A wider public has welcomed the large group of psychologists, who regard as irrelevant or unanswerable the question whether the mystical experience is actually a communion of the human spirit with the divine. This puts them out of court as critics of the mystics. If God is banished from the inquiry, or treated as a product of merely subjective imagination, we need not trouble about the mystics any more. For they are convinced that their communion with God is an authentic experience. It is for those who regard this conviction as an illusion to give their reasons for doing so. As I have said elsewhere, if a dozen honest men tell me that they have climbed the Matterhorn, it is reasonable to believe that the summit of that mountain is accessible, though I am not likely to get there myself. It is true, no doubt, that what can be handed on to others is not the vision itself, but the inadequate symbols in which the seer tries to represent what he has seen and to preserve it in his memory. Language was not meant for such purposes, and contemplatives sometimes feel that there is a kind of profanation in speaking of things which 'it is not lawful for man to utter.' It is difficult to communicate such experiences to those who have never known anything of the kind themselves. But we may listen to them with the same humility and confidence that we show to great poets and musicians. We never think of questioning their good faith.

The psychologists, however, having once for all ignored the hypothesis that the vision is a vision of ultimate reality—and this abstraction is no doubt necessary for those who are merely studying states of consciousness as such—devote too much attention to what in the older Catholic books are called mystical phenomena, and have no difficulty in showing that these abnormal experiences are familiar to students of mental pathology. As Pratt says, if the theologian is tempted to treat mysticism as a supernatural phenomenon, the psychologist is beguiled by 'the charm of the pathological.' Is it the result of indigestion, as Carlyle's melancholy was attributed to gastro-intestinal catarrh, or of excessive fasting, or is it auto-intoxication, resembling what William James felt when under the influence of nitrous oxide? Or perhaps it is a variety of schizophrenia, divided personality, or of mere auto-suggestion. If none of these theories suffices, there is always Professor Freud. Do not some female mystics show symptoms of sublimated erotomania?[1] Cannot the Oedipus complex be brought in somewhere? We are reminded that

[1] The symbol of the spiritual marriage goes back to Origen, and is found sometimes in Augustine, but it was first emphasized by St. Bernard, and became part of the common stock in the writings of the later mystics.

various methods have been adopted to induce such states. Some have gazed intently on their own navels; others have fixed their eyes on some bright object; the Indians have made a special study of these experimental methods. The experience of ecstasy, thus attained, is said to be very pleasurable. Awe and reverence are felt towards those who seem to have been possessed by a supernatural spirit. Hashish, alcohol, mescal, may be employed. Orgiastic dances like those of the dervishes produce collective excitement, culminating in exhaustion and even loss of consciousness.

All this belongs to what Dom Cuthbert Butler calls the undesirable side of mysticism. There is some excuse for the quite mistaken importance which psychologists have given to these abnormal states, because many writers on mysticism, especially in the Roman Catholic Church, have welcomed what they have regarded as genuinely supernatural visitations. Visions, locutions, auditions, and so forth, are accepted as miraculous facts. But the great contemplatives themselves have discouraged this attitude. St. John of the Cross even said of a nun who claimed to have held conversations with God: 'All this that she says: God spoke to me; I spoke to God, seems nonsense. She has only been speaking to herself.'

Those who have attributed mysticism to psychasthenia, weakness of the will, are obviously mistaken. For an intense concentration of the will is one of the chief characteristics of the mystic. As T. H. Hughes[1] says: 'When the soul is said to be passive, the passivity is not a state of inactivity or lassitude. The will is not in abeyance, nor are the various faculties inert. All the faculties are directed to one centre, so that there is a narrowing of the field of consciousness, through the intense concentration of the will to one focal point.' 'There is an openness of soul to receive what the loved one has to give, with elements of tension at times between the two.' Equally at sea are those who speak of 'divided personality.' We are all divided personalities, amphibious creatures. As I have said, we live partly in a world of ponderable things and partly in a world of imponderable values. But the aim of the mystic is to unify his personality. Mysticism, says Bastide, does not mean dissociation; it is the creation of a new ego. This is a thought of which more must be said when we come to St. Paul. More generally, it has been often pointed out that the greatest mystics have been strong and healthy persons, many of them long-lived, and some of them gifted with remarkable organizing capacities. Nothing can be further apart than the lives of the great mystics and those of drug-addicts.

Nevertheless we must not dismiss the judgments of so many able pathologists as wholly without justification. Plotinus says that the faculty for spiritual perception is one which all possess but few use. It may be true that all possess it in germ, but only a few possess it in a superlative degree. The mystic is not a common type. The greatest contemplatives are as rare as great poets, musicians, scientific discoverers. One of the commonest errors of our time, now that we are obsessed by democratism, and by a snobbish predisposition to deny all superiority, is to forget our

---

[1] *The Philosophic Basis of Mysticism*, pp. 50 and 75

Lord's words that narrow is the way that leadeth unto life, and few there be that find it. Christianity gives us a new type of aristocracy; it is utterly opposed to the notion that we can reach the truth by counting heads. Just as we go to the recognized masters of human thought in philosophy, science and the arts, so we must be content to sit at the feet of the masters of the spiritual life; and these are specialists, who have concentrated on a single aim.

The objection that mysticism is a religion for the élite must be faced. Berdyaeff, a disillusioned Communist, is not afraid to face it. The quantitative majority, he says,[1] has always oppressed the qualitative minority, that which is composed of truly spiritual individuals. History works out in favour of the average man and of the collective. It is for such that dogma and cult have been adapted. The average man has always insisted that everything should be brought down to the level of his interests. 'Christianity, a religion which is not of this world, suffers humiliation in the world for the sake of the general mass of humanity. The whole tragedy of spiritual humanity lies in that fact.'

It required some courage to say this to-day. Of course, no one would dispute Dom Butler's words that 'mysticism is within the reach of the poor and unlearned and the little ones of Christ. Mysticism finds its working expression not in intellectual speculation but in prayer.' I hope I have said nothing contrary to this obvious truth. Prayer is the mystical act, and prayer is not the privilege of the few. The tragedy is that so few use it.

Genius is often a little 'queer.' Monoideism is dangerous. The life of the cloister, which sheltered so many of the best-known contemplatives, is not wholesome for everybody. Solitude is the death of all but the strongest virtue. A man who has experienced nothing is made no wiser by solitude. There has been a morbid strain among some of those whose lives the historian of mysticism must deal with. The self-torturing of Suso, the impulse which led Madame Guyon to swallow the most repulsive filth—these and many other things make us shudder. But they are plainly aberrations. They belong to a strange perversion of the religious sense which is not integrally connected either with Christianity or with mysticism, and which has a mainly historical interest, since we rarely meet with it now. We do not find anything of the kind in the philosophical mystics, nor in the Quakers.

[1] *Freedom and the Spirit*, pp. 11 and 32.

In the New Testament the Spirit of God is the very life and energy of God, issuing from the fountain-head of Deity; the self-consciousness of God, exploring the depths of the divine heart and mind; the Spirit of the absolute truth, nay, the truth itself; the finger of God, by which His work is done in the spiritual world. The life, the consciousness, the truth, the power of God is God; God living, thinking, teaching, working. But God thus manifested is in the thought of the New Testament clearly differentiated from God in His own infinitude, the fountain of the divine life, the Father. . . . And though in His workings and gifts He is regarded as a power and a gift rather than as a Person, yet in His own divine life it is impossible to doubt that He possesses that which answers in some higher and to us incomprehensible way to personality in man.—H. B. SWETE.

CHAPTER III

MYSTICISM IN THE NEW TESTAMENT

THE cradle of Christianity was in northern Palestine, where among a people of mixed origin, ardent adherents of Judaism but not much attached to the sacerdotal hierarchy at Jerusalem, there appeared a movement of prophetic and spiritual religion headed by John the Baptist and carried further by our Lord, who was known to His contemporaries as the prophet of Nazareth in Galilee. Both He and the forerunner placed themselves in the prophetic succession; Christ lived, taught, and died as a prophet. The Gospel may be regarded as the culmination of a higher religion which in Palestine was heralded by the prophets, but which appeared almost simultaneously about the middle of the first millennium before the Christian era in China, India, Persia, Greece and Palestine. Other times of spiritual upheaval may be noted at the period when Christianity was contending with its Oriental rivals for victory in the Roman Empire, and at the period of the Reformation. Many people think that we are at the beginning of another crisis now. Such movements depend on a collective inspiration; it takes two to tell the truth, one to speak and one to hear.

For later generations the person of a founder sometimes dwarfs the contributions of his disciples. Those who have hoped to write a biography of Christ have no Boswell to record day by day the table talk and habits of his Master; our records, apart from the earliest Christmas carols in Matthew and Luke, record only the brief ministry of our Lord, which perhaps extended over several years, but comprised only a small fraction of His life. It is therefore not surprising that psychologists like William James have shrunk from discussing the character of Jesus as an example of the mystical life. There have been many modern lives of Christ, in most of which the credal and even the national predispositions of the authors have been apparent. Middleton Murry discusses the question whether He was a mystic, and concludes that 'in a great and complete mystic like Jesus of Nazareth the human organism actually becomes a new kind of organism.' This would not be universally admitted; but the words of Goguel at the close of his *Life of Jesus* are true, and justify the use of the word mystic in speaking of Him. 'The unique originality of Jesus consists in His sense of the presence of God, in that conscious and living communion with God in which He lives. To Him God is no abstract idea, but an immediate and living reality; God in Him, not a God conceived with the mind or imagined or dreamed, but a God who is experienced, felt, known.' So Renan in his not very satisfactory *Life* says truly: 'Jesus feels that He is in God, and when He speaks of His Father He is speaking from His heart.' It is the prophetic consciousness at its highest perfection. He taught as one having authority, and not as the Scribes. His authority was the supreme and ultimate authority, the

Holy Spirit of God Himself. Those who wish to trace back Christian mysticism to the fountain-head have ample warrant for doing so.

But if we regard mysticism not merely as a personal experience, but as a thought-out philosophy of life, a spiritual interpretation of reality, it is St. Paul whom we must regard as the founder of Christian mysticism. If I seem to have given too much space to his teaching, I must reply that he is an immensely important figure in Church history, and that perhaps no great man in history has been so much misunderstood and misrepresented. We know more about him than about any other character of antiquity, with the possible exception of Marcus Tullius Cicero. His letters, which were perhaps dashed off, dictated in a hurry, and certainly without the slightest expectation that they would be treasured as holy scripture, are of unique value both as revealing the character of the man, and as giving us a picture of the conditions under which the Gospel was presented in the first generation after the death of Christ to the cities of the Hellenistic world. For our present purpose much of this is irrelevant; but 'the religious experience of St. Paul'—the title of an excellent book by Professor Percy Gardner—is of quite essential importance for a historical study of Christian mysticism. There has been no spiritual revival within Christianity that has not been, on one side at least, a return to St. Paul. Protestants have always felt their affinity with this institutionalist, mystics with this disciplinarian.

I have said that he has been misunderstood and misrepresented. I am not thinking of the gross libels against his character by such men as Lagarde and Nietzsche; these are merely absurd and astonishing, for the language is that of personal animus; nor of the contemptuous tone of Renan, which is equally out of place. But the real Paul has been half buried under a Talmud of Paulinism, and no one has contributed more to misunderstanding than Martin Luther, who almost identifies faith with a feeling of confidence—*fides* with *fiducia*—a state of mind which as we know was far removed from the humble self-criticism and self-reproach of the apostle himself. We need not inquire exactly what Luther meant by reliance on the imputed merits of Christ. St. Paul's faith had a very different foundation.

In order to understand St. Paul it is wise not to rely very much on the Acts of the Apostles. The best critics, I think, refuse to follow Loisy in his extreme scepticism about the historical value of Acts, which is certainly an honest book, based in part on a genuine travel diary. But St. Luke is less virile than St. Paul. He is attracted by magic and miracle, and his mental simplicity is shown, for example, by his notion that 'speaking with tongues'—*glossolalia*—meant 'the gift of diverse languages,' as our Anglican liturgy unhappily follows him in saying. His three accounts of the apostle's conversion, which are curiously inconsistent, are more materialistic than St. Paul's own guarded references to it. The six speeches recorded in Acts are of course composed by the author; almost all ancient historians did the same.

St. Paul was not a systematic theologian like Origen and St. Thomas Aquinas. He was a travelling missionary, like George Fox and Wesley.

He grazes more than one heresy, or what the Church afterwards called heresies. There is a well-marked development in his thought, which is remarkable when we remember the short interval between his earliest and latest writings. This has been described as a gradual approach to the Hellenistic mystery religions. But, as Harnack says, 'What Gentile Christianity did was to carry out a process which had in fact commenced long before in Judaism itself, namely the process by which the Jewish religion was inwardly emancipated and turned into a religion for the world.' The change was mainly though not exclusively in the Judaism of the Dispersion as opposed to that of Palestine. But the change in the thought of St. Paul, which this change in Judaism made possible for him, is unmistakable. In 1 Thessalonians we have a naive picture of the Messiah coming on the clouds of heaven; this was part of the Pharisaic tradition; but the hope of a speedy return of Christ to earth faded, very slowly it is true, in the primitive Church. The words in Philippians, 'I have a desire to depart and be with Christ,' show a different state of mind. Messianism is not discarded even in the Fourth Gospel, but it has become an otiose feature in that treatise, and there is not much left of it when St. Paul can say, 'the kingdom of God is righteousness and peace and joy in the Holy Ghost.' It does mark a great change when in place of the Pharisaic doctrine of the two ages, the present age and that which is to come, we have the faith of Platonism in a nutshell; 'the things which are seen are temporal (or, rather, temporary); the things which are not seen are eternal.' The doctrine of the Spirit as immanent in the hearts of men makes the Parousia a present possession of the Christian, though no doubt only an 'earnest' of what we hope for when 'our earthly house of this tabernacle is dissolved, and we inherit a house not made with hands, eternal in the heavens.' More and more, the realization which was the spiritual core of the Hellenistic mystery cults, that of a corporate union between the Head and the members of a body, took possession of the apostle's mind. This 'Catholicizing' of Christianity is no doubt most pronounced in the Epistle to the Ephesians, the authenticity of which is far from certain, but it is also to be found in Colossians, which we may regard as certainly Pauline. But before assenting to the theory that St. Paul transformed the Gospel into a very un-Jewish worship of Kyrios Christos, we must remember the vast difference that the Christian 'Lord' was a historical person who had lately lived and died in Palestine. The Church never wavered in its refusal to take part in the fusion of divinities which was so marked a feature of later antiquity.

Those who quite rightly find the mainspring of St. Paul's faith in his consciousness of the presence of the Holy Spirit within him have sometimes asked why he so confidently identified this indwelling Spirit with Jesus of Nazareth, whom he probably never knew in the flesh. The cult of Jesus as the Christ had begun before the conversion of St. Paul, and must be traced back to the Easter experiences of the apostles, which convinced them that their Master was alive. To Paul the Jew it had been a shocking thing to connect the idea of the Messiah with one who had died the most shameful of deaths. The Acts leads us to suppose that the vision on the way to Damascus altered his whole life. Such visions were common experiences at the time. But it is not likely that the change was unprepared for; we should be almost sorry to think that St. Paul became an apostle instead of a persecutor in consequence of something he saw in the sky. The heroic martyrdom of Stephen, which he witnessed at close quarters, may well have raised questionings in his mind. The apparent suddenness of the mystical revelation is quite normal; Plato in his undoubtedly genuine Seventh Letter speaks of the 'leaping spark' by which divine inspiration flashes on the mind. St. Paul is very reticent about the manner in which he 'saw' Christ, when it pleased God to reveal His Son 'in' him. But he speaks of other 'visions and revelations,' of one in particular 'fourteen years ago'; he could 'speak with tongues'; and, like Socrates, he had an inner monitor, 'the Spirit of Jesus,' which on one occasion made him alter his plans. But these experiences do not seem to have been frequent; we gather that the occasion when he seemed to himself to have been caught up into the third heaven was unique. In any case, as soon as he was convinced that Jesus actually was what His disciples believed Him to be, he was overwhelmed by deep love and gratitude towards the crucified and glorified Lord, who had humbled Himself to leave His station 'in the form of God' in order to 'empty Himself,' and 'become obedient unto death, even the death of the cross,' for our sakes. Such an example could only call forth a lifetime of devotion.

We shall not fully understand the Christology of St. Paul unless we take account of a conception of history which is not familiar to us. 'It is certain,' says Wrede, 'that Jewish apocalyptic books are cognisant of a Messiah who before his appearance lives in heaven and is more exalted than the angels themselves.' This is the doctrine which we find in the famous second chapter of Philippians, with the addition that as a reward for His sufferings Christ was exalted to a yet higher dignity than He had before, namely equality with God, and was given the name of Lord (Kyrios).[1] For St. Paul, Christ was, we may say, waiting in heaven till 'the fullness of the time was come.' But he was also the archetypal man, the second Adam. History is a kind of dramatization of the eternal purposes of God, a revelation in time of a reality which is above time. Putting together this conception of history with the doctrine of Christ as the archetypal man, we see that what our old divines called the whole process of Christ, His life, death, resurrection and ascension, must be re-enacted in little in the experience of the Christian. Thus the events of our Lord's life on earth, and in particular the story of the Passion, are very closely linked with the normal process of the spiritual life. St. Paul is willing no longer to 'know Christ after the flesh,' that is, to say, as the actor in an isolated human tragedy. It is the eternal, universal, ever present Christ, who nevertheless became very man and suffered

---

[1] In spite of the opinion of Lightfoot and other scholars, I am convinced that the disputed phrase ἁρπαγμὸν ἡγήσατο, means 'counted it a light thing'; ἁρπαγμὸς or ἅρπαγμα (there is no difference in meaning), means something picked up without trouble. It was a colloquial phrase.

for our sakes, on whom his thoughts love to dwell. 'The things that are seen are temporary,' but they are the sacraments of eternal and ultimate truth. In Colossians the Son is the 'image'[1] of the invisible God, the 'fullness' of God in bodily form.

What has been rightly called Christ-mysticism is the kernel of St. Paul's religion. It is not a doctrine about Christ; it is fellowship with Christ, not with a figure in past history, but with a life giving power, a spiritual reality and energy transforming and at the same time perfecting his character, and enabling him to 'put on the new man.' Christ is 'highly exalted' at 'the right hand of God,' and yet is the indwelling Spirit, very near to men and women here on earth. 'The Lord is the Spirit,' he says. The Spirit is called indifferently the Spirit of God and the Spirit of Christ; we need not think of 'three Persons.' The same experience is meant, whether St. Paul speaks of Christ living in us, or of the Spirit dwelling in us, or of our bodies as the temple of God. The apostle dwells much more frequently on the indwelling of the Spirit of Christ than on His exaltation at the right hand of God. The formula 'in Christ,' or 'in the Lord,' occurs, says Deissmann, 164 times in St. Paul.

Such an experience, so profound a conviction, must in a thoughtful mind imply a psychology. St. Paul adopts a tripartite analysis of human personality. There is the flesh, which is our animal nature; the psychical man; and the spiritual man. He also speaks of 'the body' as the 'tabernacle' of the soul while we live here. The body must be reverenced and preserved from defilement because it is the temple of the Holy Spirit. In a sense it is a part of ourselves; for though St. Paul emphatically rejects the resurrection of 'the flesh,' which 'cannot inherit the Kingdom of God,' there is a 'spiritual body' which is prepared for us when the body of flesh is dissolved. If he speaks disparagingly of the psychical man, we may remember the tremendous words of our Lord, that we must be willing to lose our *psyche* in order to save it. It is not possible to be sure exactly what the Aramaic original of these words meant, and we must be cautious of importing the psychology of Platonism into the Synoptic Gospels; but clearly our Lord did not mean merely the risk of physical death. The psychical man, for St. Paul, is the self of our normal experience. For the Platonists, the soul is the wanderer of the metaphysical world. We are, I repeat, amphibious creatures, living partly in the world of ponderable things and partly in the world of imponderable values. The psychical man is therefore unstable. He may rise to the spiritual man, or he may sink to the carnal man, or, as most of us do, he may fluctuate uneasily between the two. The highest stage in our ascent, or we may say the highest part of our nature, is what St. Paul calls *pneuma* and the Platonists *nous*. The Greek Fathers were well aware that these two words are practically synonymous. The *pneuma* is both ourselves and not ourselves; it is the realization of what God meant us to be. We might quote several sayings in St. Paul's epistles which convey

---

[1] The Greek word εἰκών is the same that Plato uses in his words that time is the moving image of eternity. An εἰκών has much more reality than an εἴδωλον.

this doctrine. 'God hath sealed us, and given the earnest of the Spirit in our hearts.' 'If Christ be in you, the body is dead because of sin, but the Spirit is life because of righteousness.' The necessity of putting off, killing, even crucifying 'the old man' is often dwelt upon, as it is by almost all the mystics. 'He that soweth to the Spirit shall of the Spirit reap everlasting life.' The immortal part of the human person is something not belonging to the natural man to start with; we must make it our own. I do not however think that St. Paul held the doctrine of 'conditional immortality.' Such a doctrine involves an almost Manichean dualism, and contradicts the belief, common to all the best theologians, that the soul of man cannot pass out of existence into nothingness.

The chief difference, I think, between the psychology of St. Paul and that of the Platonists, is that St. Paul once speaks of defilements of the flesh *and spirit*. For the Platonist, *nous* is impeccable. We may remember that St. Paul believed in evil spirits; there is no devil in Platonism. But St. Paul does not write with the precision of a philosopher; he might have agreed that the defilements belong rather to *psyche* than to *pneuma*. He certainly held the conviction common to all mystics that there is at the centre of the soul a spiritual presence which can never consent to sin. This is the Holy Spirit, or Spirit of Christ, or the immanent Christ, who may be grieved, quenched, driven away from the impure heart, but certainly cannot Himself suffer defilement.

Before leaving St. Paul we must add that in his later epistles the thought that 'we are all made to drink into *one* Spirit' is increasingly prominent. In the spiritual life personality is not abolished, but individual separateness is transcended. This is a doctrine of very great importance. It assisted the growth of ecclesiasticism in Christianity, but it also shows us the real basis of charity. As some Indian teachers say, we ought to love our neighbours because we *are* our neighbours. We should love our neighbours as ourselves because love breaks down all barriers, even the barrier between 'me' and 'thee.'

The Epistle to the Hebrews, which in my opinion was written between A.D. 90 and 96, is notable as the only book of the New Testament which was written by a scholar for scholars, and as one of the earliest attempts at a philosophy of history. Those for whom the essay was composed were threatened with persecution, and were discouraged at the failure of the expectation, so strongly held in the first century, of an approaching return of Christ to earth. The author has done for faith and hope what St. Paul did for charity. He writes as a Jewish Christian who is also a Platonist. He combines the Jewish belief in a divine education of mankind by means of historical events with the Greek belief that all happenings in time and place are types and shadows of the eternal verities which abide for ever, pure and unchanged, in the counsels of God. This sacramental view of history is profoundly Christian. The hand of providence can be traced in history. And yet, as the Quaker Isaac Penington says, 'Every truth is shadow except the last. Yet every truth is substance in its own place, though it be but shadow in another place. And the shadow is true shadow, as the substance is true substance.'

Earth is the shadow of heaven, and we who seek a country of our own are but strangers and pilgrims on earth. The writer says to his readers, 'You are disillusioned and unhappy and tempted to give up your Christian faith. Come, let us consider what are the lessons of past history, and what faith and hope really mean.' Revelation has been gradual, historical, progressive. It has culminated in the Incarnation of the Son of God, who is the brightness of the Father's glory, who was the instrument in creation, who carries forward all things through the word of His power, and who is also the heir of all things. Here we have the doctrine of the cosmic Christ, which St. Paul in his latest epistles lays down, and which the Fourth Gospel develops with the help of the idea of the Logos. Christ as man, and man as one with Christ, are made lower than the angels, but may rise higher than they, for the greater pain and the greater gain are theirs. For what is physical death? The globe itself shall fade away like an unsubstantial pageant, but Thou, O Lord, art the same and Thy years shall not fail. Even Christ was made perfect through suffering; He was without sin, but His life had a purpose through which it may be said to be perfected. And His redeeming death is not only something that He suffered; it is something that we must do. To suffer for others is a divine prerogative; it is the glory and offence of the Cross. The chosen people lost the promised 'rest' because they lost heart and patience. *Nimis avide consolationem quaerere*—is not this the secret of failure in small things and in great? Like St. Paul, he compares the Christian course to a long-distance race. The saints and heroes of old are on the spectators' seats; Jesus is waiting for us at the goal. The men of old received not the promises, nor were they ever fulfilled quite as they hoped. The splendours and terrors of the old dispensation were only shadows of the new. But ye, he says, are come—come already—to the city of the living God. The kingdom that cannot be shaken is all about us, is ours already. Let us therefore serve God acceptably with reverence and godly fear. For it is only perfect love that casteth out fear, and we are still on the road.

The unknown author of the Fourth Gospel was probably such a man as Apollos is described, a theologian well acquainted with the Jewish-Alexandrian philosophy of religion of which Philo is for us the chief representative. He is often considered the chief exponent of mysticism in the New Testament. But we do not find in him the personal experience which made St. Paul a mystic. Rather he accepts the doctrine of St. Paul and develops it with the power of a religious genius, showing for all time the permanent meaning of the Incarnation. He writes for the third generation of Christians, and deals with the opponents of what we may already call the Catholic faith—the hostility of the Jews, which at the end of the first century was bitter and vindictive; with the beginnings of Gnosticism, which threatened to sever the tie which bound the Church to the historical Jesus, and apparently with a Baptist faction, now almost forgotten. Messianism, though not repudiated, is practically shelved; the gift of the Holy Spirit makes the dream of the second coming almost meaningless. The cosmic Christ, whose presence in the world is continued in the presence of the Paraclete, is now called the Logos, a name with a long and interesting history. It begins with Heracleitus of Ephesus, whose works unhappily survive only in meagre fragments. His Logos is a cosmic, all-pervading principle of reason, the divine reason immanent in nature and in man. In Plato and Aristotle its place is taken by the *Nous* of Anaxagoras, but the name was revived by the Stoics as the rational and generative principle out of which the world after its destruction by fire may be born anew. For the Stoic, man's duty and happiness is to live in accordance with the law of the universe. In the Old Testament and Apocrypha the Word of the Creator is personified in the poetical language of the Psalms, and in the later books the divine Kochmah or Wisdom is an analogous conception. The value of the doctrine of a cosmic Spirit, active in history, is often denied. But all through this study we shall meet with the same problem, how to connect the Godhead, who is absolutely transcendent, with the Creator and ruler of the universe. The problem can never be solved, because the Godhead 'dwelleth in the light which no man can approach unto,' a blinding light which is too much like darkness. The Fourth Gospel insists that God 'works' in the world, but He works through the Logos, who is Himself God, though not the Godhead. The evangelist, like St. Paul, makes all the theophanies in the Old Testament Christophanies, and (which is very important), makes our Lord promise that the Paraclete will reveal to the Church not only the meaning of His discourses on earth, but many things which His disciples are now unable to bear. The principle of what we should now call evolution in religion had never been so clearly stated before.

The form chosen is that of a Gospel, a 'spiritual Gospel' as Clement calls it. The divine attributes of the exalted Christ are boldly ·thrown back into His earthly life. The whole narrative is pervaded by symbolism. The miracles are acted parables; a numerical arrangement, in which the sacred numbers three and seven can be found, though not paraded, all through, was no doubt valued at the time. There is also an intense and almost harsh moral dualism, such as we find in the *Theologia Germanica* and some other mystical writings.

Although the Fourth Gospel has been rightly called the best commentary on St. Paul's epistles, there are certain differences. The Pauline doctrine of *kenosis*, the self-emptying of Christ, disappears; the Passion is part of the 'glory,' which might be the title of the third section of the Gospel, beginning at chapter thirteen. We do not find in the Gospel the necessity to slay 'the old man' in our nature.

We need not here discuss the mystical elements in the other books of the New Testament.

The union of the soul with God is far more inward than that of the soul and body. . . . Now, I might ask, how stands it with the soul that is lost in God? Does the soul find herself or not? To this I will answer as it appears to me, that the soul finds herself in the point where every rational being understands itself with itself. Although it sinks in the eternity of the divine essence, yet it can never reach the ground. Therefore God has left a little point wherein the soul turns back upon itself and finds itself, and knows itself to be a creature.—ECKHART.

The thought of death leaves me in perfect peace, for I have a firm conviction that our spirit is a being of indestructible nature; it works on from eternity to eternity; it is like the sun, which though it seems to set to our mortal eyes, does not really set, but shines on perpetually.—GOETHE.

> But that fair lamp, from whose celestial ray
> That light proceeds which kindleth lovers' fire,
> Shall never be extinguished nor decay;
> But when the vital spirits do expire,
> Unto her native planet shall retire:
> For it is heavenly born and cannot die,
> Being a parcel of the purest sky.
>
> SPENSER.

CHAPTER IV

THE PROBLEM OF PERSONALITY

I F we confine our attention to the West we shall be in danger of leaving incomplete our survey of a type of religion which, as has been said, is singularly uniform in all countries, in all periods, and in all the higher religions. If we agree with Justin Martyr that Heracleitus and Socrates were Christians before Christ, and with Augustine that what is now called Christianity was in existence from the first, we shall not have any scruple in looking outside the Churches for illustrations of our subject, whether in the religious philosophy of India or in the religious metaphysics of the Orphics and Platonists. We may find reason for agreeing with Whitehead that 'the decay of Christianity and Buddhism, as determinative influences in modern thought, is partly due to the fact that each religion has unduly sheltered itself from the other. They have remained self-satisfied and unfertilized.' We may admit this without any wish to become Buddhists or Hindus instead of Christians. In this book I have not forgotten (who can forget?) the crisis through which Western civilization is passing, and though mysticism is very independent of time and place, parts of its message have been more acceptable in some civilizations and in some climates of opinion than in others, and modern Europe has perhaps not been a very favourable field for the religion of the Spirit.

The greatest advances in civilization have been due to the interaction of two cultures. The flowering time of Greek civilization followed the fusion of the northern invaders with the Ægean inhabitants. The Jews were subjected to Babylonian, Persian, and Greek influences; Persian religion especially left a very decided mark on their beliefs. Christianity as a world religion is essentially a blend of late Hebraic and Hellenistic thought. In many parts of Western Christendom the reciprocal influence of Teutonic and Latin traditions and modes of thinking has had fruitful results.

We all know that our civilization is in great danger, and most of us agree that our only hope is in a revival of spiritual religion, with a recognition of absolute values, and a devotion to whatever things are true, just, noble, and of good report. But where shall we look for our prophets? It is not the clergy but laymen and free lances who are taking the lead, and more and more they are turning to the wisdom of the East. Radhakrishnan gives a long and imposing list of Western thinkers who have owned deep obligations to India. The list includes English, French, Germans, and, significantly, several Americans. I know no Indian languages and have not visited the country; but translations of great Indian books such as the Bhagavadgita, and able works in English by Indians, leave no doubt as to the salient features of the mystical religion which has developed in that ancient and stable civilization.

The fundamental doctrine of Indian religion is that the self-conscious ego, the subject of rights and duties, is not the real self. Consciousness is never more than a mirror of reality; it creates nothing. Its main function seems to be to supersede instinct when the environment is changing. The ego can only know itself as object, and the object is not the self.

The Spirit of man—Atman, Nous, Pneuma—is different from the empirical ego. It is timeless and deathless, say the Indians. In the famous words of the Bhagavadgita, translated by Edwin Arnold—

> Never the Spirit was born; the Spirit can cease to be never;
> Never the time it was not; end and beginning are dreams.
> Birthless and deathless and changeless the Spirit abideth for ever;
> Death cannot touch it at all, dead though the house of it seems.

The Spirit is the background of the being which we share with other persons. It is superhistorical and free from space and time. The spiritual world is our true home. Salvation consists in deliverance from the world of change and decay. 'The world passeth away and the lust thereof, but he that doeth the will of God abideth for ever.'

As for the genuineness of the superindividual presence within us, there can be no doubt whatever. The mystics all speak with the same voice. Radhakrishnan says, 'We have a direct and immediate consciousness of reality, a vision of the real, a perception of the truth. This intuitive perception is the illumination and enhancement of our being. In all of us there dwells a secret spirit, a power of freeing ourselves from the changes of time, of discovering to ourselves the eternal in the form of unchanging consciousness.' We may think that Eckhart went too far when he speaks of the 'something in the soul which is above the soul, divine, simple, superessential essence, the simple ground in which there is no distinction, neither Father, Son, nor Holy Ghost, the unity where no man dwelleth.' This recalls the extravagant language of 'Dionysius the Areopagite,' who thinks that we can enter into relations with the absolute Godhead, beyond even the distinction of the three Persons of the Trinity. But we may trust St. Augustine when he says, 'I entered into my inmost self, thou being my guide. I entered and beheld with the eye of my soul, above the eye of my soul, above my mind, the light unchangeable. . . . It was something altogether different from any earthly illumination. Nor was it above my mind as oil is above water or heaven above earth. It was higher because it made me; I was lower because I was made by it. He who knows the truth knows that light, and he who knows that light knows eternity. Love knows that light.' 'All minds partake of one original mind,' says Cudworth. Why should we regard human nature as most itself when it is least inspired? We find ourselves, says John Caird, in that which seems to lie beyond us. The unanimity of the mystics, William James says, ought to make the critic stop and think. Aldous Huxley, a convert to mysticism, is convinced that the mystics have shown that those who have been trained in recollection and meditation 'can obtain direct experience of a spiritual unity underlying the apparent diversity of independent consciousness. They make it clear that what seemed to be the ultimate fact of personality is

c

not an ultimate fact.' He goes on to say that individuals may merge their private consciousness in the greater impersonal consciousness underlying the personal mind. This would probably be accepted by most Indian thinkers, but it goes a little beyond both Platonism and Christianity. For the Christian, the love of God is certainly not a higher Narcissism; there is no loss of personality, and no worship of an impersonal Deity. Keyserling to be sure says that mysticism always ends in an impersonal immortality.[1] But impersonal is a negative word. We may doubt whether we should call God a Person, but we may say that there is personality in God, for otherwise there can be no prayer except contemplation. Plotinus, the greatest philosopher among the mystics, insists that in heaven—'yonder'—personality in man is preserved. The doctrine of the universal self, so safeguarded, goes far to reconcile the divergent ideals of self-sacrifice and self-realization. The apparent contradiction proves not, as Bradley thinks, that goodness is only appearance, but that the self-conscious ego is not wholly real. The self that is sacrificed is not the same as the self that is realized. We can never get outside ourselves, but what St. Paul calls the old man is not the real self.

The love of God, says St. Teresa, is our true self. She heard God saying to her, 'However high thou shalt go, however great a perfection thou mayest have, the higher will I stand above all, to ruin all thy perfection.' This is not pantheism, for reality is a kingdom of values, and values are always hierarchical. For the pantheist, God is 'as full, as perfect, in a hair as heart,' Pope's words, which the Hegelians are fond of putting in the pillory. Emerson, in his admiration for the Indians, sometimes does not avoid this pitfall. His stanza containing the words, 'I am the doubter and the doubt, and I the hymn the Brahmin sings,' has been wittily parodied by Andrew Lang. I do not think that any of the great mystics are pantheists. Plotinus speaks of the 'soul made spirit' as 'always attaining and always aspiring,' and Proclus says that 'all things pray, except the Supreme.' The ladder of perfection, in the phrase of Hylton, one of the most attractive of the fourteenth-century English mystics, reaches from earth to heaven.

Belief in the reality of the lower self is expressed by self-assertion, greed and sensuality. The antidotes are discipline, humility and love. In the spiritual world there is no separation except what comes from discordance of nature, but persons, though transfigured, remain distinct. If individuality is a mere illusion, the love of our neighbour fares no better than the love of God.

We cannot love our own higher selves, but neither, I think, can we love 'a valid inference.' The Catholic Neo-Thomists refuse to employ the ontological argument. Direct knowledge of the existence of God they call ontologism, and deny that it is possible. It is true that Thomas Aquinas will not use the ontological argument, but he rejects only the common travesty of it, which Kant has no difficulty in demolishing. St. Thomas was personally a mystic, as he showed by laying aside his controversial studies which he found no longer necessary after the intuitive

---

[1] Keyserling, *Immortality*, p. 175.

revelation which had been granted him.[1] When he says, *impossibile est naturale desiderium esse inane*—'It is impossible that a natural craving should be a delusion,' he admits all that the ontological argument really means. Quite strictly it is not impossible that our purest longings should be in a conspiracy to deceive us, but it is what Lotze calls intolerable. In all philosophy we reach a point where we must trust ourselves. It is a reasonable act of faith. Modern Catholic theologians are not really far away from the doctrine of the eternal self which the Indians prize so much. For instance, E. I. Watkin in his learned work, *The Philosophy of Form*,[2] which is mainly Aristotelian rather than Platonic, says, 'I am aware of an abiding Ego which persists identical and relatively changeless. To this changeless factor the measures of Time cannot apply.'

We may say perhaps that the aim of the mystic is to bring the dark background into the light, to conquer it for consciousness. It should not remain bare of contents, but he is anxious not to contaminate it with infusions from the surface consciousness, whether intellectual or affective. He wishes to interrogate the background which is still dark, and to obtain its answer. The margin of the region in twilight 'fades for ever and for ever as we move,' but the proportion of our mental life which is subliminal and irrational should diminish. The region of twilight is itself of great value, since in our present state we must always see 'as in a mirror by means of images.' This means that we must not scorn or reject our 'psychical' experience, because it is not yet 'spiritual.' We have to try to discover the spiritual meaning of which it is the sacrament. But in Indian thought the renunciation of the instrumental values is very thorough. The Bhagavadgita says:

> Seek refuge in thy soul, have there thy heaven;
> Scorn them that follow virtue for her gifts.

The intrusion of hedonism or utilitarianism into religion has been resented by those who have seen that disinterestedness lies at the heart of all higher religion. Pleasure, says Seneca, is our companion, not our guide. We delight in the good because we have chosen it; we have not chosen it because it delights us. 'If a man seeks the good life for any reason outside itself,' says Plotinus, 'it is not the good life that he seeks.' Spinoza with equal emphasis says that we must seek not the rewards of virtue but virtue for itself. How ruthlessly does Plato in the second book of the Republic tear away every prop which might help him in his argument that righteousness must be followed 'in scorn of consequence.' The righteous man may be misunderstood, vilified, tortured, and at last crucified[3]; but it is still better to be righteous than to be thought so.

The error of following the negative road, the renunciation of the natural man and his interests, as the only path to the knowledge of God,

[1] The story has been beautifully told by Robert Bridges, in the first book of his *Testament of Beauty*.

[2] Page 60.

[3] The Greek word means 'impaled'; but the two methods of execution were often combined, if we may judge from the craven prayer of Maecenas: '*Vita si superest bene est. Hanc mihi vel acuta si sedeam cruce sustine.*'

has been often exposed. It is caused partly by the desire to be invulnerable and relieved from inner discordance, which is one of the roots of
asceticism. It may for some be the shortest road to disinterestedness to
abjure all human interests; but when Plato insists that the philosopher
must come back to the cave to help the prisoners there, he half recognizes
that the true philosophy of life must be incarnational. Our path is one
of withdrawal and return, not of withdrawal only, and the motive of
both is love. This is so generally acknowledged that we need not spend
more space in rebutting a pathetic error which has brought mysticism
into discredit both in Europe and in Asia. A journey through the unreal
is an unreal journey. The heaven which we reach by scorning everything
in this world is the shoreless ocean of Nirvana. We may admit this without
falling into the vulgar error of disparaging the contemplative life. The
practical worker wants to make things happen; the philosopher, the poet
and the mystic want to understand and set a value upon what always is.
There is room for both types. 'See that thou make all things according
to the pattern showed thee in the mount.' These are the marching orders
of the true mystic. R. L. Nettleship says: 'True mysticism is the consciousness that everything which we experience is only an element in the
fact, i.e., that in being what it is it is symbolic of more.' The Atonement
means that 'God can only make his work to be truly His own work by
eternally sacrificing what is dearest to Him. Suppose that all human beings
felt permanently to each other as they now do occasionally to those they
love best. All the world would be swallowed up in the joy of doing good.
So far as we can conceive such a state, it would be one in which there
would be no individuals, but a universal being in and for another;
where being took the form of consciousness, it would be consciousness of
'another' which was also 'oneself'—a common consciousness. Such would
be the 'atonement' of the world.'

Before dismissing the method of abstraction as a pure mistake, one
fact may be remembered. Until the Reformation most of the great
mystics had agreed that we should try to think of God 'without the help
of images.' This may have been partly because the Supreme Being,
'whom no man hath seen or can see,' cannot be likened in imagination
to any visible form. The precept, approved by so many masters of the
spiritual life, must be treated with respect. But at the Counter-Reforma-
tion, says Dom John Chapman, 'the dogmatic theologians were rising
up against mystical theology. The Dominicans ignored it; the Jesuits
denied its very existence.' It was the object of Jesuit devotion not to
suppress the desire to form images but to stimulate it to the fullest extent.
Mysticism became ecstatic and violently emotional. From that time to
this, he says, there have not been many great mystics in the Roman
Church. But differences of temperament must be allowed for; some people
are visualists, others are not. One danger of unrestrained image-making
is that it sometimes leads to hallucinations. This danger is recognized
by the best mystical writers.

The language of deification, common in mystical literature, sounds
arrogant and almost blasphemous to those who do not realize how much

more stiff and personal our word God is than the Greek *Theos* as used in antiquity. Professor Gilbert Murray gives many examples of a very loose employment of the word in the Greek poets.[1] The apotheosis of the emperors, a Hellenistic importation into the West, illustrates the vagueness of the idea. Vespasian's last joke, *Vae! puto Deus fio*, would not sound so comic in Greek. The 'barbarous people' of Malta and of Galatia were ready to deify the apostles. But *theos* meant particularly an immortal, and the gift of immortality conferred deification. This notion is quite common in the Greek fathers. Theophilus says that man by keeping the commandments of God may receive immortality as a reward, and may 'become God.' That 'Christ became man in order that we might become God' is stated by Athanasius and other orthodox divines. The Hermetic texts are full of the doctrine, sometimes expressed almost materialistically.

The Church thus found the idea of deification firmly imbedded in the thought of the time. As Judaistic Christianity, Messianic and apocalyptic, faded away, the Greek idea of immortality gained ground. A favourite phrase was that Christ by His Incarnation abolished death, and brought mankind into a state of incorruption, which is sometimes called 'God-making' (θεοποίησις).

But as I said in an appendix to my *Christian Mysticism*, deification may be conceived either as essentialization or as substitution. The former was the doctrine of the Platonists—'the throne of the Godhead is the mind of man'; the latter was the doctrine of the mysteries, in which the divine element was sacramentally imparted or infused. Platonism insists that we can only know what is akin to ourselves. If there were nothing godlike in human nature we could not know God. Orthodox theology repudiated with horror the notion that man is of the same nature (ὁμοούσιος) as the Father; but spiritual union with the Logos-Christ was not inconceivable. Christian divines were only concerned to insist that the divine Spirit is not *divided* among the creatures, and that they are not essential *parts* of Spirit. Eckhart, following Plotinus in his doctrine of an impeccable soul-centre, taught that at the core of the soul there is a 'spark,' which is 'so akin to God that it is one with God and not merely united to Him.' The queer word *Synteresis*, the *scintilla conscientiæ* which is not extinguished even in the worst sinners, occurs first in Jerome. Meanwhile, the Arabian philosophers were developing Aristotle's doctrine of the Active Reason, 'separate, impassible and immortal' into a theory of an impersonal higher self, distinct from the lower soul, which, unless it can unite itself with the higher, perishes at death. Eckhart was condemned, it appears wrongly, for saying that the soul centre was uncreated. These theories are obviously in close accordance with Indian thought. The *Theologia Germanica* is non-committal. 'The true light is that eternal Light which is God; or else it is a created light, though divine, which is called grace.' It is interesting that while Plotinus taught that the higher soul is impeccable, most of his successors deserted him here. 'If the will can sin,' asks Iamblichus, 'how can the soul be impeccable?'

[1] *Five Stages of Greek Religion*, pp. 12, 13.

Between the ideas of essential immanence and of substitution of the divine life for the human comes that of gradual transformation. 'Love changes the lover into the beloved.' This is perhaps the truest doctrine. 'We shall be like Him, for we shall see Him as He is.' But this is a change not to be completed in this life.

But what is the Divine into whose likeness we aspire to be progressively transformed? Plotinus, though his heaven is the rich intelligible or spiritual world, in which our individuality is preserved, believes that on certain rare occasions the human soul may transcend even the realm of spirit, and enter into communion with the One 'beyond existence,' of whom nothing positive can be affirmed.[1] The reasons for this belief may be given shortly. First, there is the actual experience of the blank trance, in which the contemplative seems to have left behind all distinctions. Second, there is the metaphysical argument that since reality consists in the unity in duality of subject and object, perceived by the intelligence to be coextensive and reciprocally necessary, there must be an absolute unity from which Spirit and the spiritual world proceed. Thirdly, the beatified spirit must have something still to aspire to, since aspiration is part of the spiritual life. Indian thought develops this speculation to its logical conclusion. But the claim that human nature, even at its highest stretch, can apprehend the Absolute, is probably a mistake. The strange language of the mystics on this subject is enough to give us pause. 'The *Atman* is silence,' say the Hindus. The pseudo-Dionysius calls God the Father 'the absolute No-thing which is above all existence,' and declares that 'no monad or triad can express the all-transcending hiddenness of the all-transcending superessentially superexisting superdeity.' 'God because of his excellence may rightly be called Nothing,' says Scotus Erigena. 'Not this, not this,' say the Indians of every attempt to form a picture of the Absolute. 'Christ himself never arrived at the emptiness of which these men talk,' says Tauler, who nevertheless uses much the same language.

What is the connection between the negative road and 'the dark night of the soul,' the terrible experience of dereliction described by several Catholic mystics[2]? It has been suggested by Aldous Huxley that the Christian contemplative begins with a religion of personal devotion to God or Christ, and then finds that as he or she progresses in spiritual experience God ceases to be a Person and becomes as it were a climate. There is much truth, he would say, in Keyserling's opinion that extreme mysticism, whether it wills it or not, ends in an impersonal view of immortality. And it may be that the fading of personal relationship with God sometimes causes acute distress. But neither the Indians nor the Neoplatonists nor the Christian philosophical mystics seem to have had the experience of the dark night, though they followed the same road.

[1] I have elsewhere protested against the practice of modern writers on Neoplatonism who call the One, the Good, or the Supreme of Plotinus, 'God.' His whole philosophy is thus thrown out of gear.

[2] Dom Butler says: 'From the twelfth century onwards the thoughts of the mystics have been coloured by the theories of Dionysius'; it was he who introduced the language about 'the divine dark.'

I think that the misery which the cloistered mystics describe so vividly was mainly the result of nervous overstrain. Those who escaped it were not as a rule extreme ascetics. The Platonist lives in hard training, but does not 'buffet the body' like Suso and John of the Cross and other fanatical devotees of renunciation.

As for the aspiration to union with the 'One beyond existence,' I think we must follow Eckhart in distinguishing between the Godhead and God. Not, of course, that they are two Beings, but the God of religion is not the ineffable Absolute, but the God Who reveals Himself to man in the creation and in the human soul. What we know of God, apart from prayer, which is not merely a soliloquy or a spiritual dumbbell exercise, is mainly from our apprehension of His revealed nature as perfect Goodness or Love, as Truth, and as Beauty. In prayer we speak to Him as to a Being Who can hear and answer us. Such intercourse could not be held with the Godhead, the Absolute. Hooker says wisely: 'Dangerous it were for the feeble brain of man to wade far into the doings of the Most High; whom although to know be life, and joy to make mention of his name, yet our soundest knowledge is to know that we know him not as indeed he is, neither can know him. Our safest eloquence concerning him is our silence.' Critics of Plotinus often forget his warning that to aspire to rise above *Nous* is to fall outside it.

The religion of the Vedanta, says Swami Abhedananda,[1] admits that Brahman has two aspects, one without any attribute, and the other, who is called the Ruler of the universe, with attributes. The latter is the personal God, who is the first-born Lord of the world. He is the efficient cause of all phenomena. All things live and move and have their 'being' in him, and he can be loved and worshipped. While the Absolute is the transcendent divine, God is the cosmic divine. The God of religion is the Absolute in the world context. He is personal in the sense that He has an environment on which He acts. The Absolute is evidently super-personal. It may be said that to the mystic God ceases to be an object and becomes an atmosphere; but does the mystic ever cease to pray to One who is not himself? Far from it.

This distinction between the Godhead and God may seem to identify the God of religion with the Soul of the world, an immanent pantheistic Spirit whose life is bound up with the time process. This notion of God has been very widely accepted in modern thought, for more than one reason. Metaphysics tends to be monistic, morality dualistic, aesthetics pluralistic. For the moralist the world is an arena in which good and evil are contending for supremacy. One of the problems of philosophy is that while the metaphysician, especially if he adopts the shallow Hegelian optimism that 'the real is the rational,' often arranges experience in a hierarchy of 'degrees of reality,' all of them with positive signs, the moralist knows that he must admit minus as well as positive signs. The bad is not merely appearance; in our experience it is as real as the good. Either then the Creator must be the author of evil as well as of good, or He is engaged in war with a power not Himself. In other words, the

[1] *Contemporary Indian Philosophy*, p. 57.

moralist, as moralist, is more than half a Manichean. God, as the moralist knows Him, is a limited struggling power, Who needs our assistance to carry out His wishes, perhaps even to 'realize Himself.' This moralistic argument is reinforced by the world-view of those thinkers who, like the late Professor Alexander, wish to 'take Time seriously.' For them the cosmic process is a real movement, and for most of them a movement towards perfection. They are still infected by the great superstition of the nineteenth century. God therefore is gradually coming into His own; He is 'emerging' or, with Alexander, He has given notice that He is about to emerge. If the doctrine of entropy, 'the principle of Carnot,' is true, and the universe is slowly running down like a clock, this God is under sentence of death, though He may have a long time in which to realize Himself; for without the world, according to these thinkers, He is nothing.

This theory, avowed by many philosophers and accepted though not emphasized by many others, is far from satisfying the religious consciousness. Even if we could believe that the good was on its way towards a complete victory in Time, that would not content us. The object of our worship 'sitteth above the waterflood and remaineth a King for ever.' 'Before the mountains were brought forth, or ever the earth and the world were made, thou art God from everlasting and world without end.' Coleridge expressed the divergence between Christianity and modern philosophy neatly by saying, 'If G. equals God, and W. equals the world, then for these philosophers $G—W=O$, whereas for Christianity $G—W= G$.' Our real self is not the captive of Space and Time; still less can this be believed of the object of our worship. And yet while we are in the flesh we are 'workers together with God,' as the moralist tells us. Because we are 'amphibious beings,' there are and must be ragged edges in our beliefs.

The doctrine of rebirth has had a long history. There is much in natural science which seems to support it. The germ-plasm is potentially immortal. What looks like unconscious inherited memory is common in the animal creation. Who taught the chick to break out of its egg? Who taught the spider to spin and the rooks to build? Why are our horses terrified at the smell of a menagerie lion? Why are we afraid of snakes? There are countless examples of faculties which it is difficult to account for except on the hypothesis of a long series of former existences. For Eastern thought death is part of a recurring rhythm in the history of the individual. In answer to the objection that there can be no self without a body, many Indian thinkers, like St. Paul, postulate a 'spiritual body' made of some fine ethereal substance, which is the vehicle of the soul, though 'flesh and blood cannot inherit the Kingdom of God.' This conception is welcome to modern spiritualists, but it seems to me to be one of those intercalated categories which commend themselves to our wavering and nebulous imagination of the eternal world.

The doctrine of rebirth was held by some Gnostic sects and by the Manicheans. Origen accepted it. More recently, Giordano Bruno, Van Helmont, Swedenborg, Krause, Goethe, Lichtenberg,

Lavater, Schopenhauer, Ibsen, Maeterlinck, Robert Browning, McTaggart, were among the believers. Hume declared that it is the only doctrine of the kind worthy of the attention of a philosopher. The strongest argument for it is that our present lives are manifestly inadequate to determine our eternal destinies. I think we must be content to say that we do not know and cannot expect to know.

For the Greeks it was obvious that pre-existence and survival stand or fall together. Pre-existence and survival were fundamental tenets of the Orphics and Pythagoreans, and of their disciple Plato. For Plato the soul, instead of being an unsubstantial phantasm, is the man's real self. It is the most real thing we have and the most truly our own; it makes us all what we are. When we die, this immortal part of each of us goes to the gods to give an account of itself. Souls after death pass through an intermediate state of rewards and punishments, and then are reincarnated in a form suited to their merits or demerits in previous lives. Only the worst men are hurled into Tartarus for ever; the majority undergo a long purification in successive lives. Both for Plato and Aristotle eternal life is a prize which we win, 'as far as possible,' by thinking immortal thoughts, 'ascending in heart and mind,' as our collect says, to the timeless and changeless eternal world. For Aristotle the self-conscious ego perishes at death; what survives is the Active Reason, which is impersonal. Such at least seems to be his meaning, as Averroes for example believed, though it has been much disputed.

Reincarnation and Karma do not necessarily imply each other. The origin of the theory of Karma is the almost universal desire to justify the ways of God to man. Whatever a man reaps, he must have sown. This in India seems to be more thought of than the converse that what we sow we must some day reap. It is characteristic of the nebulous character of all eschatology that belief in exact retribution for good and evil in this world, for all actions done here, is combined with belief in posthumous and extramundane rewards and punishments, as indeed it is in Plato. The doctrine of Karma is said to appear first in the Upanishads, not in the Vedas. It was therefore not very old when it was adopted by Buddhism. It is difficult not to think that it should have no place in Buddhism, which denies the existence of a substantial soul. Universal justice and universal causality are affirmed by Buddhism, but strictly there is no continuity between the subjects of the rewards and penalties ordained by Karma. Probably the pious Buddhist does not ask whether it is himself who will receive the reward of his deeds. Those who labour for posterity do not ask this question.

Even in the Hindu version of the doctrine, does anything survive for a rebirth except the bare form of identity and its liabilities? The criticism most often made is that since there is no memory of previous existences there is no real survival of the personality and no real justice. This objection does not seem to me to carry weight. Apart from the fact of unconscious memory, which is perhaps the essence of instinct, how much of our present lives is lost to us, while yet 'what we have been makes us what we are.' Our sins which we have forgotten are not therefore forgiven, perhaps they are not forgiven because they are forgotten. If our past sins have become, as Julian of Norwich says, 'No longer wounds but worships,' that is because we have risen on stepping-stones of our dead selves to higher things; the question is whether we are still the same persons. Keyserling says too boldly that he can accept no personal responsibility for anything that he did more than fifteen years ago. H. G. Wells, in his contribution to the American volume called *Living Philosophies*, says that though he often echoes St. Paul's words, 'Who shall deliver me from the body of this death?' he cannot feel his identity with the youth who once bore his name. Even if the link between successive incarnations were no more than that between successive generations of the same family, who shall say that there is no real continuity, no sense of obligation and no fellow-feeling?

The real objection to the doctrine of Karma applies also to the Greek version of the theory, and I fear to popular Christian theodicy. Reward and punishment for moral merit and demerit ought surely to be *in pari materia*. It is not a fitting recompense for an evil life to be reborn blind, or a cripple, or a brute. This last notion is ridiculous; it was rejected by the later Neoplatonists, and can hardly have been held seriously by Plato and Plotinus, though it was seriously upheld by the Indians. 'The stealer of food shall be dyspeptic, the scandalmonger shall have foul breath, the horse-stealer shall go lame, stealers of grain and meats shall turn into rats and vultures, the thief who took dyed garments or perfume, shall become a red partridge or a muskrat.'[1] The doctrine was intended not so much as a prediction of the future as an explanation of the present condition of men. Whatever a man now reaps, he must have sown. The whole doctrine of rebirth is best regarded as a myth, which gives expression to a perhaps unwelcome truth, that we cannot form any picture of the survival of personality in time unless the soul has a concrete vehicle in the shape of a real body of flesh and blood. The ideas of 'intelligible matter,' and of a 'spiritual body' do not help us to realize future existences, though as symbols they may be defended.

The question about the legitimacy of hopes of reward and fears of punishment in the religious life must not be shirked, and it is not a little embarrassing. It is made much more difficult on the hypothesis that the self-conscious ego is the real person, for we cannot help thinking that almost all our neighbours as we know them, and perhaps we ourselves, are 'overbad for blessing and overgood for banning.' If the bad man's soul is lost, it is not the soul which would have been his if he had not been a bad man. The difficulty is this. Some of the saints are recorded to have wished that heaven and hell were blotted out, so that they might love God for Himself alone. Is not this the only state of mind which accords with the religion of love? Is not love notoriously incompatible with mercenary motives? Do we not agree with Spinoza that virtue is and must be its own reward, and with Plotinus that 'If a man seeks the good life for anything outside itself, it is not the good life that he is seeking'? A. C. Bradley in a remarkable passage quoted by Pringle

[1] Tylor, *Primitive Culture*, II, 8.

Pattison, says: 'The ideas of justice and desert are, it seems to me, in all cases untrue to our imaginative experience. This is a point of view which emerges only where, in reading a play, we slip, by our own fault or the dramatist's, from the tragic position, or when in thinking about a play afterwards we fall back on our everyday legal and moral notions. But tragedy does not belong, any more than religion belongs, to the sphere of these notions; neither does the imaginative attitude in presence of it.' And yet Christian theology has always insisted on future retribution as an ever-present hope and fear. It has pictured man as a pilgrim on his way to the realm of perfect bliss and happiness, in constant anxiety not only to obtain this prize, but to escape a fate of unimaginable horror. If we say that these are only crude images intended to entice and to terrify the half-converted, who would be deaf to appeals addressed to their higher motives, many would perhaps accept this compromising justification; but these hopes and fears are by no means absent in many spiritually minded Christians, and we cannot get over the fact that they are freely appealed to in the Synoptic Gospels. It would be very arbitrary criticism to argue that as Christ was above the heads of His reporters, they put into His mouth words and counsels which were more adapted to their unregenerate hearts than to the sublime purification of motive which He wished them to receive from Him. We cannot go behind our earliest records, which seem to appeal to two quite different motives; for in spite of the frequent references to rewards and punishments, it would be absurd to deny that we find true disinterestedness in the Gospels.

The evidence has been collected in a hostile spirit by Westermarck, and with candour and reverence by Bishop Kirk of Oxford in his Bampton Lectures. The Bishop points out that 'There are two strains of thought in the New Testament which appear to contradict and neutralize each other beyond all hope of reconciliation.' Complete disinterestedness is insisted on in many places; but the hope of reward is held out quite as plainly in many others. It would not be worth while to quote these passages: they are too numerous and too plain to be evaded. It is not surprising that opponents of Christianity have made the most of them.

Von Hügel has also discussed the subject at length in the second volume of his *Mystical Element in Religion*. He regards the so-called mercenary appeals in the Gospels as 'the traditional layer' in Christ's teaching. It is not agreeable to have to accept pre-Christian Jewish ideas, supported by the authority of Christ, on such a subject, though von Hügel, with his love of institutionalism, prefers the Synoptic Gospels, in parts of which such ideas are to be found, to the theology of St. Paul and the Johannine books. It is notorious that the Jews in many books of the Old Testament are preoccupied with the question, 'Shall not the judge of all the earth do right?' and that their theodicy demanded, at least ultimately, happiness and prosperity for the righteous, misery or destruction for the wicked. The book of Job is characteristic. After a profound treatment of the terrible problem of evil, it ends unexpectedly like a Victorian novel, with the restoration of Job's fortunes, and a new wife and children who apparently did as well as the old. But this is not the way we are dealt with in this world, and it would be a very poor account of the good tidings of great joy to say that our Lord, like Canning, 'called a new world into existence to redress the balance of the old.' It is easy to say that the rewards promised in the Gospels are such as would not appeal to a sensual or selfish man; but ought we to serve God for the sake of rewards, however we interpret them? There is very much in the Gospels in which what we cannot help thinking a deeper note is sounded.

The famous controversy between Bossuet and Fénelon turned on the possibility of pure love and disinterestedness. Fénelon was no Quietist, and Bossuet really had much sympathy with mysticism. Discreditable motives were undoubtedly at work in the attacks upon Fénelon and the devout if unwise Madame Guyon.

But the advocates of disinterestedness often went too far. It is not true that we ought to have no concern for our own salvation, or that our will ought to be quiescent for the Holy Spirit to work upon. There is no short cut to 'pure love,' and the way to it is by active participation in the duties of our calling. Many extravagant expressions have been collected from the writings of the quietistic mystics which justify the alarm which the movement excited in the ecclesiastical authorities. It is not likely that heaven and hell ever had very much influence on conduct, because irreligious persons seldom really believe in them. But undoubtedly these threats in former times enabled the hierarchy to extort large sums of money as a kind of spiritual fire-insurance, and some persons of unstable intellect have actually been driven insane by them. We cannot help wishing that a few passages even in the New Testament had been expunged.

Without in any way claiming to have solved the difficulty, I think the psychology of the New Testament, understood as I have done in this chapter, may give some help. Our Lord's great saying, 'He that would save his *psyche* shall lose it, and he that is willing to lose it shall save it,' must be given its full value. The psychical man claims justice, or asks for mercy, for himself. He reasons as an individual, and is inclined to think that the tangible advantages of which he has been deprived, or of which he has deprived himself from a sense of duty, in this life, ought somehow to be made good to him hereafter. The dark side of the picture occupies him less, and there is a widespread revolt among religious people against the belief in vindictive and endless punishment, as well as against the belief that hell is a place of physical torture. But when the 'psychical man' has become a 'spiritual man,' he has left behind the world of claims and counterclaims. In so far as he lives in the realm of the eternal values, and through them enjoys the vision of God, he no longer clamours for justice to himself. The self that he has found in place of the *psyche* that he has left behind,[1] has surrendered its separateness, and therewith its claim for reparation in kind. The same truth may be expressed in other words. Clement of Alexandria finds that there are three stages in the ascent of the soul to God. 'Faith is a compendious

[1] So Origen says: 'By putting off our psychical existence we become spiritual.'

knowledge of essentials, while knowledge is a sure and firm demonstration of the things received through Faith, carrying us on to unshaken conviction and scientific certainty. There is a first kind of saving change from heathenism to Faith, a second from Faith to Knowledge; and Knowledge as it passes on into Love begins at once to establish a mutual friendship between the Knower and the Known. Perhaps he who has reached this stage is equal to the angels.' Love makes no demands for payment; it gives freely and is its own reward. Clement hints that human nature can hardly reach this perfection. Since this state is what we aim at, the morose accusation of mercenary motives may be dismissed. He who loves God, even imperfectly, does not want to keep a *meum* and *tuum* account with his Maker, any more than with those whom he loves on earth. I think it is significant that though we may sometimes say of those whom we have loved and honoured upon earth that they are gone to their reward, we never think of saying so about ourselves. It is much more normal for the dying Christian to say, 'Lord, now lettest thou thy servant depart in peace,' or with the dying Christ, 'Father, into thy hands I commend my spirit.'

To return to the teaching of our Lord in the Synoptic Gospels. The apostles to whom these precepts were addressed were simple peasants, brave and loyal men, but not saints, mystics, or philosophers. They were sometimes strangely obtuse in understanding what seems to us plain teaching. If, as we believe, the ascent to higher things must be gradual, and by no means only by stripping off all ideas that are contaminated by association with the world of sense, we can perhaps understand that our Lord fed them with milk and not with strong meat, as St. Paul says, while at the same time He often told them things which they might hope to understand later. It is of course quite possible that they failed to assimilate or remember some of the more purely spiritual parts of His teaching. These may be more fully represented in the discourses of the Fourth Gospel, which is an interpretation of the eternal significance of the Incarnation. Nevertheless, we must not twist the recorded words of Christ to suit our own ideas.

'You can never find out the boundaries of the soul, so deep are they.' So said Heracleitus, and it is true. Our personality is in a state of flux, never wholly immersed in its lower affinities, and never possessed of all that it has in it to become. An 'amphibian' must think amphibiously. Hence the necessity of constantly using myths and symbols, the inadequacy of which we perceive ourselves when we think seriously. Even philosophers think and write mythically, Plato consciously, many others unconsciously. We can hardly go beyond the words of the First Epistle of St. John, 'Beloved, now are we the sons of God, and it doth not yet appear what we shall be. But we know that when he appears we shall be like him, for we shall see him as he is.' Or in the words of St. Paul, 'Though our outward man perish, the inward man is renewed day by day.' The words of Augustine, which I have already quoted, *Quod Deo non perit sibi non perit*, are a great comfort to me.

I saw Eternity the other night,
Like a great ring of pure and endless light,
All calm as it was bright;
And round beneath it Time in hours, days, years
Driven by the spheres
Like a vast shadow moved.

H. Vaughan.

If Time be taken exclusive of all those particular actions and ideas that diversify the day, merely for the continuation of existence or duration in abstract, then it will perhaps gravel even a philosopher to comprehend it.—Bishop Berkeley.

With thee stand the causes of things that are here so unstable: with thee abide the origins of all things that here abide not; with thee live the eternal reasons of all which is here unreasonable and temporal.—Augustine.

St. Augustine's point, in discussing the meaning of *saecula saeculorum*, is that the eternity of God is no mere unifying or synthesizing of the time-process, but something different in kind, to which the moments of the time-series stand as subjects.—Welldon.

Time doth but measure other things, and neither worketh in them any real effect nor is itself ever capable of any. The very opportunities which we ascribe to Time do in truth cleave to the things themselves wherewith Time is joined; as for Time it neither causeth things nor opportunities of things, although it comprise and contain both.—Hooker.

We become more sure of the super-temporal unity of our being in proportion to the deepening of our personality.—Holtzmann.

Both heaven and hell have their foundation within us. Heaven primarily lies in a refined temper; in an internal reconciliation to the nature of God, and to the rule of righteousness. The guilt of conscience and enmity to righteousness is the inward state of hell.—Whichcote.

The eschatology of a nation is always the last part of its religion to experience the transforming power of new ideas and new facts.—Canon Charles.

CHAPTER V

TIME AND ETERNITY

I HAVE given my reasons for refusing to treat mysticism in religion as a branch of psychology or of psychopathology. Mysticism deals not with states of consciousness, but with ultimate reality, or it is nothing. It belongs to philosophy, if with the ancients we define philosophy as the art of living and add that the unexamined life is not worth living. It is the art of living, for those who believe that the affirmations of the religious consciousness are the most real things in our experience. Problems arise when we try, as we must, to correlate our religion with the rest of our knowledge, the world of ultimate values with the world of things and instrumental values. We have considered one of these problems, the meaning and value of personality. We cannot neglect another, one of extraordinary difficulty, the problem of Time. For though the absolute values are timeless and changeless, they are actualized for us in the changing world of Time and Space in which our present lot is cast. In attacking this problem I have tried to avoid technicalities; but the subject itself is so difficult that the treatment of it can hardly be made easy.

It has been said that the character of a philosophy is determined by its attitude to Time, and also that the status of Time in reality is the most difficult of all philosophical problems. I am not so presumptuous as to hope that I can make any contribution to its solution, but everyone who is interested in ultimate problems must try to make up his mind about the meaning and value of Time. He has not even the right to say that the problem is for him insoluble, until he has used such wits as he possesses in the endeavour to come to a conclusion.

Plato's famous definition is that Time is the moving image of eternity. What eternity means we shall have to discuss presently. For mystics it is the character and quality of the Real, which is perfect and therefore unchanging. How then can Time, which is the form of continual change, be the image of that of which constancy is the chief attribute? An image must resemble that of which it is an image; a copy must reproduce the features of its archetype. Thus Plato's definition requires much consideration.

Although Plato has not solved the problem, he has the great merit of distinguishing Time as it is in itself from our awareness of Time, and from events in Time. The confusion caused by not making this distinction has been the cause of the impasse to which many philosophers have been reduced. Plato says that the Creator wished the creation to resemble the spiritual world as far as possible. We do not know why the temporal and spatial world was created, but the suggestion is made that, since God is good and feels no jealousy, He wished all possible levels of existence to be actualized. The resemblance of the created image to its archetype consists partly in its goodness and beauty, to which some Oriental philosophies are blind, and partly in the belief that the universe has no beginning or end. Everlastingness is the moving image of eternity. The theory that Time and the world were created together, so that the universe had a beginning, was adopted by St. Augustine and by many others. To my mind it is unsatisfactory, if we assign an unknown but real date to the creation. It depends on the belief, very widely held, that empty Time is unthinkable. Unless we confuse Time with our awareness of Time, or with events in Time, there is no difficulty in thinking of empty Time or of empty Space, any more than in thinking of a blank sheet of paper. If the world was created at a date which we could name if we knew it, the question what preceded the creation is reasonable and unanswerable. Kant agrees that we can think of empty Time, but that the thought is empty, as of course it is.[1]

The notion of the creation of Time at the beginning of a temporal series in no way resolves the famous 'antinomy' emphasized by Kant, though the alleged contradiction in the idea of an infinite series is said to have been disposed of by the philosophical mathematicians Cantor, Dedekind, and Broad. But to say that a mathematical series has a beginning, with 0 or 1, does not seem to me any argument for a beginning of Time. Leibniz thinks that though the world may be limited in spatial extension, it may be unlimited in temporal duration. 'If it is the nature of things in the whole to grow uniformly in perfection, the universe of creatures must have had a beginning.' The *ignis fatuus* of perfectibility has worked havoc in this problem. To those who are free from this modern superstition the arguments in favour of the perpetual existence of the universe are so convincing that Aquinas is plainly uneasy at having to reject them as contradicted by revelation. *Mundum incepisse sola fide tenetur.* It does not occur to him that the revelation of such a fact as the creation of the world at a remote date could hardly be made. Averroes believed that Time had no beginning.

Nevertheless the idea of infinite time is almost equally unsatisfactory. Windelband says, 'it is difficult to say which idea is the more intolerable, that of an absolute rest, or that of a never-ending restlessness of the will. Both elements have their emotional value in relation to the finite time-aspects of empirical reality and our varying experience of it. At one time rest is welcome after long unrest, though it is tolerable only if it does not last too long. By others the struggle, even if it does not attain its end, is gladly welcomed; yet if such a state of things is conceived absolutely, it threatens to make the will itself illusory. Thus we see that the things that are certainly real in the finite world of experience become impossibilities the moment they are converted into absolute realities by metaphysical thought.'

It is interesting that St. Augustine, unlike the Schoolmen who were seldom in doubt, frankly despaired of solving the difficulties about Time. 'What is Time? If no one asks me, I know; if I wish to explain it to another,

_____
[1] Kant, however, agrees with Leibniz that a series may have a beginning but no end.

I know not.' So Berkeley says:[1] 'For my own part, whenever I attempt to frame a simple idea of Time abstracted from the succession of ideas in my mind, which flows uniformly and is participated in by all beings, I am lost and entangled in inextricable difficulties. I have no notion of it at all.' St. Augustine accepts the Platonic doctrine that Time and the world are coextensive, without noticing the great difference which the Hebrew-Christian doctrine of creation in time makes. But he sees clearly the error of identifying Time with our standards of measuring Time. Time went on just the same while the course of the sun was miraculously suspended in the valley of Ajalon. The present is an unextended point; what moderns have called the specious present is a compound of memory and anticipation. The temporal order is the medium for the actualization of values which transcend the temporal order. For God, past and future do not exist as such. *Futura iam facta sunt.*

Plotinus is as diffident as Augustine in approaching this question. 'Some of the blessed ancients must have found the truth.' Although Eternity is the sphere of Spirit, and Time of Soul, we must not separate them dualistically. 'Things that are born are nothing without their future,' and 'all things that are Yonder (in heaven, we may say) are also Here (on earth).' Particular things exist in the spiritual world, including personal lives: they remain distinct, though not separated. Plotinus will have none of a spatialized heaven, or of a despiritualized earth. The warning is given in quaintly simple language by the author of that beautiful medieval mystical treatise, *The Cloud of Unknowing*, 'Be wary that thou take none example at the bodily ascension of Christ for to strain thine imagination in the time of thy prayer bodily upwards as thou wouldst climb above the moon. For it should in no wise be so, ghostly. For heaven ghostly is as nigh down as up, behind as before, before as behind, on one side as another. Inasmuch that whoso had a true desire to be in heaven, then that same time he were in heaven ghostly.' Eternity is the atmosphere in which spiritual beings live. Perpetuity is the time-form of eternity, and therefore things that are born yearn to continue in existence. It is possible that Neoplatonism exaggerated the 'upward striving' of the creatures which in truth is by no means a universal fact. Plotinus rejects the Aristotelian definition that Time is 'the measure of motion according to earlier and later.' Unless the last words are used in a spatial sense, which would be 'to confound Time with Space,' they explain nothing about Time in itself, which is not merely subjective. To say that Time is measured by motion would be unobjectionable. Time is natural; it had to be. That is to say, it is given us *a priori*; we must accept it without trying to account for it. The Spirit and even the Soul transcend it; but it is for us a necessary form of thought. We cannot think it away, though we may think things away from it. As for creation, he says that 'Time, still non-existent, reposed in the bosom of Reality,' until Nature, or the Soul of the world, being restless and desiring to exert its active powers, 'took upon her the form of a servant and the likeness of a creature

---

[1] Quoted by Gunn, *The Problem of Time*, p. 69. I am indebted to this learned treatise for some other quotations and references.

D

of Time, and made the creation subject to Time in all things.' Of course he does not mean that there was a time when Time was not. Time is the form which the Soul creates when it wishes to translate the eternal ideas into vital laws. Time is 'the span of life proper to the Soul,' 'the activity of an eternal Soul exercised in creation.' Real time, the external life of the universal Soul, is uniform and steady, as Newton said.

Time is the form of willed change, the will being that of the World Soul. One of the objections against those philosophies which deny any reality to Time is that they give us a world in which nothing really happens, and in which nothing seems to be willed either by God or man. For Plotinus, the world 'Here' was called into being by the Soul, who wished to actualize, in a lower medium, the vision which it had seen in the world 'Yonder.' To carry out a purpose, duration is needed, and therefore in the soul-world duration is real. Time, therefore, is not merely the measure of the impermanence of the imperfect; it is, at least in part, a teleological category, within which our aspirations for progress operate. The ends for which we strive belong to the spiritual, not to the psychical world. They are striven for in Time, but they are not themselves in Time. It is fair to say that in the Platonic school, though this character of Time as the form of the will is acknowledged, it is less emphasized than the view, more congenial to the East, of the phenomenal world as a polarization of a timeless and changeless reality.

Boethius in the sixth century was much read through the Middle Ages. His definition of Eternity as 'the completely simultaneous and perfect possession of interminable life' had great influence. He also introduced the conception of *aevum* as a mean between Time and Eternity. As this was accepted and developed by Aquinas, some consideration of it is necessary. '*Aevum*,' says Aquinas, 'is intermediate between Time and Eternity, participating in both, since, while Time has a before and after, and Eternity has not, *aevum* has not a before and after, but they can be conjoined to it.' 'Spiritual creatures as regards their affections and intellections, in which there exists succession, are measured by Time; as regards their natural being they are measured by *aevum*; as regards their vision of glory they participate in Eternity.' It is perhaps not easy to discern in this conception anything more than the tempting but almost always futile expedient of intercalating intermediate stages between two conceptions which we cannot reconcile. Von Hügel suggest that Aquinas is groping after something like Bergson's *durée*. It is not the way of the Angelic Doctor to grope, and I do not think he would have approved of Bergson, whose *durée*, it seems to me, is lifted out of the Time series. Bergson's reputation was higher when von Hügel wrote than it is now. Nevertheless, the life of the soul on earth does 'participate' in both Time and Eternity, so that the conception of *aevum*, whatever its metaphysical value, does harmonize with our experience. Eckhart emphasizes the amphibious life of the soul here. He also says, 'he who stands continually in a present Now, in him God the Father begets his Son without ceasing.'

Royce and others regard Eternity as an infinite 'specious present.' It is suggested that God, in contemplating the course of Time, is aware of earlier and later, but not of past and future, which have no meaning for Him. Duration would then be for God a motionless order of externality; it is not a time order. Or we might call it a temporal order without transiency, a valuable conception, since it rebuts the error that the past has now no existence. Duration becomes a real order only when it includes valuation.

Newton is often criticized for his canon that Time 'in itself and in its own nature flows equally without reference to anything external.' I venture to think that Newton was right. He uses 'duration' as an equivalent for Time, and perhaps the words 'Time flows' may be objected to. But he postulates an absolute equably 'flowing' Time, even though 'it is possible that there is no perfectly equable movement which can serve as an exact measure of Time.' We must therefore distinguish between Time as it is in itself from our measurements of Time. This distinction is of the utmost importance in view of the recent Time-philosophies based on the new discoveries or theories of mathematical physicists. Have the modern theories of relativity much metaphysical significance? Are they not essentially, including the Space-Time theories of Minkowski and his followers, methods for measuring distances and movements more accurately? Einstein[1] deprecated treating them as affecting our knowledge of ultimate reality. I have never quite understood why, for example, the number of miles traversed by the earth in its yearly journey round the sun should not be regarded as an absolute measurement. But I readily admit my incompetence as a mathematician. I do however think that 'Time in itself' is quite other than our measurements of things in Time. That Time is merely subjective, in the sense that individuals have different times, equally legitimate, I cannot believe.

Hegel said long ago that the contrast of idealistic and realistic philosophy is of no importance. Bosanquet and Alexander have said the same. The main cleavage now seems to be about the status of Time and history in reality. Bosanquet thinks that history is of small importance to the philosopher; for the Italian new idealists, Croce and Gentile, reality is historical through and through. This controversy suggests the question whether the Time series is theoretically irreversible. It seems to us to be so, and it is generally assumed that our opinion is correct. It is defended both by moralists and by modern science. The moralist protests that if the process may be traced either way, like a problem in mathematics, nothing ever really happens. There is nothing new under the sun. Will is an illusion, since it can change nothing in the future. Can we believe that our actions have no result either in Time or in Eternity? Can we measure Time as we measure Space, without any notion of purpose? Does not this destroy the very idea of Time as the form of willed change?

[1] 'As far as the laws of mathematics refer to reality they are not certain, and as far as they are certain they do not refer to reality.' Quoted by Gunn, p. 231, who also quotes Sellien as saying: 'In the problem of space-time what we are concerned with are questions of measurement, and not questions relating to space and time as forms of intuition.' F. J. Sheen (*God and Intelligence*, p. 72), quotes other authorities to the same effect. 'An increased degree of accuracy' is all that Einstein and others aim at. Bertrand Russell says, 'The principle of relativity does not have such far-reaching philosophical consequences as is supposed.'

If, as has been suggested, God recognizes earlier and later, but not past and future, this means that He views the Time series from a point outside it, but still as a series. It does not seem to follow that He does not recognize real change within a finite process. When the mystics say that He views the creation in an everlasting Now, that only means that the unreality of the past and future is negated, and that His apprehension is immediate, not, like ours, a blend of memory and anticipation. It does not mean that the future is foreordained, but only that it is foreknown.

From the point of view of science, an irreversible process is an awkward exception in the mathematically ordered universe. The reason for believing it is the well-known 'principle of Carnot,' according to which the universe is running down like a clock. Ten years ago I collected the opinions of eminent men of science for and against this theory,[1] and I do not think that any important new evidence has come to light since. The prevailing view was then, and I believe still is, that the reasons for accepting the second law of thermodynamics, which pronounces the ultimate doom of all life in the universe, are incontrovertible. The time will come when all movement will cease. Heat will dissolve in radiation, and all heavenly bodies, including our sun and our earth, will be as dead as the moon, if indeed anything is left of them at all. Attempts have been made to find some opposite principle, by which the elements may be reassembled and the order of nature as we know it reconstituted. It has been suggested that the cosmic rays may be the vehicle by which first hydrogen and then the heavier elements may be generated. But these theories seem to have failed to win acceptance, and Sir Arthur Eddington tells us bluntly that anyone who doubts the law of entropy puts himself out of court as a man of science. At the same time he says candidly that the theory is incredible, because it implies that the whole cosmic process started 'with a bang' at some far distant date, and that the configuration from which the slow movement towards dissolution began was almost infinitely improbable. This certainly seems like an impasse, and the attempt to escape from it on the lines of outmoded Berkeleyan idealism cannot be admitted as legitimate. To start with stars and atoms, regarded as concrete realities, and to end with subjective idealism, almost obviously requires a *salto mortale* which we have no right to make. Some have objected that the progress of humanity and indeed the appearance of life in the world are examples of a reversed process. This argument seems to me worthless, in view of the rarity of life, and the geologically recent date of its appearance. But it cannot be denied that an irreversible process is difficult to reconcile with the panmathematicism which some of our scientists wish to establish as the ultimate structure of the cosmos. If a layman may venture the opinion, the cosmology of natural science has not yet reached its final form, and new discoveries may relieve the perplexity which none feels more strongly than our physicists themselves.

We might have expected that the principle of Carnot would have been specially unwelcome to believers in a cosmic law of progress, since it finally destroys all hope of unending advance towards perfection. But

[1] In my book, *God and the Astronomers*.

on the contrary it was sometimes welcomed as giving the quietus to the theory of cyclic recurrence, which these visionaries regarded as pessimistic. Nevertheless, vigorous protests were heard. Wundt says: 'There is one idea which would be for ever intolerable though its realization was thought of as thousands of years distant; it is the thought that humanity with all its intellectual and moral toil may vanish without leaving a trace, and that not even a memory of it may remain in any mind.' And Arthur Balfour wrote: 'Man will go down into the pit, and all his thoughts will perish. Matter will know itself no longer. Imperishable monuments and immortal deeds, death itself, and love stronger than death, will be as though they had never been. Nor will anything that *is* be better or worse for all that the labour, genius, devotion and suffering of man have striven through countless generations to effect.'

But do not these eloquent laments miss the mark? Long before entropy was thought of, men had realized that we have only a lease of this planet. Who ever supposed that our race would live on earth for ever? It is needless to say that Christians have never held such an opinion. The splendid lines of Lucretius were famous in antiquity:

> Quorum naturam triplicem, tria corpora, Memmi,
> tres species tam dissimiles, tria talia texta,
> una dies dabit exitio, multosque per annos
> sustantata ruet moles et machina mundi.

By what right do we assume that the past is non-existent, and obliterated from the mind of God? What a strange conception of eternal life do such regrets imply? Apart from the refutation of the perfectibility theory, which did not deserve to be taken seriously, why is the prediction of a state when nothing can ever happen any more unwelcome? It is because current philosophy has so entangled God with the Time process that if that process comes to an end God Himself will die, or pass into a state of unconsciousness and inertia, 'lost to Time and use and name and fame.' If we reject this view of Deity, which is quite unchristian, God could survive the universe and live without it. Such a thing is possible, no doubt; but if the creation is a necessary result of God's will and purpose, is it credible that it should cease to be so? Or can we be satisfied with the idea, popular among religious people, that eternity is a never ending state which will follow the end of Time?

One solution, which satisfied Origen and has met with some acceptance since, is that though the existing world order may come to an end, God may create other universes in which to carry out His purposes. If this only means that the universe probably contains and will contain many other abodes inhabited by intelligent beings to whom the Creator and Christ as Logos may make themselves known, there can be no objection to a thought which Alice Meynell has drawn out in a well-known poem. But this does not dispose of the law of entropy, which is supposed to threaten the whole universe together. And the hypothesis of the creation of new universes is liable to the objections which make the theory of a creation in time so unpalatable to natural science.

To the Platonist the doctrine of entropy is very unwelcome. He does not believe that God is entangled in the fate of the world, but he does believe that the perpetuity of the universe is the Time form of the eternity of the Creator, and the question, Why should God wish to destroy what He has made? cannot be answered. There can hardly be any single purpose in the vast diversity of worlds; but an entire cessation of activity on the part of the Creator seems hardly credible. We may therefore hope, and perhaps even believe, that there is some constructive agency in the universe to counteract the disintegration which the physicists believe to be in progress. After all, the clock has been wound up once, and whatever power wound it up once may presumably wind it up again. There is however, a lurking suspicion in my mind that we shall never be able to construct a closed system. 'There is a crack in all that God has made,' says Emerson. The phenomenal universe, not being fully real, cannot be rounded off satisfactorily. There will always be leakage somewhere; the 'living garment of God,' as knowable by us, will always have ragged edges.

Of Bergson Janet says quite truly that he 'divinizes Time,' and in so doing takes 'la durée' out of Time altogether. The same criticism, I cannot help thinking, applies to Alexander's fantastic Gnosticism, in which the Aeons Space and Time contract an ill-assorted marriage, quite in the manner of ancient theosophy. His 'emergence' is much the same as Bergson's 'élan vital.' The universe is history; Mind is a form of Time; Time is the mind of Space; all existences are complexes of motion; Time is restless; it begets God, who, it seems, is preparing to 'emerge.' I cannot think that the new measurements give any countenance to this strange mythology. I agree with Urban that 'this packing of Time or Space-Time with meanings and values is the only thing that gives to modern doctrines of emergence the apparent intelligibility they seem to have.' 'There is no element of direction in Space and Time, and without direction they are ultimately meaningless and unintelligible.' 'Space and Time are the warp and woof of the canvas on which the meanings of the world are spread out.'

Whitehead also postulates an 'impetus,' which may be compared with Plotinus' ἔφεσις. Except in the human soul, desiring to identify itself with its higher faculties, I can see no justification in nature for this cosmic theory.

Gunn quotes from Bertrand Russell a passage which evoked an indignant protest from Alexander. 'There is some sense, easier to feel than to state, in which Time is an unimportant and superficial characteristic of reality. Past and future must be acknowledged to be as real as the present, and a certain emancipation from slavery to Time is essential to philosophical thought. The importance of Time is rather practical than theoretical, rather in relation to our desires than in relation to truth. Both in thought and in feeling to realize the unimportance of Time is the gate of wisdom.'

'The uniformity of Time's course' says Schopenhauer, 'and its independence of the will, give it the authority of objectivity.' I should say that it is objective in the sense that all *a priori* judgments are objective. Bradley contends that the idea of Time is self-contradictory. If there is a contradiction, it may be because, as Haldane says, 'we are at once in Time and out of it.' But I entirely agree with Bradley's words: 'If there be no supreme spiritual Power which is above chance and change, our own spiritual interests are not safeguarded. But with any such Power it seems to me nonsense to talk of the absolute reality of Time.'

In reading Bradley we are confronted with the difficult theory of degrees of reality. A hierarchy within a purely existential system is not an easy conception. If however reality is a kingdom of values, the difficulty disappears, for valuation is essentially hierarchical.

If the exhortation to take Time seriously, as a constituent of ultimate reality, were merely the sequelae of the dying superstition of ineluctible cosmic progress, we might dismiss it as a product of wishful thinking, encouraged by the material gains in western Europe and America in the period before the two Great Wars. But there is more in it than this. Time is the form of the will, and unless the will effects something in the real world it is a delusion. Are we to believe that the Creator 'planted in us vain hopes,' as Aeschylus says, in order that we may subserve the purposes of a Nature which has no care for us? Christianity makes Hope one of the three great virtues. 'We are saved by hope.' The Hebrew race owes its indomitable tenacity to its power of 'believing in hope, even against hope.' Even if, as the Epistle to the Hebrews says, the heroes of the old dispensation 'received not the promise,' it was because God had prepared 'some better thing' for their successors. No pure hope shall wither, except that a purer may spring out of its roots. Have we then any right to accept a view of the real world as a world in which nothing ever really happens, a world in which human effort has no result outside the shifting and perishing phantasmagoria of mere appearance? To do this would be to deny the validity of one of our deepest convictions.

The two worlds are not entirely sundered. Is not this transformation just what the spiritual life is or should be? As Professor Taylor says, 'in proportion to its moral worth it is a life which is undergoing a steady elevation and transmutation from the mere successiveness of a simply animal existence to the whole and simultaneous fruition of all good which would be the eternity of the divine.'[1] Those who advance in the spiritual life live more and more 'under the form of eternity.' But eternal life is a life of fruition, not of striving. Aristotle would say that it may still exercise 'activity,' directed outwards, but without further inner change. Morality as we know it is always a struggle against evil. When therefore evil is overcome, morality as such has done its work. We might say that it has passed into religion, of which the culmination is not virtuous action but the vision of God.

The Time series contains within itself an infinite number of finite purposes, each having a beginning and an end. When each of these is achieved, it does not pass out of existence, but takes its place in the

---

[1] Professor Taylor would certainly have admitted that this is an ideal goal to which finite creatures can never attain.

eternal order, of which the temporal order is not merely an imperfect copy, but, we may say, a sacrament. Our wills are not always and necessarily striving after the unattainable. They can realize what they aim at, and in so doing they pass out of the arena of moral conflict. The pursuit of temporal and secular good fails to satisfy the moral sense itself, which is a sign that even disinterested work to improve merely environmental conditions is not a fulfilment of the highest demands of our nature. Still, we must never forget that the dutiful performance of the 'civic virtues' is the first stage in the 'purification' which must precede 'enlightenment.' As for the future of humanity, there will almost certainly be flowering times of civilization, not less glorious than the culminating periods of past history. But we must not hope for unbroken progress. As St. Bernard says, *Habet mundus iste noctes suas et non paneas.*

'We feel and know that we are eternal.' This is the famous profession of faith of Spinoza, a profoundly religious man; though we may be surprised at Goethe's judgment that he was 'most emphatically a theist and a Christian.' Eternity in Spinoza is without any compromise lifted out of the Time series. It is qualitative, not quantitative, and therefore belongs to the kingdom of values. But neither Spinoza nor the Platonist can accept a dualism of fact and value. A fact which has no value is no fact; a value which is no fact is no value. How to relate them is the perhaps insoluble problem of philosophy, for the problem is created by the ambiguous status of the finite individual.

Can we be content with the time-honoured solution that God surveys the whole temporal process as present—as a *totum simul*? This is a kind of extension of the idea of a 'specious present' to infinity. It has been objected that an unending series cannot be seen all at once. But this is to reimport the form of Time into a realm where by hypothesis it does not belong. It has also been objected that a series from which past and future have been banished, while the recognition of earlier and later remains, would be a neutral Time, which could be read as well backwards as forwards. I am not quite convinced that the series is necessarily irreversible; and in any case the objection seems to confound God's foreknowledge with predestination. Can we in any sense admit duration as an element in reality? We must I think admit that non-successive duration contradicts our idea of Time, and that successive duration, especially in the Bergsonian form, contradicts our idea of eternity. As for the notion that Space and Time are finite, a theory which is supposed to be confirmed by recent calculations of mathematicians and physicists, I cannot help agreeing with Professor Hallett: 'I do not expect ever to stand at the ultimate edge of space, with room behind me but with none before; nor at the last moment of time, with the past behind me and with no future to come; nor do I believe that anyone, whether finite or infinite, will ever do so.'

The notion of a partially eternized duration is intellectually most unsatisfactory. We say to ourselves, what would the history of the world look like if we could 'stand out and look at ourselves'; if we could survey all durations and all spaces from a point not in the series? This is not really to view the world 'under the form of eternity,' for though 'we know that we are eternal,' we are certainly not in full possession of eternity, nor can we even in imagination see as God sees. Duration cannot be excluded from our view of reality. If we exclude it, we are left only with the inert and frozen world of lifeless forms, against which Plato, in a famous passage of the *Philebus*, protests so vigorously.

The question whether Spinoza believed in 'personal' immortality has not the same meaning for his philosophy as it has for modern 'personal idealists.' For him as for the Indians and the philosophical mystics, there is no fixed personality. The soul is the wanderer of the metaphysical world. We are or will be what we may become: we are what we attend to, what we care for, what we love. Hallett says that for Spinoza 'it is not the whole mind that is eternal; there is a part that perishes at death; and it is possible for a man so to live that what perishes is of small importance in comparison with what is eternal.' This is approximately the faith of most of the mystics. The word 'personal' may mean very different things. The indwelling Spirit, the Holy Ghost of the New Testament and of Christian theology, is super-personal. It is not strictly part of ourselves. The soul is the self. But the soul may be so transfigured as to 'participate,' as Plato says, in the super-personal nature of Spirit. In this 'transformation of the spirit of our mind,' as St. Paul says, using the philosophical term *Nous* as an equivalent of his own chosen word *Pneuma*, the individual nature of the soul is not lost or absorbed in the Absolute. Plotinus is emphatic that individuality, though not separate individuality, is preserved in the word 'Yonder,' and I am convinced that Spinoza (though it has been denied) believed the same. Those who accuse Platonism of irreconcilable dualism of course see an inconsistency here, and they can find abundant justification for this view in the writings of ecstatic mystics. But this is a fundamental misunderstanding of the Platonists, whose heaven is much richer, not emptier, than our earth. The loss of individuality is even more irreconcilable with Christianity, for absorption is the end of love.

Anthropologists have proved that belief in some kind of survival, though not universal, is so general as to be impressive. They have accounted for it after their manner, assuming that a tree is known by its roots, not by its fruits, by the reactions of the savage to the mysterious phenomena of dreams, by the difficulty of realizing that a human life has been really extinguished, and above all, on biological grounds, because the belief was favourable to those who held it. We may allow some importance to these alleged grounds. Primitive animism is still alive. The dead are so much in the survivors' thoughts that necromancy meets an emotional need. Belief in survival has a moral and therefore a beneficial social effect. But as a historical fact, the belief in immortality among the higher peoples is not even continuous with primitive animism. It was not so among the Jews, nor among the Greeks. Partly it has sprung from mystical religion, and partly from the moral demand for just recompense from the Deity. Popular theodicy has usually taken a materialistic and cruel form, but in my opinion it has never been very strongly believed. It has been said that ninety-nine people out of a hundred profess that they believe in heaven and hell, and only one out of a hundred acts as if he believed in them.

The late Dr. Schiller has discussed the 'half-beliefs' which play a considerable part in the world of opinion. Full beliefs become half-beliefs when we cease to be interested in them. Fancies become half-beliefs when we play with them, as even philosophers may do if, like Hume, they 'leave their theories behind in their study.' Most often they are beliefs accepted on authority, which we were forbidden to question, and therefore prevented from understanding. Dr. Schiller and other members of the Society for Psychical Research drew up a questionnaire, to which they received about three thousand answers. The questions were as follows: 'Would you prefer to live after death, or not? Do you desire a future life whatever the conditions might be? If not, what would have to be its character to make the prospect seem tolerable? Would you (e.g.) be content with a life more or less like the present life? Can you say what elements of life (if any) are felt by you to call for its perpetuity? Can you state why you feel in this way as regards questions I and II? Do you now feel the question of a future life to be of urgent importance to your mental comfort? Have your feelings undergone change? If so, when and in what ways? Would you like to know for certain about the future life, or would you prefer to leave it a matter of faith?'

The result of the inquiry was that many promised to answer but did not, which seems to imply either indifference or uncertainty. A surprisingly large number answered that the subject did not interest them; they had no time to think about it. A few resembled Frederic Myers' churchwarden, whom he asked what he really believed would happen to him after death. The reply was, 'I suppose I shall go to everlasting bliss, but I wish you would not talk about such disagreeable subjects.' Some, as might be expected, expressed a horror of the idea of annihilation; a few expected to be 'absorbed in the Absolute.' Some indignantly repudiated any wish for survival. Necromancy had made a few converts. Two classes of affirmative answers seemed to Dr. Schiller to 'ring true.' Those whom he calls the mystics replied more or less in the manner of Spinoza: 'we feel and know that we are eternal.' They were satisfied that a conviction which seems to spring from the core of our being cannot be a delusion. The other class consisted of the bereaved, who could not face the possibility that they would never see their dear ones again.

These two grounds of belief may be rejected by many as obviously wishful thinking. But I do not agree. In every philosophy, as I have said, we come to a point where a man must trust himself. This is the real basis both of the ontological argument for the existence of God, and for its corollary, the belief in human immortality. When the rejection of a belief is 'intolerable' it is a reasonable act of faith to accept it, with all reservations as to the form of the belief which we can make vivid to ourselves, and which we can relate to the rest of our knowledge. I dislike Pascal's well-known words that the heart has its reasons which the intellect knows not of, because 'the heart' in modern usage seems to be the seat of irrational emotionalism; but the Spirit, whether we call it *Nous* or *Pneuma*, has its reasons which the logic-chopping faculty (*Dianoia* in Greek) cannot fit into its scheme. We must however remember that immortality for the mystic may mean something very different from survival in Time under conditions not utterly different from our ordinary experience. The hope of reunion after death is seldom contradicted; to try to destroy such hopes would be heartless. But here also is there not something deeper than an affection which cannot bear to think of final separation? 'Love is as strong as death. Many waters cannot quench love, neither can the floods drown it. If a man would give all the substance of his house for love, it would utterly be contemned.' Love brings us into the heart of reality as nothing else does. There is a very deep meaning in the simple words, 'God is love.'

> Love's not Time's fool, though rosy lips and cheeks
> Within his bending sickle's compass come,
> Love alters not with his brief hours and weeks,
> But bears it out even to the edge of doom.
> If this be error and upon me proved
> I never writ, nor no man ever loved.

So says our greatest poet, and such is the experience of humanity. But this hope favours no particular theory as to the how, when, and where of its realization. It is an affirmation of one of the ultimate values, which stand in their own right, and cannot be explained or justified by anything outside themselves, nor even by each other.

Some aspects of immortality as traditionally pictured were not represented in these answers. Although the Church has usually taught that only a minority are saved, and that the fate of the lost is horrible in the extreme, none of the writers shows any sense of *fear*. The disappearance of fear as an abiding sensation was a feature of western civilization until the two wars shattered our security. The fear of hell has evidently almost vanished, and in these replies there are very few references to the joys of heaven. Apart from this, the apparent indifference of many among them need not be a sign of frivolity. Spinoza thought that 'a free man' will seldom think of death. 'Death does not count,' was a saying of the Balliol philosopher Nettleship. What Clough called a Stoic-Epicurean acceptance was until lately a common frame of mind. An Epicurean *tetractys* sums up the gentle and amiable creed of this sect. 'Nothing to fear in God. Nothing to feel in death. The good, easily won. The bad, easily borne.' In reading Lucretius one sometimes fancies that death was more dreaded in antiquity than it is now; but he may be only painting in strong colours the terrors from which he thinks that 'the man of Greece' can deliver us. We are even more surprised by the words of the Epistle to the Hebrews (ch. ii, 15) that Christ died to 'deliver them who through fear of death were all their lifetime subject to bondage.' Could this be said of anyone in our day, even of those who dislike the thought of resigning 'this pleasing anxious being'? No doubt there are many who can say with the Frenchman, 'pour être mort, malheureusement il faut mourir.' It is the process of dying, not the prospect of being dead, that makes them uncomfortable. Some good and brave men, like Samuel Johnson, have admitted that they feared death; many who were neither good nor brave have faced it with equanimity. But there are some things which almost all of us would rather die than do. This fact is enough to prove that the continued existence of our self-conscious ego is not our supreme interest.

The traditional Christian eschatology is certainly an amazing thing. It is not primitive. The nations to which we owe most, the Hebrews, the Greeks and the Romans, were very late in developing a religious doctrine of the soul. The Hebrew Sheol was outside the jurisdiction of Yahveh. The denizens of the Homeric Hades would gladly exchange their condition for the meanest serfdom on earth. Even in Plato's Republic, when a young Athenian is asked whether he has not heard that the soul is immortal, he replies in the negative. In Latin the Di Manes have no singular number. But Orphism knew of a hell for the wicked, and even in Buddhism an ingenious system of tortures after death established itself. It is universally admitted that all eschatology must be symbolic, and in a syncretistic religion like Catholic Christianity it is not surprising that an unintelligible conflation of local, temporal, and materialistic symbols was stabilized. Here we need only notice the inappropriate character of the reward, which is conceived as a state of static fruition accompanied by interminable songs of praise, a prospect which if it were taken literally might deter many persons from the practice of virtue; the bisection of the human race into the saved and the damned; and the horrible cruelty of the punishments. Attempts to prove that hell has only a sub-tropical temperature; that it is tenanted only by Judas Iscariot and a few others; that all will be saved at the last; that the wicked are not tormented but annihilated, have never been sanctioned by orthodox theologians. We must be content to say that in popular teaching our Lord made use of the current doctrines of His time, explicitly rejecting only the Sadducean view that the individual is extinguished at death. This example may perhaps teach us to deal tenderly with traditional beliefs.

But nothing can prevent us from being shocked when St. Thomas Aquinas coolly says: 'That nothing may be wanting to the felicity of blessed spirits, a perfect view is granted them of the torments of the damned.' Dante has no doubt that Justice and *Love* created the Inferno. During the greater part of Church history, preachers, both Catholic and Protestant, have gloated over descriptions of eternal punishment, and no subject was so popular for wall paintings in parish churches. That such doctrines are profoundly dishonouring to the God who in Christ revealed Himself as Love can hardly be disputed; and now it appears that they have simply faded away, carrying with them, too often, the blessed hope of everlasting life which they so long disfigured. Would it be too much to say that immortality is now rarely referred to in the pulpit, and that words expressing a belief in it are chiefly reserved for consolation in bereavement, or in comforting the dying? The hope has been secularized; it has lost its religious character, and therewith its credibility.

The notion of progress in a future state is not Christian, but perhaps the only objection to it is that progress is a temporal conception. The same difficulty applies to purgatory, which perhaps most Protestants as well as Catholics now substitute for hell. We must frankly admit that no revelation on such subjects has been or can be given. 'Eye hath not seen nor ear heard, neither hath it entered into the heart of man to conceive,' what awaits us when we are quit of 'the body of our humiliation.'

Does this frank confession of agnosticism in a matter of transcendent importance contradict the act of faith which is the heart of Platonism and mysticism, that 'the fully real can be fully known'? This can hardly be affirmed, when we remember how freely Plato resorts to myths when he is dealing with ultimate problems He does not pretend that his myths have factual reality; but 'something of the kind' must be true. 'Opinion' is one thing, and perhaps most people must be content with it; 'knowledge' is another, and knowledge can be won only by strict moral discipline, straight thinking, and earnest desire to be 'immortal, as far as man may.' But it is part of knowledge to recognize its own limits. We have convictions which cannot be rationalized, and when we try to relate these with the rest of our experience, we must use the language of myth and symbol. They are pictorial representations, translated into the forms of space and time, of supertemporal realities.[1] This is the subject of my next chapter.

[1] Milton makes Raphael say to Adam:
> The secrets of another world perhaps
> Not lawful to reveal. Yet for thy good
> This is dispensed, and what surmounts the reach
> Of human sense I shall delineate so
> By likening spiritual to corporeal forms
> As may express them best, though what if earth
> Be but the shadow of heaven, and things therein
> Each to other like, more than on earth is thought?

The whole meaning, importance and value of life are determined by the mystery behind it, by an infinity which cannot be rationalized but can only be expressed in myths and symbols.—BERDYAEFF.

Nature is a world of symbolism, a rich hieroglyphic book; everything visible conceals an invisible mystery, and the last mystery of all is God.—LUTHARDT.

Of true religions there are only two: one of them recognizes and worships the Holy that without form or shape dwells in and around us; the other recognizes and worships it in its fairest form. Everything that lies between these is idolatry.—GOETHE.

Nature viewed materialistically is only an abstraction for certain purposes, and has not a high degree of truth or reality. The poet's nature has much more. The process can only cease when nature is quite absorbed into spirit.—BRADLEY.

> Cease then, my tongue and lend unto my mind
> Leave to bethink how great that beauty is
> Whose utmost parts so beautiful I find;
> How much more these essential parts of his,
> His truth, his love, his wisdom and his bliss,
> His grace, his doom, his mercy and his might,
> By which he lends us of himself a sight.
>
> SPENSER.

> This, this is what I love, and what is this?
>   I asked the beautiful earth, who said "Not I."
>   I asked the depths, and the immaculate sky.
> And all the spaces said, "Not he but his."
> And so, like one who scales a precipice,
>   Height after height I scaled the flaming book
>   Of the great universe, yea passed o'er all
> The world of thought, which so much higher is.
> Then I exclaimed, "To whom is mute all murmur
>   Of phantasy, of nature and of art,
> He than articulate language hears a firmer
>   And grander meaning in his own deep heart,
> No sound from cloud or angel." Oh to win
> That voiceless voice, "My servant, enter in."
>
> ARCHBISHOP TRENCH, *after* AUGUSTINE.

The religious man values what he sees chiefly as an imperfect shadowing forth of what he is incapable of seeing. The concerns of religion refer to indefinite objects, and are too weighty for the mind to support them without resting a great part of the burden on words and symbols, by a process whereby much is represented in little, and the infinite Being accommodates Himself to a finite capacity.—WORDSWORTH.

> The outer world is but the pictured scroll
>   Of worlds within the soul,
> A coloured chart, a blazoned missal-book
>   Whereon who rightly look
> May spell the splendour with their mortal eyes
>   And steer to Paradise.
>
> ALFRED NOYES.

CHAPTER VI

SYMBOLISM AND MYTH

THE conviction that all or most of our knowledge is in some sense 'symbolic' is more general than it was a hundred years ago. Philosophy, which aims at resolving all contradictions, is biased in favour of monism. At one time mind is explained as an epiphenomenon of matter, at another matter is explained as an epiphenomenon of mind. The latter theory, subjective idealism, is now viewed with favour even by physicists and astronomers. 'We are coming,' says Sir James Jeans, 'very near to those philosophical systems which regard the universe as a thought in the mind of its Creator, thereby reducing all discussion of material creation to futility.' Theology, now prepared to come to terms with its old enemy, is coming to recognize that the value of historical dogmas is symbolic, since as events in time and place they are within the domain of natural science, and when taken out of their religious context can hardly be treated as arguments for spiritual truths.

And yet neither subjective idealism nor naturalism can satisfy us. We live in two worlds, which are so far related to each other that if we deny all reality to either of them, the other fades away or loses all its determining features. If mind is only an epiphenomenon, it becomes as otiose as the gods of Epicurus, and we are left with a naïve realism which cannot be seriously treated as a picture of reality. If the visible world is a mere phantasmagoria, we are left with an empty heaven, like the Nirvana of Indian thought. In grasping at infinity we arrive only at zero.

The general view taken in this book is that reality is primarily a kingdom of values. The ultimate values which have been revealed to us are Goodness or Love, Truth, and Beauty. These are attributes of the nature and character of God, that is to say, of the Godhead in his relation to the world. They are known to us *a priori*; we cannot get behind them. They are therefore not symbolic; in them, so far as we n make them our own, we are in contact with reality. These three ultimate values are a triple star whose light often seems to mingle, a threefold cord not quickly broken. They cannot be reduced to each other, or treated as means to anything beyond them. There seems to be no fourth, to our knowledge. The concept of the Holy, emphasized by Otto and others, is not another value but a sense of the 'numinous' which is elicited by the contemplation, in the spirit of a worshipper, of any of the three values named as ultimate.

Christianity undoubtedly gives a kind of primacy to 'Love,' a word which it prefers to Goodness. Goodness in the sense of moral conduct belongs to our life here in a state of probation. In its outer manifestations it is the sacrament of the spiritual life, and it is inextricably involved in an internecine war against the powers of darkness. In the eternal world this antagonism is transcended. But Love is a divine thing. As Hartmann says, 'Personal love touches, like a soft light, the primal source of spiritual life, and it raises the spiritual source into consciousness. A life of love is a life spent in the knowledge of what is best worth knowing, a life of participation in the highest that is in man.' I agree with the late Professor de Burgh that when we say that God is Love we may make this affirmation not merely 'analogically' but directly. In other words, love as we know it differs from divine love in degree, but not in kind. As Clement of Alexandria says in his admirable analysis of spiritual growth, which I have already quoted, faith leads to knowledge and knowledge to love. In this final stage 'the knower and the known are united.' So St. Bernard in a beautiful sermon on the symbolism of the Canticles says: 'The perfect correspondence of wills makes of two one spirit. We need not fear that the inequality of the two should make this harmony imperfect; love knows not reverence. Love is the great reality. It is the only affection of the soul in which the creature is able to respond to the Creator, though not on equal terms, and to repay like with like. Although being a creature the soul loves less, because she is less, nevertheless if she loves with her whole self, nothing is wanting where all is given. He that is joined to God is one spirit.' Although St. Bernard speaks only of love to God, pure human love, as the sacrament of this, is the fulfilment of the law of love in our earthly life. 'When thou seest thy brother thou seest thy Lord.'

Is our love of God reciprocated? Spinoza, as is well known, says No. The One of Plotinus is exalted above all passions. But Origen, though in other places he seems afraid of the heresy called Patripassionism, says finely (in *Ezek. Hom.* vi, 6), 'The Father himself and God of all is long-suffering, merciful and pitiful. Has he not then in himself passions? The Father himself is not impassible; he has the passion of Love.'

We are not cut off from knowledge of things as they are. The Spirit of God dwells in us, and the vision of God, imperfect and shadowy but authentic as far as it goes, is within our reach. There is therefore a knowledge which is not symbolic, though in the expression and interpretation of it we must use as symbols those forms of thought which belong to our experience as denizens of a temporal and spatial world. The spiritual life must be lived before it can be interpreted in words.

In giving to value the primacy even over 'existence,' we are safeguarding the validity of the spiritual sense. For value is essentially hierarchical. The notion of degrees of reality is perhaps impossible to understand except in terms of valuation. In mere existence, abstracted from valuation, one thing is not more real than another, and in mere existence there are no minus signs; the lowest term, if we attempt to distinguish higher and lower, which we have no right to do apart from valuation, must be nothing, or the all-but-nothing, the 'no thing,' of the Platonic substratum which we call by the misleading word 'matter.' But in valuation we find minus qualities; evil is certainly not the mere privation of good. Those philosophers who have regarded evil as something merely privative, something which needs only to be supplemented and rearranged to bring it into harmony with the Absolute, are contradicting our experience of evil; and, as Mcneile Dixon says, 'If we abolish hell, the gates of heaven also shut with an ominous clang.' I would further maintain that we cannot exclude valuation without reducing perception to mere sensation. Perception always includes some measure of judgment.

I differ from those moral philosophers who identify value with what 'ought to be,' and who insist that all value must be value for a person.[1] Moral valuation no doubt speaks in the imperative, but this cannot be said of truth or beauty. In our homage to these two supreme values we are seeking to know what is, not what ought to be. Nor must value always be value for a person. We do not create values; we apprehend them.

A symbol is the representation of some moral or spiritual truth under the forms of natural things. Its object is suggestion or insight, it is a kind of language. Images are taken from natural relations and used to express more universal or ideal relations. The symbol is the indirect presentation of a concept which cannot be presented directly. In religious symbolism events in space and time are endowed with greater value and significance than belong to them as events in history. We need symbols because we belong to two worlds. I have said that we need a bridge to take us across from the temporal to the eternal, from the visible to the invisible, from appearance to reality, from shadow to substance. These words, which are all symbolic or metaphorical, picture to us different aspects of the duality of soul-life in this world. It is the function of symbolism to unite, not to separate, the two worlds. We do not always need this bridge. The contemplative, who aspires to the vision of God, discards one image after another, and at last, it may be, achieves his desire to apprehend spiritual reality 'without images.' He fears, rightly or wrongly, that any mental pictures drawn from the visible world may contaminate the purity of his communion with the Supreme, 'alone with the Alone.' At the other end of the scale, when we are dealing, by abstraction, with the empirical world, which in isolation has no meaning beyond itself, we forget to look for a vision of the infinite in the finite. There is no beauty, says E. I. Watkin, where the entire meaning is obvious. There are also many persons who, as St. Paul says, mind earthly things only. They do not need a bridge because they choose to remain on the nearer side. Their philosophy, if they have one, is naïve realism.

In order to link together the two worlds, there must be a resemblance between the symbol and the thing symbolized. The Platonists express this by saying that the lower 'participate' in the higher. As they were fond of saying, we could not see the sun if there were not something

---

[1] Hartmann (*Ethics*, Vol. I, 241, English translation), says: 'The relation of ontological to axiological determination is an old point of dispute. Many thinkers have given precedence in their systems to values over being; pre-eminently Plato; likewise Aristotle; so, too, the Stoics; and even Kant, as well as Fichte and Hegel.' But as a moralist Hartmann insists that there are values which without our co-operation remain unactualized. This is true, but in 'actualizing' the values in the phenomenal world we do not create them.

E

sun-like in ourselves. The mere fact that we are conscious of our limitations shows that there is something in us which can transcend them.

The facts are absolute, though our knowledge of them is relative. Some philosophers, such as the Russian Berdyaeff, distinguish between realist and idealist symbolism. The latter, exemplified for instance by Kant, immerses us in subjectivity, refusing to believe that we have knowledge of objective reality. The same objection is taken to the *symbolo-fidéisme* which at one time was popular in France. It sees no necessity in the symbols, which in consequence are not true symbols, since they fail to connect the two worlds. Realist symbolism is incarnational. Now we see as in a mirror, by means of symbols, but the mirror reflects real objects. The true mysticism, says R. L. Nettleship, in a passage which I have already quoted, is that everything, in being what it is, is symbolic of something more.

The distinction between a symbol and a sign has been insisted upon by many great writers. Goethe says: 'That is true symbolism where the more particular represents the more general, not as a dream or shadow, but as a vivid instantaneous revelation of the inscrutable.' And again: 'Of the Absolute in the theoretical sense I do not venture to speak, but this I maintain, that if a man recognizes it in its manifestations, and always keeps his eye fixed upon it, he will reap a very great reward.' The wrong kind of mysticism, says Emerson, consists in the mistake of an accidental and individual symbol for a universal one. Ruskin's distinction between fancy and imagination aims at the same truth. 'There is reciprocal action between the intensity of moral feeling and the power of imagination. The powers of the imagination may always be tested by accompanying tenderness of emotion. Imagination is quiet, fancy restless; fancy details, imagination suggests. All egotism is destructive of imagination.' Plato gives a lower place to imagination (*phantasia*). He would not have agreed with Wordsworth that imagination is 'reason in its most exalted mood.' We have to wait for Philostratus for the contrast between imitation (*mimesis*) and imagination. Imagination, says Philostratus, is a more cunning craftsman than imitation; for imitation portrays what it has seen, imagination what it has not seen. We may, I think, admit that imitation is not a happy word for the creation or use of symbols; but Plato is not to be saddled with a crude theory of copying. Music, for example, to which he attaches great importance, is not a representation *in pari materia* of anything visible. Good music is 'an imitation of a good soul.' (*Laws*, 812). Music and painting (*Cratylus*, 423), are *languages*. In an interesting passage of the *Statesman* he says that some things have sensible images, which are readily known, but that the greatest and highest truths have no outward images visible to man; immaterial things, which are the noblest and greatest, are shown only in thought and idea. This may seem to distinguish between myth and symbol; the myth, which aims at visualizing the greatest and highest truths, creates its pictures for the purpose; it does not find them in nature. Harnack shows that a symbol in its proper sense implies a sacrament, or, as the Greeks called a sacrament a mystery. 'What we nowadays understand by symbols is a thing which is not that which it represents; at that time (in the second century,) it denoted a thing which in some kind of way is that which it signifies; but on the other hand according to the ideas of that period the heavenly element lay either in or behind the visible form without being identical with it.' The symbol was never a mere type or sign, but always embodied a mystery. Justin Martyr uses 'to speak symbolically,' and 'to speak in a mystery,' as interchangeable terms. The doctrine of sacraments as 'efficacious signs' is no doubt dangerous, as bordering on sympathetic magic; but even Aristotle says that 'in all natural things there is something marvellous, as Heracleitus is reported to have said, Here, too there are gods.' Nature, he says elsewhere, is marvellous or superhuman (δαιμονία), but not divine; it half conceals and half reveals God. A mystery, for the ancients, is not something inexplicable; it is something revealed, truly though inadequately, in a lower medium.

A symbol is not a conventional sign. The Union Jack makes us feel patriotic; the smell of incense makes some of us feel religious; but there is no essential connection between the sign and the thing signified. Most of our linguistic symbols are only conventional; a dead metaphor is not symbolic, because it is dead. But poetical language sometimes suggests that which it describes. Homer's line, αὖτις ἔπειτα πέδονδε κυλίνδετο λᾶας ἀναιδής suggests the stone of Sisyphus bounding down to the plain. Virgil's 'quadrupedante putrem son tu quat t ungula campum' suggests a horse galloping. Rather less obvious in their suggestiveness are Milton's lines, 'The trumpet spake not to the armed throng,' or 'Swinges the scaly horror of his folded tail,' and Tennyson's 'His heavy-shotted hammock-shroud Drops in his vast and wandering grave.' Our language is exceptionally rich in words which suggest their meanings, words like crash, boom, hiss, stop, thunder. Some modern philosophies have I think, gone too far in explaining thought as based on linguistics.

The line between sign and symbol is not easy to draw. A crown is a sign of royalty, an aureole of saintliness or spiritual dignity (in some Byzantine pictures even Satan has a nimbus), but these are conventional signs. And yet the suggestions which they convey, like those conveyed by eloquence or poetry, are much the same as those suggested by what we classify as real symbols. The changes of the seasons remind us that mortal a facta peribunt—in all literature the decay of vegetation at the approach of winter is a symbol of human mortality. A flowing river is a picture of 'the stream of time.' The Anglo-Saxon noble, in a famous passage of Bede, who compared the life of man to the flight of a bird which darts through a lighted hall from darkness into darkness again, is felt to have found a striking symbol, although, as I shall say presently, light and darkness are themselves only symbols of life and death. Arbitrary and accidental signs are useful as language, but symbolic mysticism postulates a real resemblance between the symbol and the thing symbolised. When St. Paul says that the invisible things of God since the creation of the world are seen, being understood from the things that are made, I have demurred to the word 'clearly' in our versions, which is not in the Greek, but otherwise the words express the faith both of Christianity and of Platonism.

If we believe that the world of time and space, which necessarily supplies the forms under which we picture reality, and the language in which we express our thoughts, is an image or reflection of the real or spiritual world, we must recognize that, except when we are concerned with the absolute values, and even then when we try to interpret them to ourselves, we cannot dispense with symbols. The mystic, whether Christian or Indian, tries to realize the inadequacy of the temporal and spatial symbols. But the 'negative way' has its limits; we may cease to think as children, but we must always think as men.

In our thoughts about God we remember the Psalmist's warning, 'Thou thoughtest wickedly, that I am even such an one as thyself,' and very many of men's thoughts about God, not only in backward races but in the Old Testament and among modern Christians, are open to this reproach. But when, in our anxiety to escape from anthropomorphism, we identify the God of religion with the Absolute of philosophy, we find that a Being stripped of all limiting attributes is not a possible object of worship. We must be content, I think, to say that God has revealed Himself to us as perfect Love, Wisdom, and Beauty, and that He has given us the presence in our souls of His Holy Spirit, through Whom we may have communion with the eternal world beyond space and time. The world around us is full of traces of His presence, reflected, as it were, in an imperfect medium, and brought into fuller light by contrast with an evil principle which for us is equally real, and which no philosophy, in my opinion, has been able to explain. In mystical ecstasy some have thought that we may be for a moment aware of the source of all being; but the God of religion is not the Absolute of whom nothing positive can be said without denying it in the same breath.

In what sense, and to what degree, is dogmatic theology symbolic?

The part of symbolism in belief is very far from simple. Goethe says, 'That is true symbolism, where the more particular represents the more general, not as a dream or shade, but as a vivid instantaneous revelation of the inscrutable.' This does not cover the whole field. Minds are differently constituted. Some men, like Kepler, 'wish to perceive the God whom I find everywhere in the external world, in like manner also within me.' Others, who feel the presence of God within them, seek to find evidence of His activity in the world outside.

Symbolism is not always an interpretation of the general by means of the particular. Those, for example, who distinguish between substance and shadow, or reality and appearance, are using optical symbols which perhaps are no more adequate than the spatial and temporal symbols of popular theology. It is, I think, helpful to divide symbols under two heads. There are the symbols behind which we can see, and the symbols behind which we cannot see. In speaking of the attributes of the Godhead, we are aware that our expressions are true only *per excellentiam*, though we shall not go so far as Scotus Erigena, and think that *nihilum* is the most respectful way of thinking of Him. I have said already that in saying that God is Love we are 'speaking no proverb' ; but when we speak of the wrath of God we may be very doubtful, and to speak of the eye or the hand of God is of course not serious anthropomorphism. Poetical and artistic symbolism is of a rather different kind. The almost universal use of metaphor in poetry is noted by Aristotle. We can hardly picture anything to ourselves without saying that it is like something else. Ritual, whether religious or secular, works by association. It is a very natural impulse to honour the Deity with the finest products of human art that we can devise. At the back of this impulse is the recognition that Beauty is one of the ultimate values, the revealed attributes of God, and that as we honour God as Truth in science and philosophy, as we honour Him as Goodness by righteousness and love, so we honour Him as Beauty by making all our handiwork, and especially whatever is specially dedicated to His service, as fine as we know how. This kind of symbolism needs no further explanation.

But there are other religious symbols which are not opaque, and it is here that controversy becomes acute. Goethe says rather brutally, 'The incurable evil of religious controversy is that while one party wishes to connect the highest interest of humanity with fables, the other tries to rest it on things that satisfy no one.' A mere fable or allegory, like Bunyan's *Pilgrim's Progress*, may have great religious value, but there is no ambiguity about its character. Great religious poems, like the Divine Comedy and Paradise Lost, are based on what the poets believed to be literal facts. It is known that Milton rejected his first plan of writing about King Arthur partly because he had doubts about the historicity of the Round Table stories. There is very little allegory or symbolism in either poem. The case is more complicated when we consider St. Paul's attitude towards the earthly life of Christ. He makes it clear that he regards what our old divines called the whole process of Christ as a dramatic revelation of the spiritual life of the Christian. We also have to die to sin, to crucify the old man, to be buried and rise again to newness of life, seeking those things which are above, where Christ sitteth at the right hand of God. But although for the author of the Fourth Gospel the Incarnation was primarily a dramatic revelation of the love of God to mankind, for St. Paul it had other qualities. The Passion, on which his interest is mainly concentrated, was a sacramental act; it not only symbolized but effected something, and therefore had an essential importance as an event. Moreover, the resurrection was far from being an isolated occurrence in the past, for the glorified Christ is still living and active in the world. What is called Christ-mysticism is, as I have said, the kernel of his personal faith.

It is these historical facts, these happenings in time and place, which Liberal Christianity regards as symbols, but as symbols which it can see behind. The determination of the Catholic Church to make no terms with the Modernists, who honestly hoped that by the method of symbolism they had raised the dogmas of the Church to a secure position above high water mark, was due to the fact that neither they nor their opponents really regarded the historical dogmas as symbols. The traditionalist, who has accepted his creed on authority, and thinks it impious to call it in question, is indignant if the factual occurrence of the events in his creed is tampered with. The Liberal Churchman, on the other hand, does not really need them even as symbols. He has his own opinion as to what actually occurred in Palestine two thousand years ago, and he would never have invented such dogmas as the virgin birth and the bodily ascension to vivify his faith. He acquiesces in them as symbols for other people, and the other people have no use for them as symbols. The partial justification of the ecclesiastical authorities is illustrated by the course followed by some of the protagonists of Modernism after the rejection of their methods by the Church. It has even been maintained that Christianity might survive if its Founder were proved to be as mythical a personage as Hercules, a theory which no scholar could accept for a moment. This would in fact have one of two results. It might divinize the actual political Church, which, as Loisy argued, was obliged, in order to survive, to become what it has been; or it might leave, of Christianity, only mystical piety, which is almost independent of denominational forms. Church history is terribly unedifying. A theocracy must stoop to persecution, to unholy alliances, to fraud and a policy of obscurantism. It is not always the enemies of spiritual religion who are driven to exclaim with Gambetta, 'clericalism is the enemy.' And as for unattached mysticism, it is perhaps a melancholy reflection that the Society of Friends is numerically the smallest of all religious associations. Moreover, a religion which is no religion in particular is like a speech which is no language in particular. Esperanto and pidgin English do not carry us far.

This is not the place to remind my readers how difficult the position of a preacher now is, when so much of the old scaffolding of the building is no longer secure. The preacher wishes to help his people by 'speaking to their condition,' as the Quakers say; but he also wishes to preserve his own intellectual integrity, and not to use language which does not correspond with his own convictions. A sermon is always like a bucketful of water dashed over rows of narrow-necked vessels. A still better comparison would be with the perplexity of an optician, who has to provide a hundred myopic patients each with a pair of spectacles best suited to his defect of vision; and the religious teacher must try to help them to see the invisible! There can be no standardized orthodoxy to suit both the learned scholar and his kitchen-maid. We shall best understand what seems so strange in traditional eschatology if we remember that for many people religion is chiefly valued as providing an absolute sanction for good conduct. To the earnest moralist life appears in silhouette. The choice before him is not between the good, the better, and the best. It is between right and wrong, between good and evil. The importance of the alternative is infinite—to save his soul or to lose it. Hence he pictures the result of choosing rightly, or wrongly, in the most vivid colours; no imagination can exaggerate what it means to him. We are often told that the priests draw these crude pictures in order to entice or terrify the half converted. Too often this has been true; but it is seldom realized that auto suggestion plays a great part, and that conscience will have no dealings with half measures.

It is accepted that Christianity made its way in the Hellenistic world as a mystery religion, and some consideration of the symbolism characteristic of this type will not be out of place. The official cult of the pagan gods, linked with city and family, was still carried on, but it had withered in the hearts of men. In its place came the moral teaching of the philosophers, and an individual longing for what was already called salvation. These devotees united in communities. They were promised, as the reward of ascetic discipline and due observance of sacramental rites, release from care and trouble in the present life, and a blessed immortality or deification in the world to come. The pagan mystic, however, was still oppressed by fears of the malign influence of the stars, or by an impersonal fate pictured as Ananke (Necessity) or Tyche (Chance). The Church promised deliverance from these terrors.

There were two philosophical theories which underlay the symbolism of the mysteries. The materialistic pantheism of the Stoa lent itself to a doctrine of occult sympathies running through all nature. This doctrine obviously opens the door wide to astrology, magic, and superstitions of all kinds. The Church discouraged 'Chaldean' science; but just as the Plotinian doctrine of divine immanence degenerated into the theurgy of some later Neoplatonists, so the similar teaching of the school of Eckhart was followed by the fantastic speculations of Cornelius Agrippa and Paracelsus. The same phenomenon is observable in our own day. It is said that our *materia medica* still retains a few relics of the 'signatures' which it was believed that some plants display as an indication of their usefulness as drugs.

The other theory was that of allegorism. This method was practised, before Christianity, both by Jews and Greeks. There is no other way of making archaic stories about the gods, and archaic sacred books, acceptable to a more critical and reflective age. The legends about the Greek gods were by no means edifying, and Homer makes fun of the Olympians, or some of them, as Scottish folk-lore turned the Devil into a comic character. But where such levity is precluded, there is the choice between turning narrative into allegory, and justifying—perhaps even holding up for imitation, the capricious and cruel actions recorded of an archaic tribal deity. The former method, however absurd from the point of view of scientific criticism, is much less objectionable than the latter. A good example of the method of allegorism in paganism is Plutarch's essay on Isis and Osiris. Apuleius is able to derive spiritual exaltation from the sacramental worship of Isis, with which he concludes a very dirty novel. Philo applies allegorism without scruple to the Hebrew Scriptures, and St. Paul follows him much more cautiously. One branch of allegoric symbolism, it was thought, was cryptic and unconscious prophecy.

Religious symbols often lose their value, when changing climates of opinion either diminish men's interest in the thing symbolized, or prevent the symbol from any longer suggesting what it was framed to represent. For instance, many of our authorized prayers, in which we humble ourselves before the throne of grace, and deprecate the wrath of an all-powerful ruler, do not express the relation in which citizens of a free country wish to stand with our heavenly Father. The wrath of God is a symbol of something which many people think it unworthy to attribute to the Deity. A scientific age is most unwilling to accept the theory of supernaturalistic dualism, of occasional interventions and breaches of natural law. This reluctance makes a large class of traditional symbols unacceptable. For those who reject the belief in what Catholic theologians call analogy, the belief that the creation reveals, though imperfectly, the attributes of the Creator, events in time become mere occurrences with no meaning beyond themselves. As bare facts they belong to the sphere of nature, and whether they are true or false have no bearing on religion. Simple folk still cling to them, without realizing that, when taken out of their context, they have no value for faith; and vulgar rationalism assumes with equal thoughtlessness that miracle is not, as Goethe said, the dearest child of faith, but its parent. The traditional symbols of Christianity are in part the legacy of an unscientific age, and in part the compromise which great Churches have to make for the sake of the uneducated majority. But faith must be allowed to speak its own language, which is not the language of science.

This discussion would not be complete without some consideration of a few conceptions which are certainly symbolic, but so natural and so universal that we seldom think of them as in any way artificial. It is curious that though most people wish to be immortal, no one wants to be ubiquitous. Our spatial symbolism is not that of dwellers in Flatland; it pictures reality as higher and lower. Perhaps there is no nation which has not envisaged the Deity as 'high and lifted up.' Perhaps there is no language in which words like 'sublime,' 'exalted,' 'superior,' 'high,' are not honorific epithets, and 'low,' 'base,' 'inferior' terms of dispraise. Some peoples have identified the Supreme Being with the sky; more commonly the sky has been his residence. Sun-worship combines the symbolism of height with that of light. Aristotle believed that the outer envelope of the universe was composed of a fifth element, æther, finer than the four elements known on earth, a doctrine which already appears in the *Epinomis*, probably a genuine work of Plato in his old age. God Himself, according to Aristotle, was not in space at all; but the æther, of which he thought the stars are made, and the *pneuma*, a material but very tenuous substance which was not yet equivalent to our 'Spirit,' were nearer to the divine than we are. The Stoics brought God into the universe by identifying Him with the element of which the outermost circle was composed. The Platonists rejected this materialism, but not the spatial metaphor. The Epicureans located the gods in the *intermundia*, but practically banished them from the universe.

Munro, in defending Lucretius, prefers even his cosmology to the 'rotund and rotatory God' of the Stoics. Apart from the notion that the Deity has His residence in the sky, the observation of the heavenly bodies produced in the ancients, as it did in Kant, a feeling of awe. George Meredith, in one of his finest sonnets, suggests that even Lucifer was so affected.

> Around the ancient track marched, rank on rank,
> The army of unalterable law.

It is probable that the majority of Christians still believe, or half believe, in a geographical heaven which might be reached in an aeroplane if we knew the way. I once got into trouble with one of our most intelligent bishops by saying that he did not believe in a spatial heaven. He protested that he had only said that it was not 'over our heads.' He must have known that the earth rotates. It was a remarkable illustration of the reluctance even of educated men to admit that Christian eschatology is, and must be, purely symbolic. If our traditionalists are asked whether they believe heaven to be within or without the solar system, they do not answer. Galileo was perhaps not speaking seriously when he hoped that his opponents would see Jupiter's moons 'on their way to heaven,' but we cannot be sure. Whichcote, the Cambridge Platonist, said that 'heaven is first a temper, then a place'; even he did not dare to say that it is not a place.

The notion of 'a new heaven and a new earth' belongs to a conflation of the forms of time and space. The old expectation of a millennium on earth, the 'days of the Messiah' of apocalyptic Judaism, had a shadowy survival in the dream of human perfectibility, the secularized apocalyptic of the 'century of hope.' The belief in a local hell in the centre of the earth hardly exists any longer; it gave a plausible explanation of volcanic eruptions. The Roman Church, it is true, still maintains that a local hell beneath our feet has the support of the best ecclesiastical authorities, and that the flames are not to be explained away symbolically; but it is certain that educated Romanists do not feel themselves obliged to accept this.

Spatial ideas are our clearest ideas, and it is very difficult not to clothe any idea which we wish to picture clearly in spatial forms. Bergson has shown how constantly time is spatialized in our thought. Plato in the seventh book of the *Republic* ridicules the notion that astronomy 'compels the soul to look upwards.' 'I cannot conceive,' he says, 'that any science makes the soul look upwards, unless it has to do with the real and the invisible. It makes no difference whether we gaze stupidly at the sky or downwards at the ground. So long as we are observing sensible objects our souls are looking downwards.' If it is true that Plato before the end of his life abandoned the geocentric theory of the universe, he may have guessed that there is no real up and down in space. But he allows us to 'look up' when we are contemplating invisible reality. All through the history of religion we find a fluctuation between 'both-and' and 'either-or.'

God is 'in heaven,' but He is 'closer to us than breathing and nearer than hands and feet.' 'His centre is everywhere, His circumference nowhere'; and yet 'God is in heaven and thou upon earth, therefore let thy words be few.' It is interesting that Augustine at first 'did not know that God was a Spirit, not having limbs.' He came to know that 'God dwells deep in my being as my innermost self, and is higher than the highest that I can reach. He is above my soul, but not in the same sense as the sky is above the earth.' The mystics, who had learnt from the Neoplatonists that God is a Spirit (Tertullian never learnt this,) taught that to ascend to God means to withdraw into the depths of ourselves. Abelard says that the exalted Christ does not occupy any position in space, but has an 'equal dignity' with the Father. Many modern theologians are more timid. Martensen on the Continent and Canon Mason in England actually suggested that the body of Jesus was raised for some distance above the ground. It suggests some stage contrivance. And yet the instinct which makes many of us reluctant to repudiate a religious symbol as pure fiction must be regarded with respect. Our knowledge, whether of earthly or of heavenly things, or of the relation between them, cannot be rounded off completely while we live here.

Greek mythology and philosophy preferred spatial to temporal myths. 'Here' and 'Yonder,' rather than present and future, expressed their consciousness of the difference between the seen and the unseen, between fact and value.

The symbol of Time is dealt with in another chapter of this book. No one can hope to solve the immense difficulties which surround the problem of Time. Those who argue that Time is real say that we must answer three main questions: (1) Ought we to think of God as above time in the sense that for Him there is no movement from past to present, no after or before? I answer that 'earlier and later' are quite different from 'past and future.' God, we may suppose, is aware of the successive stages in the development of every process, but for Him there is no past and future, since it is quite wrong to say that past and future are non-existent. (2) Are we to think of the time-process as a whole, ordained to realize a purpose the full meaning of which can be understood only when the purpose reaches completion? I answer that an eternal purpose is eternally frustrate. To speak of 'an endless process realizing a divine purpose,' and of a time-process '*succeeded* by a timeless state' is nonsense. It is almost impossible to imagine any real unity between events on this planet and those in another world a million light-years away and a million of our years apart. It is better to think of God's purposes in creation as finite and independent, each having a beginning and an end. When they are achieved, they take their places in the eternal order. (3) How far can human spirits, whose life is immersed in time and space, experience timeless eternity, either now or after death? I answer that many of our thoughts, not only in religion, are fixed upon timeless objects, and that the absolute values, of which we have a *priori* knowledge, are above time, though they are reflected in the time-process. Value, says Höffding, is not absolutely dependent on its own conservation. 'It is not always estimated by dates. Should it be the fate of the good and beautiful to perish, would it therefore be less good and beautiful? The more full of content life is, the more we forget time.'

We have a right to believe that no value perishes out of existence. 'Nothing that really *is* can ever perish,' says Plotinus. God is love, and love is stronger than death.

The present trend of opinion, while ready to consign spatial images to the category of symbols, claims a much higher degree of reality for Time. Spinoza, as is well known, was of the opposite opinion, though for my own part I cannot reconcile the privileged position which he gives to extension with the rest of his philosophy. Bergson and Samuel Alexander, as I have said, almost divinize Time. The causes of this movement, which sets modern philosophy in sharp divergence from Hellenic as well as from Indian thought, are rather complex. Voluntaristic philosophy, which in this country was favoured by Coleridge and has since his time found powerful supporters, especially, as is natural, among moralists, cannot tolerate a view of reality which makes the will otiose and process imaginary. There must be real change —epigenesis in some form—and not merely evolution, which means the unpacking of what was there already in germ. Such words as emergence and organism come into favour, words which assert and deny the reality of change in the same breath. Vitalism, discreetly camouflaged, is rehabilitated. This wishful thinking is supposed to be supported by the newest physics. Time and Space are somehow mixed together. Time as it is in itself and our measurement of Time are confused; Bergson psychologizes Time under the name of 'la durée réelle,' and even calls Newtonian Time artificial. These thinkers are pleased to find that the sciences which deal with life are not content with nature as pictured by chemistry. Panpsychism is expanded to cover the unaccountable behaviour of electrons. There is free will everywhere, perhaps chance; at any rate the indeterminate. Things happen, according to William James, which administer a shock even to the Creator. If there is a God, He is more like the president of an American republic than an eastern king. He needs our co-operation, perhaps our advice. Thus contingency, which needs time, is brought into the heart of things.

The dream of perfectionism has helped greatly in the same direction. Time, for the ancients, was neutral, or, when the world was on the downgrade, an enemy. *Damnosa quid non imminuit dies?* The slow pulsation of the universe swung backwards and forwards like the pendulum of a clock. The Church in the dark ages had no hopes for any mundane future. But the ideal, which had once taken wings into the Platonic world of Forms, now came back to earth, and took shape as the future, which, as Anatole France says, is a good place in which to store our dreams. So vehemently was this hope cherished that the old theory of recurrence was spurned as 'absolute pessimism,' and the real pessimism, the fate of the universe according to the second law of thermodynamics, was almost welcomed as proving that processes are irreversible. Let us live in a world where things really happen, even if we and our God are under sentence of final annihilation.

If Christianity is a historical religion, it would seem that certain events in time have a greater importance than the Greek conception of this world could allow them. No one disputes that the religious movement in Palestine at the beginning of our era has had an enormous influence on history from that time to this. The author of the Fourth Gospel regards the Incarnation as a revelation of the eternal counsels of God, though even here the tendency to prefer 'both-and' to 'either-or,' shows itself in the few verses which imply the simpler view common among believers. Eternal life is equated with the knowledge of God and Christ; it is something into which we may enter while we live here. This Gospel is full of symbolism. It is arranged in triplets and sequences of seven. Jesus proclaims Himself the living water, the living bread, the light of the world, the resurrection and the life. In St. Paul the life, death, and resurrection of Christ are a drama to be re-enacted in little in the life of the Christian. Thus the Gospel story is a revelation of timeless reality made 'in the fullness of time'—that is to say at the earliest possible moment. A crucified Messiah was to the Jews a stumbling-block; St. Paul's preaching seemed to the Athenians foolishness; but by the time of the Apologists, and still more in the school of Alexandria, in the Cappadocian Fathers, and in Augustine, faith and philosophy joined hands. The difficulty which many feel now is that the symbolism which St. Paul acknowledges in the famous words of 1 Corinthians xiii is associated with physical miracles which at that time seemed to follow naturally from the unique position which the Church assigned to its Founder, but which to us are not a support and proof of religion, but for many Modernists a stumbling-block which they would be glad to get rid of. When the scientific type of explanation is accepted in everyday matters, but is excluded from points which religion claims to exempt from natural law, there arises what Höffding calls a bastard conception called miracle. If the reported events are true, we can never discover that there is no natural cause for them; if they are not, our faith is not injured, since miracles are not for us natural symbols of spiritual truths. 'Miracle is a bastard which neither party can afford to own.' Nevertheless, the conception of special 'acts of God' is valued as contradicting the theory that events follow each other blindly and meaninglessly. Above all things we must beware of an irreducible dualism of fact and value. In this way for many believers miracles are symbolic, a safeguard of precious truths. What I think we may say is that when symbol hardens into dogma, and becomes a mere fact in the time-series to be accepted as such without question, it loses some of its meaning as a religious symbol, and possibly prevents the creation of new symbols which might be more in accordance with what I have called modern climates of opinion.

The only possible solution to the difficulties of the time-relation, says Höffding, lies in the direction of inwardness. If our picture of eternity is the expression of the permanence of value through the changes of time, the externality of the time-relation disappears. I think that this is true;

but the problem remains very thorny, and we must be content to say that in this life we must not expect to solve it. Eternity in the full sense belongs to God only. We can justify the use of symbols, because religious feeling is not content until the infinite is presented in the form of the finite. If we are forbidden to do this we must be dumb.

Next to spatial and temporal symbolism, that of Light is the most natural and the most universal. Plato in his famous Seventh Epistle compares the sudden inspiration of the mystic to 'a leaping spark,' and the same comparison has been made independently by many others who have had the experience. In the myth of the cave, the real world is a realm of light outside the cave. The symbol is indeed so obvious that no explanation of it seems necessary. Greek Christians spoke of baptism as 'enlightenment,' the German equivalent of which was used in the eighteenth century of a very different illumination. The savage naturally associates darkness with mystery, evil, and danger, and early religious literature, as in the Old Testament and in the Persian religion, is full of the antagonism between darkness and light. The Platonists valued the symbol of light partly because it seemed to them to represent the unilateral activity of God, Who imparts Himself without losing anything of His substance. For Christians, the Logos was a reflection of the glory of the Father. In the First Epistle of John we even have 'God is Light, and in him is no darkness at all.'

We may turn to less universal types of symbolism. When our Lord bade His disciples to consider the lilies, He gave His sanction to the mysticism based on natural objects. Those who have seen the hillsides of northern Palestine ablaze with scarlet anemones in early spring will agree that no royal robes can equal them in splendour. The parables in the Gospels, suggested by almost every detail of rural work and industry, show how, in the mind of Christ, earth is the shadow of heaven, so that everything in our daily life may remind us of our duty towards God. It is not an accident that so many scenes in the life of Christ are recorded as taking place on hill-tops. On one occasion Christ spent a night on the summit of a mountain in solitary prayer. 'I will lift up mine eyes to the hills, from whence cometh my help.' We shall hardly find this particular source of inspiration so clearly indicated till we come to Wordsworth.

In Bradley's great book, *Appearance and Reality*, which shows a real sympathy with mysticism, we read: 'Nature viewed materialistically is only an abstraction for certain purposes, and has not a high degree of truth or reality. The poet's nature has much more. Our principle that the abstract is the unreal moves us steadily upward. It compels us in the end to credit nature with our higher emotions. The process can only cease when nature is quite absorbed into spirit, and at every stage of the process we find increase in reality.' Complete absorption would of course mean the disappearance of symbols, an ecstatic state which some mystics claim to have experienced; but for us the poet's vision is enough; we cannot get beyond it.

Poetry is a representation of the invisible under visible forms. I am fond of this stanza by William Watson:

> Forget not, brother singer, that though Prose
> Can never be too truthful nor too wise,
> Song is not Truth, nor Wisdom, but the rose
> Upon Truth's lips, the light in Wisdom's eyes.

The nature-mystic knows that even poetry is fettered by the inability of language to express all that he feels. Just as the musician finds in Beethoven glimpses into reality which no speech can describe, so Wordsworth knows that nature will permit no inventory to be made of her charms. There were even times when 'thought was not,' and many when he was impatient with the 'loose types of things through all degrees,' in which fancy labours to clothe imagination.

The Greek Fathers, though they show a regrettable want of appreciation of the artistic treasures which the dying civilization of paganism had left to them, were fond of calling attention to the glories of nature as a revelation of God. It was an unfortunate legacy of Semitism that the early Church did not recognize the quite legitimate symbolism which the Jews called idolatry. Some of the pagans, who watched the destruction of irreplaceable works of art, have left pathetic protests against the notion that they deified material objects of wood and stone. There was a belated revival of this barbarism after the Reformation.

I have said, in my published Hulsean Lectures at Cambridge, that there has been a strong Platonic tradition in English literature, and especially in our poetry. Spenser's Hymn of Heavenly Beauty is a very beautiful example of pure Platonism, and there are equally fine specimens in Sir Philip Sidney. But the contemplation of nature ought not to bring 'loathing of this vile world and these gay-seeming things.' This is the dualistic Gnosticism against which Plotinus protests so strongly. What can be more beautiful, he asks, than the visible world except the world above? And when Shelley in famous lines says that Life like a dome of many-coloured glass stains the white radiance of eternity, he seems to bid us to look away from the visible instead of through it. There is a spiritualistic monism which at last defeats itself.

Wordsworth is a natural Platonist, thoroughly Greek in his dread of giving rein to the strong emotions which, as he tells us, were a temptation to him. His great importance to the student of mysticism is that it was at first hand, not literary or speculative. The Prelude, as Legouis and Cazamian say, 'is the most admirable record of a soul's progress towards the full possession of self, which is implied in the apostolate of a poetic calling.' Wordsworth's faith was lived as well as thought. Few men have disciplined themselves more severely. Few have renounced so consistently the seductions of money and fame, and have accepted so willingly the loneliness which is the price of the pioneer's devotion to his vocation.

There is, however, one difference between Plato's mysticism and that of Wordsworth. It is true that Beauty for the Greeks was not merely æsthetic. It included nobility of character, which for Plato was the higher kind of beauty. Still, for Plato the lover of wisdom begins with admiration for beautiful forms, especially in the human body, and rises through them to the invisible forms of spiritual beauty. For Wordsworth, nature symbolized not so much beauty as universal life. He hated the materialism of the science of his day, but he looked forward to a time when 'the dull eye' of science, 'dull and inanimate, no more shall cling chained to its object in brute slavery.' 'If the time should ever come when that which is now called science shall be ready to put on as it were a form of flesh and blood, the poet will lend his divine spirit to aid the transformation, and will welcome the being thus produced as a dear and genuine inmate of the household of man.' In order to fit himself for this inner vision, he resolved, in words which remind us of Spinoza, to confine himself to 'such objects as excite no morbid passions, no disquietude, no vengeance and no hatred.' He is determined to reject all fanciful analogies. The value of natural objects is not that they remind us of something that they are not, but that they help us to understand something that they in part are. 'This earth is the world of all of us, in which we find our happiness or not at all.' This attitude separates him very decisively from many mystical contemplatives. The faculty which thus sees the divine in nature is imagination, which helps us to perceive 'the forms whose kingdom is where time and space are not.' Wordsworth's contemplation of nature perhaps required more solitude than would have been congenial to a Greek.

For it is not true that this kind of contemplation is a faculty which 'all possess, though few use it.' I do not think that nature speaks to most of us as it did to Wordsworth. Most of us feel at times the sublimity of high mountains, and of 'the moving waters at their priest-like task of pure ablution round earth's human shores,' the sea which, as Euripides says, 'washes away all human ills'; but too often when we are alone with nature, we make her speak our language instead of learning hers. She smiles or frowns according as we are happy or depressed. To many people she is dumb; they crave for human intercourse. Strange as it may seem to those whose mind to them a kingdom is, there are some who are only happy in a crowd. We must not despise them. Our neighbours, our 'even Christians' as Julian of Norwich calls them, are the noblest part of nature. The 'human face divine,' when not marred by sin and folly, is a clearer reflection of the God of love than any inanimate scene. 'When thou seest thy brother thou seest thy Lord.' It is perhaps significant that the poet's vision so often exhausts itself in youth, leaving bitter regrets that the 'spirit of delight' now comes so rarely.

Wordsworth's famous *Ode* moves us more deeply than the noble philosophy of the *Prelude*, because the latter is emotion remembered in tranquillity, written, as he says himself, to rescue thoughts which might otherwise be forgotten. But in the *Ode* we have poignant grief at the loss of a great consolation. It is almost like the Dark Night of the cloistered mystics. It is not merely the passing of buoyant youth into middle age.

Mark Rutherford was, I think, the first to note that Wordsworth was subject to fits of deep dejection, and I fancy that those who have recourse to inanimate nature for comfort have often been troubled in this way. There are some who think they are attracted by nature, or by God, when they are only repelled by man. The poet was not repelled by man, but he was deeply disillusioned by politics. He remained something of a radical to the end; in his last years he confessed to some sympathy with the Chartists. But the outcome of the French Revolution, which, like his friends Southey and Coleridge, he had welcomed with enthusiasm, filled him with horror. His first reaction was almost like an attempt to stabilize puerile animism; in philosophy it approached pantheism. But this is not the real tendency of mysticism. In later years he became more genuinely religious and Christian. It was a normal development of character, though the poetic inspiration failed.

It would be easy and tempting to dwell on the vein of mysticism in other English poets, and to show how strong this idealistic strain is in our nation. Tennyson not only understood mysticism, as he shows in his fine poem, *The Ancient Sage*, but he had genuine mystical experiences himself. Robert Bridges seems to me to reach his highest level in such mystical poems as his *Joy*.

> And having tasted it I speak of it,
> And praise him thinking how I trembled then
> When his touch strengthened me, as now I sit
> In wonder, reaching out beyond my ken,
> Reaching to turn the day back, and my pen
> Urging to tell a tale which told would seem
> The witless phantasy of them that dream.

But there is one nature-mystic whom I do not wish to pass over, the young seventeenth-century contemplative, Thomas Traherne, whose writings have quite lately come to light by an accident, after being long completely forgotten. The two volumes, *Poetical Works* and *Centuries of Meditations*, edited by the discoverer, Mr. Bertram Dobell, are now well known. It is to be hoped that such entire neglect of an important writer does not happen often; though when we think of the lost treasures of classical literature which the dark ages allowed to perish, while they preserved tons of dreary trash, we cannot be very confident. Traherne is not quite in the first rank, but he is worthy to stand as a third with the two Welshmen, George Herbert and Vaughan, whose sacred poetry has delighted many generations of readers.

As a nature-mystic Traherne is entitled to special attention. The contemplatives of the cloister were often indifferent to the revelation of God in His works around us. The author of the *Imitation of Christ* says: 'Thou hopest perhaps to subdue desire by the power of enjoyment, but thou wilt find it impossible for the eye to be satisfied with seeing or the ear to be filled with hearing. If all visible nature could pass in review before thee, what would it be but a vain vision?' The message of Traherne is quite different; he gives us something which we miss in the stern detachment of Thomas à Kempis. 'Your enjoyment of the world is never right till every morning you awake in heaven, see yourself in your Father's palace, and look upon the skies, the earth and the air as celestial joys, having such a reverent esteem of all as if you were among the angels. The bride of a monarch in her husband's chamber hath no such causes of delight as you. You never enjoy the world aright till the sea itself floweth in your veins, till you are clothed with the heavens and crowned with the stars, and perceive yourself to be the sole heir of the whole world, and more than so because men are in it who are every one sole heirs as well as you. Till you can sing and rejoice and delight in God as misers do in gold and kings in sceptres, you never enjoy the world.' We should 'perfectly hate the abominable corruption of men in despising it that you would rather suffer the flames of hell than be guilty of their error. There is so much blindness and ingratitude and damned folly in it. The world is a mirror of infinite beauty, yet no man sees it.' We may remember how Plotinus blames the Gnostics for not seeing that there can be no more beautiful world than this, except the world 'yonder'. One quotation from his poetry will show that he did not rest content with the visible world.

> For giving me desire,
> An eager thirst, a burning ardent fire,
> A virgin infant flame,
> A love with which into the world I came,
> An inward hidden heavenly love,
> Which in my soul doth work and move,
> And ever ever me inflame
> With restless longing, heavenly avarice
> That never could be satisfied,
> That did incessantly a paradise
> Unknown suggest, and something undescried
> Discern, and bear me to it; be
> Thy name for ever praised by me.

Even more than Wordsworth, Traherne 'averts his eyes from half of human fate.' But joy is one of the fruits of the Spirit, and those who are happy have a good reason to give—the fact that they are so. Traherne must have been a very pleasant companion. 'You are as prone to love as the sun is to shine, it being the most natural and delightful employment of the soul of man, without which you are dark and miserable.' The radiance of a loving heart illuminated, for Traherne, the whole of nature, and made his life, which was cut short at the age of thirty-eight, a constant hymn of praise. There is the same temper in St. Francis of Assisi and his immediate disciples. The bridegroom of my lady Poverty must be always merry. St. Augustine noticed, before his conversion, the bearing of his Christian friends, '*serena et non dissolute hilaris.*' In these sad times the deep happiness of Christians, 'sorrowful yet always rejoicing,' when our religion was fresh from the mint, must not be forgotten.

F

CHAPTER VII

GREEK MYSTICISM

WESTERN civilization owes more to Greece than to any other country; and though Christianity had its source in Palestine, the Gospel of Christ was rejected by His own countrymen, as India rejected Buddhism. In the event, Christianity won Europe and lost Asia. The personal and spiritual religion which may be called mysticism, even when it acquired a distinctively Christian character, was affiliated to the mystical tradition in Greece and its colonies; it won its early victories as a mystery-cult not generically different from the rivals with which it successfully competed. This being so, I have thought that my book would be incomplete without some account of the movements which a theologian might say prepared the way for a fuller revelation. The Alexandrian and Cappadocian Fathers, and Augustine, were willing to admit obligations which cannot be denied. In this chapter I shall not follow the course of history further than the Stoics, reserving Plotinus for a separate study. After the third century the Church carried off most of the honey to its own hive.

The mystical tradition appears to us as an undercurrent in Greek thought, for the surviving literary sources, until we come to Plato, are very scanty. We have fragments of prayers and hymns, mutilated inscriptions and papyri, emblems, frescoes, ruins of chapels, with scattered references and quotations. The mysteries, like Freemasonry, were not to be divulged. There is a little in Pindar; there is the *Bacchae* of Euripides, who was not an Orphic; there are references in Aristophanes, the comic poet; Herodotus is ill-informed, tracing Orphism to Egypt. As for Plato, he can tell us a great deal; but our scholars are so prepossessed with the idea that the Greeks were genial realists with both feet firmly planted on the earth, that they regard Plato as a freak, not a typical Athenian at all. To distrust and disparage the phenomenal world and all that it contains, to advocate abstention from public life, asceticism and contemplation, is this the way of the Greeks, who warmed both hands before the fire of life? But this is a mistake. Spirituality and idealism were never foreign to the Greek character, though the State religion was strangely superficial and often barbaric. It could not absorb mysticism, as the Christian Churches and the Indian religions have done. The Greek cities were tolerant of everything except disloyalty. When Justinian closed the schools of Athens, he marked the end of a thousand years of free thinking on all things sacred and secular such as the world has never enjoyed since.

I have made it clear that the nature of personality, or as the Greeks said of the soul, the destiny of the individual, the status of the phenomenal world in relation to ultimate reality, and the place of myth or symbol in religion and philosophy, are the problems which constitute the intellectual

90

side of mystical religion. The vision of God is the end of the quest; self-discipline is the road which leads to it.

In the Homeric poems the soul is not the man. The Iliad begins by saying that the wrath of Achilles sent many souls of heroes to Hades, but the heroes themselves he gave to be food for dogs and vultures. Our once popular and very heathenish hymn professes the same doctrine. 'Soon will you and I be lying each within his narrow bed. Soon our souls to God who gave them will have sped their rapid flight.' The soul is a pale and weak shadow of the living man, doomed to undergo a pitiful existence in Hades, an existence less enviable than that of the poorest serf, so that the soul of Patroclus laments for her fate, leaving manhood and youth. The soul of a living man is not mentioned, except when it quits the body during unconsciousness.

There is no mysticism so far. It is not till the sixth century before Christ that Orphism, a spiritualizing and moralizing of the old Dionysian religion, first appears in Greece and her colonies. Orphism, says Macchiero was 'a primordial mystical activity of the human spirit, originating through an immanent activity of our thought. It accompanied the Greek people along all the stages of their evolution.' It had its impostors, of course, the charlatans who moved Plato's indignation and the mirth of Aristophanes; but Miss Harrison speaks of it as 'a faith so high that it may be questioned whether any faith, ancient or modern, has ever outpassed it.'

Some scholars think that it came from Persia, with which the Ionian colonies were in contact. Others have found a strong resemblance to Indian thought. Pythagoras, who revived Orphism in South Italy, has been claimed as an Indian sage. Is not his name clearly a corruption of 'Pitta Guru,' the Sanskrit for 'father-teacher'? This need not be taken seriously. The affiliation of ideas is not very important; and I have pointed out that the religion of the Spirit appeared almost at the same time in China, India, Persia, Greece and Palestine. I do not think the hypothesis of borrowing is necessary. Rohde says that while in the popular Greek religion 'humanity and the divine Being are locally and essentially separate and distinct,' 'there appears in Greece the thought of the divinity of the human soul, and of the immortality resulting from this its divine nature. This thought belongs entirely to mysticism, a second kind of religion which, but little noticed by the popular religion, created a field for itself in isolated sects, influenced certain philosophical schools, and was able thence to convey to far-off posterity in the West and in the East the doctrine of the essential unity, of the union to be striven for by religion, between the divine and the human spirit, of the divine nature of the soul and of its eternity.' The soul, on coming at death to the other world, declares (in an authentic Orphic tablet, 'I am a son of the earth, and of the starry heaven, but my race is from heaven.' 'Out of the pure I come, pure queen of those below.' 'I have flown out of the sorrowful weary wheel' (of transmigration). The soul is not to approach a spring there— the well of forgetfulness, but to go near to the lake of memory, and to beseech the guardians to allow it to quench its thirst.

Belief in reincarnation was very old, and before 'Orpheus' was not connected with anything like the Indian Karma. Socrates on the day of his death calls it 'an ancient story,' and one of his arguments is that if things did not 'go round in a circle,' but in a straight line, a time would come when nothing will happen any more. This is the modern problem of entropy and an irreversible process. Aristotle says that the Pythagoreans believe that it is merely 'a chance' what bodies the soul inhabits during its successive reincarnations. But the doctrine was moralized, both in Greece and in India; whatever we have sown we reap; whatever we now sow we shall reap.

Nature is all of a piece. The same law which directs the changes of day and night, of summer and winter, and the revolutions of the heavenly bodies, operates in all mortal things. Life and death alternate; nature waxes and wanes, and returns upon herself. 'Shall not I also learn to think soberly?' says Ajax in Sophocles. But some of the ancients, like Catullus, find a melancholy contrast between the recuperative powers of nature and the dismal fate of men. 'Suns may die and come again; for us, when our brief day is past, there remains only one eternal night.' But this is not the Orphic doctrine. The wheel of birth and death is governed by the same law which directs the circling of the stars. The soul in its nature belongs to the divine world, but as the penalty for some sin is condemned to enter the 'sorrowful weary wheel' of births and deaths. Life on earth is a purgatory; the soul may at last expiate its fault. But the process is not endless in nature itself. At the end of the Great Year— ten thousand of our years—the present world-order finishes its course, and a new world is born. It is interesting that this doctrine was held by Origen, and some may think that it is a possible way of reconciling the dismal prospect which the second law of thermodynamics offers us with the belief that if time is the moving image of eternity, perpetuity must be the time-form of eternal life. At any rate the theory of cycles prevailed throughout antiquity, and has influential supporters even now.

All who have reflected on the dual nature of the soul find an analogy in the contrast of light and darkness. The moralist is always tempted to believe in a cosmic dualism, and if he holds that reality is spiritual, and that ultimately there must be a single principle at the root of things, he is in a difficulty. The monist is always tempted either to make the world of values an ineffectual 'epiphenomenon' or to reduce the visible world to a vain shadow in which nothing really happens. The pre-Socratic philosophers puzzled themselves over the quest for a first principle, and one of them, Heracleitus of Ephesus, belongs, according to Cornford, to the 'mystical tradition.'

Among all the irreparable losses which the age of decadence inflicted upon civilization, few are more to be regretted than the disappearance of the works of the 'obscure philosopher,' whose doctrine of the universal flux reminds us of Bergson, while his scornful aphorisms sometimes recall Nietzsche. He pours contempt upon the scientific curiosity of the Milesians; a man is made no wiser by accumulating knowledge. Reality is becoming; 'mortals are immortals and immortals mortals; the one living the other's death, and dying the other's life.' There is one reason (*logos*) for everything; particular things are only partial symbols. 'Wisdom is willing and unwilling to be called by the name of Zeus.' (He uses the form 'Zen,' which is 'life.') 'Nature is like the lord of Delphi, who half reveals and half conceals his meaning.' The world is a myth; visible things have only a symbolic truth. There is no real change; all things pass in and out of existence. 'War is the father of all things; all things exist by opposing tensions, like that of the bow and the lyre.' In yes and no all things consist, as Böhme said. Heracleitus has only contempt for the 'night-walkers and mystics' of his day, meaning the Orphics; and he rejects Pythagoras and all his works. He is a lonely thinker, who despises his fellow-men too much to wish for disciples. But his great saying, 'you cannot find out the boundaries of soul, so deep are they,' and the equally famous, 'I sought in myself,' mark him of the mystical family. Like Nietzsche he holds that 'God is beyond good and bad.'

It is usual to regard Parmenides, who taught that reality is a finite, motionless, continuous plenum, as at the opposite pole to the apostle of universal flux. But extremes in philosophy sometimes meet. Both systems threaten to issue in acosmism, the denial of reality to the phenomenal world. If Heracleitus anticipates Bergson, there are some very Parmenidean sentences in Bradley.

The Orphic brotherhoods have been compared to our nonconformist sects, and it has been pointed out that the votaries of the various independent cults grudged no expense in maintaining their forms of worship. They lacked the steadying influence of a great Church, and as we see in Protestant Europe and America, grotesque superstitions flourished like a green bay tree. Plutarch argues that 'religion' avoids two extremes—atheism and superstition (*deisidaimonia*)[1], and he denounces the mischief done by superstition as bitterly as Lucretius inveighs against *religio*, by which he means much the same thing. We must not condemn mysticism for its perversions, which have been many and great, and we must give the Church due credit for checking the belief in astrology and other absurdities. The Olympians made a poor struggle for survival; in the spiritual awakening which broke like a new dawn upon the world, wheat and tares sprang into life together.

Before discussing Socrates and Plato, who to us are the great founders of mystical philosophy, I will try to summarize the main characteristics of the mystery religions as they seem to have been among the Greeks. Our information, as I have said, is much less complete than we could wish.

The forms of initiation into the mysteries—allegory and myth, dramatic representation, sacramental actions—were intended, as Aristotle says, not to convey information but to stimulate devotional feeling. The original dramatic acts and representations were connected with the

[1] I know of no place where this word is used except in a disparaging sense. The Authorized Version is not far wrong in making St. Paul tell the Athenians that they were 'too superstitious,' or, rather, 'somewhat prone to superstition.'

natural mysteries of generation, and though they were purged of their grossness, enough of their primitive crudity remained to cause offence and arouse suspicion in unsympathetic or ill-informed minds. As long as the old forms are retained there is a danger that unworthy associations may re-establish themselves. Even in the Christian sacraments magic and materialism often 'destroy the nature of a sacrament.' Ovid complains that the lustrations of the mysteries are used to quiet a guilty conscience.[1] This error was very easy for the ancients, who believed in what has been called cosmic consciousness, a kind of panpsychism animating the whole universe. A network of sympathies runs through the whole world. 'We could not see the sun,' says Plotinus, 'if there were not something sunlike in ourselves, nor could a soul which has not become beautiful have any knowledge of beauty.' This is indeed the central principle of mysticism as a rule of life. Cosmic sympathy was as much a Stoical as a Platonic belief. 'All things are intertwined,' says Marcus Aurelius; 'there is practically nothing alien from other things, since all things have been set in order, and make up the one cosmos. For there is one cosmos and one God through all, and one substance and one law and one common reason and one truth.' The conviction that there is a unity underlying all diversity is an article of faith with all mystics; it is an ultimate truth which in our imperfect state must be apprehended by faith, not by sight. Panpsychism becomes dangerous and even absurd if we hold that the Deity is *equally* manifested in all phenomena. This error, which is destructive of morality and of belief in values, which are always hierarchical, does not concern us in this chapter. Man is a microcosm, with affinities with all grades of existence from the highest to the lowest. So Stoics and Platonists agree in saying.[2]

When, under the influence of mystical religion, men began to be conscious of the importance of personality, they asked whether it was not possible to establish sympathy not only with the manifestations of universal life in nature but with the Deity himself. The Olympian religion certainly regarded the gods as personal—human and all too human— but they were heartless. When the dying Hippolytus in Euripides takes leave of the goddess Artemis he says, 'You feel no sorrow at this end of our long friendship.' Aristotle's God exercises a magnetic attraction on the world, but feels no more than a magnet. So Spinoza says that though we must love God we must not expect Him to love us in return. Aristotle records with satisfaction that when the people of Elea consulted Xenophanes whether they should mourn for Leucothea and sacrifice to her, the sage replied, 'if you think her a goddess, do not mourn for her; if you think her a woman, do not sacrifice to her'; a saying which has

---

[1] Graecia principium moris fuit; illa nocentes
   Impia lustratos ponere facta putat.
   A! nimium faciles, qui tristia crimina caedis
   Fluminea tolli posse putatis aqua.

[2] Manilius, who is so seldom read, expresses this belief very finely:
   'Quid mirum noscere mundum
   Si possunt homines, quibus est et mundus in ipsis,
   Exemplumque Dei quisque est in imagine parva?'

pleased some critics of orthodox Christianity. The Church has condemned 'Patripassionism,' since God the Father cannot suffer; but the divine Christ 'has borne our griefs and carried our sorrows.' 'We love Him because He first loved us.' The mystery religions for the first time familiarized the Greeks with the idea that the spiritual life of man should be a replica of the life of the god, who also suffered, died and rose again. 'Alarm and terror and sweet hope,' Plutarch says, were aroused by the passion-play exhibited in the mysteries. The suffering was sometimes real, if we may trust the beautiful frescoes of the recently discovered villa outside Pompeii, where the mistress of the house, who is being initiated, kneels down with bare back to be whipped. In Asia, as is well known, the self-inflicted 'buffeting of the body' had a more sinister character. But at the end the priest could say, 'Rejoice, ye mystics; the god is saved. To you too will come salvation from your troubles.' Union with the god, and therewith immortality, was promised to the initiate; others, it was declared, have to expect a much less agreeable future. The rapture of communion with Isis is beautifully described by Apuleius. Our authorities mention either three or five stages in initiation. The first was disciplinary purification. Then followed the delivery of the sacred emblems. Contemplation and ecstatic vision came next, and the abiding feeling of blessedness.

Ecstasy meant, as Rohde says, the freeing of the soul from the hampering confinement of the body, conferring new powers of which it knew nothing before. It is now able to behold what only the eyes of the spirit can behold, the eternal reality beyond time and space. Enthusiasm meant properly the God-given side of the same experience; the two need not be sharply distinguished; both words mean that in the mystical vision the soul is transfigured and, in St. Paul's words, caught up into the third heaven. When Tertullian, who was not a mystic, says that most men apprehend God by means of visions, we realize how natural it seemed to the ancients to believe that these experiences were a genuine and by no means unusual revelation.

Aristotle tells us that no special knowledge was imparted in the mysteries, but this can hardly be said of the later developments, in which knowledge (*Gnosis*) was certainly promised, and in which what the New Testament calls knowledge falsely so called was claimed by the 'Gnostics,' against whom not only the Fathers of the Church but Plotinus wrote. The belief that knowledge of divine things can be imparted only by revelation grew in strength. There was an esoteric doctrine, the possession only of the initiated. What the Church called the *disciplina arcani*, the necessity of reserve in explaining the highest truths to the multitude who have not undergone the indispensable training, might appeal to the warning in the Sermon on the Mount, 'cast not your pearls before swine.' Plato was well aware of this. In the Timaeus he says, 'to discover the Maker and Father of the world is a hard task,[1] and when we have found him it is impossible to speak of him to all.' But Gnosticism was a barbarized and Orientalized Platonism; its adepts were arrogant rather than

[1] Not 'past finding out,' as Jowett unfortunately translates it.

spiritual. Clement and Origen tried to save Gnosis while rejecting Gnosticism. Plato's own reserve was quite justified. It is not true that there can be a standardized orthodoxy suited both to the professor and his kitchen-maid.

The sacramental meal is one of the debts which the Church owes to the mysteries. The guilds which became so common held banquets in which the departed members were supposed to be present. The cult-deity was there as the invisible host. Men were invited to dine 'at the table of the Lord Sarapis.' St. Paul contrasts 'the table of the Lord' with these feasts, and some have perversely attributed to him a grossly materialistic view of the Christian sacrament. As if any Jew could think without horror of literally drinking blood! The table of a god was not a table at which his flesh was eaten, it was a table over which he presided as host and fellow-guest.

The symbolism of a sacred marriage between the deity and a female initiate goes back to very primitive nature worship, and was an unfortunate legacy which religious conservatism could not repudiate. There is little doubt that objects were displayed in the Eleusinian mysteries which we should consider indecent, though Plutarch, as far as I am aware, is the first to express disgust at what he saw in Egypt. The Hermae at Athens and the scarecrows in Roman gardens show how little squeamishness about male nudity there was in antiquity. Catholicism still consecrates virgins as 'brides of Christ.'

Christianity owes to the mystery-religions not only the primary emphasis on personal religion as opposed to civic ceremonies, but the elaboration of ritual in public worship. Matins and vespers, conducted by priests in white canonicals, with liturgical prayers and hymns, were part of the worship of Isis. The Church at this time was hospitable; the twenty-fifth of December was the birthday of the Invincible Sun. The mystery religions, says Cumont, 'offered, in comparison with previous religions, more beauty in their ritual, more truth in their doctrines, and a superior good in their morality.'

It is a pity that we have so few specimens of the prayers of the worshippers, for what we have is very beautiful. Reitzenstein quotes from the Hermetic literature a dialogue on regeneration between Hermes and his son Tat. Tat has renounced the world and begs his father to tell him the secret, which Hermes says can only be made by divine revelation. This Tat receives, and can now declare: 'My spirit is illuminated. To thee, O God, author of my new creation, I offer spiritual sacrifices. O God and Father, Thou art the Lord, Thou art the Spirit. Accept from me the spiritual sacrifices which Thou desirest.' He quotes from another prayer: 'We give thanks to Thee, most High, for by Thy grace we have received the light of knowledge. Having been saved by Thee we rejoice that Thou hast shown Thyself to us wholly, that Thou hast deified us in our mortal bodies by the vision of Thyself.' Besides formal prayer, the votaries were instructed to spend many hours in silent meditation; the little chapels probably remained open for those who wished for a quiet place in which to practise contemplation.

We need not discuss here why the Church succeeded where these pagan cults failed. They were handicapped by their association with astrology, magic and theosophy, and by the survivals of a gross symbolism which I have already mentioned. But they were genuine parts of a great religious revival, and if they were partially discredited by crass superstition and imposture, the same may be said of all religions, not excluding our own.

'To few men,' says A. E. Taylor, 'does the world owe a heavier debt than to Plato. He has taught us that philosophy, loving and single-minded devotion to truth, is the great gift of God to man and the rightful guide of man's life, and that the few to whom the intimate vision of truth has been granted are false to their calling unless they bear fruit in unwearied service to their fellows. All worthy civilization is fed by these ideas, and whenever our Western world has recaptured the sense of noble living it has sought it afresh in the Platonic writings. . . . If we sometimes underestimate our debt to Plato, it is because Platonic ideas have become so completely part and parcel of our best tradition in morals and religion.' I think this is more true of our nation than of any other part of Europe. And it is Plato the religious mystic, not the creator of political utopias, who has inspired us, and exercised an influence second only to that of the Founder of Christianity.

We need not join in the discussion about the relation of Plato to Socrates. When Plato tells us that he has given the world nothing of his own, that is only the self-effacement of the Indian disciple with his *guru*, and we may add of St. Paul towards 'Christ crucified.' Plato has given us a great deal of his own, though we may mention here that Socrates was a mystic, subject to prolonged trances, and conscious of an inner 'voice' which spoke within him from time to time. Philosophy for him was what its name declares—not wisdom but the love of wisdom, or according to the old definition the art of living. With some modern philosophers it has been little more than an interesting game; for Socrates it was something that a man will die for. Modern philosophies are much concerned with epistemology, the theory of knowledge; Plato's search, and that of his master, was for the knowledge which saves the soul, the truth which reveals God. He rested on an act of faith—for such things cannot be proved—that the ultimate reality is also the supreme good. The two are one; like all Greek thinkers he could not accept an ultimate dualism. Further he held that 'the fully real is fully knowable,' though this wisdom can be won only by a life of discipline. If we live as we ought we shall see things as they are, and if we see things as they are we shall live as we ought. The two are inseparably connected.

One of the worst blunders which critics make about Plato is to accuse him of what they call intellectualism. This is partly a mere mistake in scholarship. The Platonic Nous, which is the whole personality acting under the guidance of our highest faculty, has been translated 'reason,' for which the Greeks have another word. 'Spirit' is the best English word for Nous, though in English it does not sufficiently suggest the activity of the mind. But in part we have to deal with what Plato called misologism, hatred of intellect, a very prevalent heresy in our day, as we see by the popularity of pragmatists like William James. A modern Platonist has called this blasphemy against the Holy Ghost, and I have reminded my readers that the Seven Gifts of the Holy Spirit are wisdom, understanding and the rest. If we demur at the saying that all sin is ignorance, would it not be true to say that the greatest crimes —not necessarily the wickedest actions—in history have been the work of men who 'know not what they do'? The Sanhedrin in condemning Jesus to death believed that they were 'doing God service.' Ignorance armed with power is a terrible thing.

If this is intellectualism, the same charge may be brought against Aristotle, Aquinas and Kant. Aristotle says that 'everyone chooses what he thinks good, but only the good man thinks good what really is good.' Aquinas says that 'every sin arises from a kind of ignorance. A man's will is only secure from sinning when his understanding is secured from ignorance and error.' Plato is emphatic that 'we shall be better and braver if we think that we ought to enquire than if we fancied that there is no knowing.' 'I should deem him a coward whose heart failed him before he had examined difficulties from every side, and either discovered the truth or accepted the best of human theories as a raft on which to sail through life—not without risk, I admit, if he cannot find some word of God which will more safely carry him.' 'There are two kinds of ignorance: there is simple ignorance, and double ignorance, which is accompanied by a conceit of wisdom.' 'When a man supposes that he knows and does not know, this is the real ignorance.' Plato knows that there is nothing 'irrational' in knowing the limitations of our knowledge, and also that there can hardly be certainty without divine revelation. This certainty may be granted to us as the reward of diligent seeking.

Our secularized apocalyptism has blinded us to the error of packing Time with values which do not belong to it. A chastened meliorism is not an unreasonable attitude; but the horror with which many of our writers regard the theory of recurring cycles would have been unintelligible to the ancients, who believed that they were living in a downgrade period. In any case the hope of a goal of evolution does not satisfy the religious mind. What we long for is not a static condition of monotonous fruition, which to a creature of time would be intolerably boring. Mere perpetuity is no release from the 'sorrowful weary wheel'; the wheel would cease to rotate, but we should still be chained to it. When in a favourite hymn we sing, 'Change and decay in all around we see; O Thou who changest not, abide with me,' we pray for a deliverance not from life but from death. What timeless life would be like we cannot imagine, but we know that in the realm of the ultimate values, and (so the Pythagoreans and Platonists thought) in the arid heights of mathematics, in which there are no irreversible processes, time and change are transcended. This longing has been felt by all mystics; it is naturally strongest at times when earthly hopes burn dimly. I will quote two very beautiful little poems in which the vision of the eternal world,

a glorious light casting no shadows, shines upon the poet's mind. Sir Philip
Sidney writes

> Leave me, O love which reachest but to dust,
>   And thou, my mind, aspire to higher things.
> Grow rich in that which never taketh rust:
>   What ever fades but fading pleasure brings.
> Draw in thy beams and humble all thy might
>   To that sweet yoke where lasting freedoms be;
> Which breaks the clouds and opens forth the light
>   That doth both shine and give us sight to see.
> O take but hold! Let that light be thy guide
>   In this small course which birth draws out to death,
> And think how ill becometh him to slide
>   Who seeketh heaven and comes of heavenly breath.
> Then farewell, world! Thy uttermost I see;
>   Eternal Love, maintain thy life in me.

Ronsard writes:

> Si notre vie est moins qu' une journée
> En l'éternel; si l'an qui fait le tour
> Chasse nos jours sans espoir de retour;
> Si périssable est toute chose née;
> Que songes tu, mon âme emprisonnée?
> Pourquoi te plaît l' obscur de notre jour,
> Si, pour voler en un plus clair séjour,
> Tu as au dos l'aile bien empennée!
> Là est le bien que tout esprit désire,
> Là le repos où tout le monde aspire,
> Là est l'amour, là le plaisir encore!
> Là, O mon âme, au plus haut ciel guidée,
> Tu y pourras reconnaître l'idée
> De la beauté qu' en ce monde j'adore.

'The fully real is fully knowable.' But how? Natural science can never
penetrate beyond the phenomenal world, which for Plato is only a shadow,
'a true shadow in its own place' as Isaac Penington says in words which
I am fond of quoting—but only a shadow of eternal reality. Urwick in
his excellent book *The Message of Plato*, in which he shows the close
resemblance between Indian thought and the Platonic tradition, contrasts 'the two paths' which are open to our choice, the path of divine
knowledge and the 'path of pursuit' which the Indians think the Western
nations have chosen to follow. The upper path brings into play powers of
the soul which are dormant on the lower. These powers are often ignored
or refused a hearing. 'Our thought is so little religious, it is concerned so
wholly with the path of pursuit, in attainments and achievements and
satisfactions in this world and the things of it, that we are almost content to
identify religion with the goodness of the lower path—a religion of morality
touched with emotion and linked to occasional worship, which satisfies
us because it can be made compatible with a virtuous worldliness.'

Aristotle rather surprises us when he says that the lover of myths is in his way a philosopher. So Réville says, 'The human mind when it works spontaneously is a philosopher, as the bee is a mathematician.' Myth is the poetry of religion, and poetry, not science, is the natural language of religion.

I have given a chapter in this book to symbolism, but a short discussion of the place of myth in Plato may not be out of place. The myth is an integral part of Plato's message, not a mere extraneous embellishment. Spiritual truths cannot be adequately set forth in the language of science, nor established by logic. It has often been objected that Plato's arguments for the immortality of the soul are unconvincing, and insufficient to account for the conviction which he undoubtedly had that the soul has a place in the eternal world. The same objection applies to the classical 'proofs' of the existence of God. The 'moral argument,' which Kant accepts, rests on our immediate recognition of one of the ultimate values. The other proofs do not lead us to the God of religion, unless we transform the ontological argument, as I think we may do, into the reasonable faith that our purest hopes and desires are not in a conspiracy to deceive us. Plato uses myth when he speaks of human immortality.

Westcott distinguishes between myth and allegory. In allegory the thought is grasped first, and then arranged in a particular dress. In the myth, thought and form come into being together; the thought is the vital principle which shapes the form; the form is the sensible image which displays the thought. The parable is distinct from both. In the Gospels, the Sower is an allegory, the Prodigal Son a parable, the Sheep and Goats a myth. In Plato, while the choice of Heracles is an allegory, the speech of Diotima about love is a legend which passes into an allegory, and the allegory into a myth. Plato is not fond of the word *mythos*; he prefers *logoi*, 'stories'; they are not pure fiction, but, he would perhaps say, have a sacramental meaning. Is the connection with concrete fact essential? An awkward question which Plato is not very ready to answer. He is in fact rather unscrupulous; a work of the imagination—he is not afraid to call it a pious fraud, may in time be believed. This is in truth the way that myths degenerate. They first congeal into flat historical recitals, and then evaporate, because they no longer bridge the gulf between the natural and the spiritual.

This disintegration of myth is so universal that we may wonder whether it can be avoided. The Russian theologian Berdyaeff in a very remarkable passage says: 'Christianity, which is a religion not of this world, suffers humiliation in the world for the sake of the general mass of humanity. By entering the world in order to save it, it is always running the risk of becoming weakened and losing its true spirit. The whole tragedy of spiritual humanity lies in this fact.' Religious symbolism is fundamentally opposed both to naïve realism and to subjective idealism. In his more serious myths Plato would have us believe that 'something like this must be true'; and if this seems to us to go too far we may remember the very impressive confession of F. H.

Bradley in his *Essays on Truth and Reality*: 'I find myself taking more
and more as literal fact what I used in my youth to admire and love as
poetry.'

The whole psychology of Platonism, with its tripartite division of
human nature into body, soul and spirit, is mythical in form. The famous
'Forms' become mythical when we hypostatize them, and we mythologize
when reality falls asunder into Here and Yonder, or into the Present and
the Future life. The Western Catholic partition into natural and supernatural events is another example, which is discouraged, Berdyaeff tells
us, by the Eastern Church.

All that Plato says about the future life is mythical, but there can be
no doubt that he believed in personal immortality, though Hegel thought
otherwise. But we must remember that the Greeks had no word for
personality, and needed none. I have said that our belief in human
immortality stands or falls with our belief in God, and also that the soul,
for the Platonists, is 'in the making,' *capax deitatis*, but only potentially a
sharer in the divine, immortal nature. If there is a want of definiteness
in his beliefs, so there is in ours. Christian eschatology is a mass of contradictions; but we accept these pictures, or some of them, as symbols of
a state of being of which we may say with the Johannine writer, 'it does
not yet appear what we shall be.' Coleridge, in commenting on Wordsworth's famous Ode, says that it was 'intended for such readers as had
been accustomed to venture at times into the twilight realms of consciousness, and to feel a deep interest in modes of inmost being to which
they knew that the attributes of time and space are inapplicable.' He
thinks that neither Wordsworth nor Plato really believed in pre-existence
'in the ordinary interpretation of the words.' Plato however, like most of
the Greeks, believed that pre-existence and survival stand or fall together.
He did not invent his eschatology. He went for it to the Orphic religion,
which through him has become part of Christianity. Though we may
regret the lurid pictures of lost souls which have too often lost their
symbolic value and become crude predictions, we may agree with what
Farnell says about the religion which Plato found in the mystery religions.
It familiarized the world with the conception of the divine element in the
human soul, with the kinship between man and God. It quickened this
sense by means of a mystic sacrament, whereby man's life was trans-
cendentally fused with God's. It strongly marked the antagonism between
flesh and spirit, and preached with insistence the doctrine of purity, a
doctrine mainly ritualistic but containing also the spiritual idea of the
purity of the soul from the taint of sin. It divorced religion from the State,
making it the pre-eminent concern of the individual soul and the brotherhood. Finally, its chief end and scope was other-worldliness, its mission
was the preaching of salvation, of an eschatology based on degrees of
posthumous retribution, purgatory, and a succession of lives through
which the soul is tried, and it promised immortal bliss through purity
and sacrament. Augustine in an often-quoted passage says that the
Incarnation was the only Christian doctrine which he did not find in
the Platonists. We can hardly consider too carefully the meaning of

these words, and especially of the exception which brought Augustine into the Church of Christ.

In this book we are concerned with Plato as a religious mystic, not as a political reformer. He has been called a pro-Spartan, a Communist, a Fascist, and an Inquisitor. His antecedents were really rather Whiggish, but he is not a keen politician, and his ideal commonwealth in the *Republic* is, from the standpoint of a practical statesman, full of absurdities, as he must have known. Rather too much has been made of his famous words that the philosopher must return from contemplation to take part in public life. The principle of 'withdrawal and return' is most valuable; but Plato's sage returns not to serve but to rule, and what likelihood is there that any city would invite a philosopher to rule over it? Perhaps the best of his provisions is that the power of the purse should be in the hands of men who have no temptation to use it either to feather their own nests or to bribe the citizens. But we need say no more on this subject.

There is no sense in which dualism can be attributed to Plato. He contrasts the higher and the lower path, undoubtedly, and he knows that evil is not merely a defect of good. But he does not make 'matter,' which for him is nothing ponderable, but practically what we call empty space, an evil principle. It was a mistake, on the strength of one ambiguous sentence, to suppose that he believed in 'an evil world-soul.' He taught, like St. Paul, that our citizenship is in heaven; we are to fly to our dear country; but the flight is neither from one place to another, nor from the present world to a future world.

'Thou shalt renounce, renounce,' says Goethe. 'This is the eternal song which every hour hoarsely sings.' But does Plato go all the way with the Indians and some Christian mystics on the path of renunciation? He does not. The 'political virtues' must be learned and practised first. In order to renounce, we must know what we are renouncing; we cannot devote ourselves without having a self to devote. Worldly affairs, he says in the *Laws*, are not worth taking very seriously; the misfortune is that we have to take them seriously. The Platonic lover begins by loving a beautiful body; then he loves a beautiful soul, and by degrees learns to love spiritual or absolute beauty. He does not begin by denying all goodness, truth and beauty to the visible world. If the world of time and space has no meaning and no value; if its multiplicity cannot even be a symbol of the shoreless ocean of the absolute, heaven itself is deprived of all contents; God may in very truth be called *Nihilum*. The world of sense is sacramental, its value consists in the fact that it points us beyond itself. The Platonist is never a hermit or a yogi. He lives in fairly hard training; a Platonist who is not something of an ascetic is a dilettante; but he loves all beautiful things.

J. A. Stewart, in an interesting essay on Platonism in English poetry, distinguishes personal from traditional Platonism, and advises us to seek for the former in Wordsworth's *Prelude*. By personal Platonism he means 'the mood of one who has a curious eye for the endless variety of this visible and temporal world, and a fine sense of its beauties, yet is haunted by the presence of an invisible and eternal world behind, or when the mood is most pressing within the visible and temporal world and sustaining both it and himself—a world not perceived as external to himself, but inwardly lived by him, as that which at moments of ecstasy, or even habitually, he is become one. This is how personal Platonism may be described in outline.'

Every religion, every philosophy, every system of ethics, every mode of living, is determined by its scale of values. Nicholas of Cusa defined God as *valor valorum*, and I believe this is what Plato meant by his Idea of the Good, on which he gave a famous lecture which he refused to publish because the supreme good can only be understood by living into it. Is not Christianity essentially the acceptance of a scale of values, a way of walking, not a way of talking? What we love and care for, that we are. *Boni vel mali mores*, as Augustine said, are at bottom *boni vel mali amores*. What are the things you would wish for if a fairy gave you the choice? What is your highest good? What are the things you would die rather than do? The whole scheme of ascent, for Platonism and for Christianity, is a sublime act of faith, an experiment which ends in an experience. The one great addition made by Christianity was the raising of Love to the first place. The ancients distrusted the emotions; the Stoics said that only weak eyes weep at other people's misfortunes. The Christian rejoices with those who rejoice, and weeps with those who weep. Ancient culture, it has been said, was 'icily cold.' Plato knew that, as a German proverb says, 'without sorrows no one is ennobled'; but Christianity is perhaps the only religion which does not promise to make us invulnerable. '*Souffrir passe*,' the Frenchman Bloy says, '*avoir souffert ne passe jamais.*' Family affection, especially the love of husband and wife—neither Plato nor the mystics of the cloister realized that in denying themselves this they were sacrificing something far more valuable than bodily comfort. Earthly attachments must be loosened; Aldous Huxley speaks of 'non-attachment' as the supreme duty; but a life without human love is maimed. Rudyard Kipling says: 'Down to Gehenna or up to the throne he travels the fastest who travels alone.' It may be so; but if we want to be free from worries, a hard heart and a good digestion will do more for us than any philosophy. Of such a man Euripides says: 'He suffers less, but we cannot envy his happiness.' This is my one criticism of what Milton calls 'a fugitive and cloistered virtue.'

It is not quite a simple question. In renouncing the values of the lower path for ourselves, ought we to busy ourselves in obtaining them for other people? Ought we to be keenly interested in what are called social services, by which I do not mean primarily a polite name for the redistribution of the taxpayers' money? The law of love must provide the answer. But on the whole it is true that other-worldliness alone can cure the sickness of the world, the world in the New Testament sense— a system of co-operative guilt with limited liability. I do not think that the practice of contemplation is often barren of results. Bosanquet says truly: 'The presence of adequate ideas which are inoperative in moral matters is vastly exaggerated.' 'Pure love,' says Ruysbroek, 'frees a man from himself and his acts. If we would know this in ourselves, we must yield to the Divine, the innermost sanctuary of ourselves. Hence comes an urgency to active righteousness; for love cannot be idle.'

I have said elsewhere that the Platonic tradition in English theology has been strong and fruitful. I will end this chapter with a few more sentences from the sermons of John Smith, the Cambridge Platonist of the seventeenth century. Plato himself would have been delighted with them.

'To seek our divinity in books and writings is to seek the living among the dead. No, seek after God within thine own soul.' 'Such as men themselves are, such will God Himself seem to be. There is a double head as well as a double heart.' 'Divine love and purity reciprocally exalt divine knowledge, both of them growing up together. This life is nothing else but God's own breath within him, and an infant Christ formed in his soul. But this knowledge is here but in its infancy. Here we can see but in a glass, and that double, too. Yet this knowledge, being a true heavenly fire lighted from God's altar, begets an undaunted courage in the souls of good men' 'Heaven is not a thing without us, nor is happiness anything distinct from a true conjunction of the mind with God.' 'As we cannot truly love the first and highest good while we serve a design upon it, and subordinate it to ourselves, so neither is our salvation consistent with such sordid, pinching and particular love.'

The worldling converts instruments into ends, and ends into instruments. So all our society is out of gear, and no political alchemy can bring golden conduct out of leaden instincts. This is what Plato is really driving at in his *Republic*, which in spite of his deplorable 'nocturnal council,' the prototype of Torquemada and the Inquisition, has been not unfairly called Christianity before Christ. It is the inside of the cup which must be cleansed. 'Unless the cup is clean, whatever you pour into it turns sour.' So Horace tells us; so Plato tells us; and we ought to have learned it from the Gospels.

CHAPTER VIII

PLOTINUS

I AM asking you to accompany me in a visit to an age of decadence The third century was not dark, like the dismal interlude, five or six hundred years long, which divides the sunset of ancient civilization from the first streaks of dawn which heralded the renaissance. It was not dark; but it was an age of lengthening shadows and waning light. So we think; and so, on the whole, thought those who lived in it. 'The world has grown old.' 'This is indeed the *fin de siècle*' (*ipsa clausula saeculi*). 'Humanity is at its last gasp.' Pagans and Christians are equally pessimistic. To both alike, civilization seemed to have no future. This feeling of hopelessness is intelligible. The government of the Empire had fallen into anarchy. Septimius Severus was the last emperor for eighty years to die in his bed. There were seven puppet emperors, set up and deposed by the army, between 235 and 249. The only possible end to these disorders was that which actually ended them—the cast iron Oriental despotism of Diocletian. The arts and sciences were in decay. The population was dwindling, and the long blockade of civilization on the north and east could only end in the capture of the fortress.

But this is not the whole story. May there not be catabolic and anabolic ages—generations which are glorious spendthrifts, and generations which are storing force for some new development? And may not political calamities actually liberate philosophy and religion, by compelling them to attend exclusively to their own business? This kind of liberation, I think, actually occurred at the period to which I am inviting your attention. We are witnessing, if you like to put it so, the last sighs of classical antiquity, and the birth of Catholic Christianity. But the second was the child of the first. The Christian Church is not the beginning of the Middle Ages; it is the last creative achievement of classical antiquity, which may be said to have died in giving birth to it. In the history of ideas, death in childbed is the rule rather than the exception. Think of the limitations of the Hebrews, with their tribal religion, their Bedouin morality, their blindness to art and science. But in their pure desert air arose the prophetic religion, which culminated in the Galilean Gospel, and at last shattered the mould into which it had been poured. And consider how in the same way Hellas had to die in giving birth to Hellenism—to that Hellenistic civilization the significant facts of which we are now trying to recover, and under the influence of which we are living even to this day. Rome too was dying in giving birth to Romanism. It is in the very period which we are now dealing with that the great Roman lawyers laid down the principles of jurisprudence under which half the civilized world is still ordered, and that the Roman Church began to formulate its claims to universal spiritual empire.

No, we are not assisting at the funeral of ideas. There was to be real retrogression, a real barbarizing, later. But now we are invited to look at religion liberated for the first time, disentangled from fetishism and idolatry, emancipated from nationalism and from politics. We are to look at it as now universal and individual, embracing in thought the whole universe, but worshipping a Deity whose throne is the inmost shrine of the human soul; we are to observe how it has struck a close alliance with its old enemy philosophy, which, after being cosmocentric with the Ionians, and anthropocentric with the post-Aristotelian schools, is now content to be theocentric, yet without renouncing one jot of its reverence for the great unbroken tradition which, from Thales to Proclus, spans the longest period of unfettered thought which the human race has yet been permitted to enjoy.

In the sphere of religion, the rivals were the Oriental mystery-cults, now naturalized in the Empire, and the Christian Church. In philosophy, the Greek schools, now coalescing into what is called Neoplatonism, were winning an easy victory over the Gnostics, who represented a barbarized Platonism. Behind these controversies, there was a deep cleavage between those who wished to preserve the classical culture as a whole, and those who, at first indifferent to it, had been provoked to hostility. This was indeed a tragic conflict, which need not have arisen. There were faults on both sides; but by far the largest share of the blame rests with the stupid and obstinate policy of the Roman Tsars, who after instigating a series of sporadic and futile pogroms against the Christians, who were never politically dangerous, made a systematic attempt to extirpate the new faith when it was much too strong to be attacked. The concordat under Constantine shows how easy a conciliatory policy would have been, and the transference of Neoplatonism almost entire into Christian theology how slight comparatively were the religious and intellectual differences between the two sides. The Edict of Milan signalized the defeat of the Empire by the Church, but the Church was the Empire under a new form.

Plotinus is by far the greatest figure of this age of transition. His Christian contemporary, Origen, was a learned Biblical scholar, and a theologian of remarkable independence; but as a thinker, though he deserves to be treated with great respect, he is not to be compared with Plotinus. Modern scholars are beginning to realize that Plotinus is one of the great figures in the history of thought. Vacherot calls the Enneads 'the vastest, richest, and perhaps the most powerful synthesis in the whole history of philosophy.' Whittaker calls Plotinus 'the greatest individual thinker between Aristotle and Descartes'; Drews 'the greatest metaphysician of antiquity.' 'No other thinker,' says Benn, 'has even accomplished a revolution so immediate, so comprehensive, and of such prolonged duration.' Eucken speaks of the *weltbeherrschenden Geist des Plotin*, and says that he, though a Pagan, has influenced Christian theology more than any other thinker—a judgment which does not seem absurd to those who have traced the ideas of Plotinus in the Cappadocian Fathers, in Augustine, in Erigena, in Eckhart, and in the whole series of Christian Platonists to our own day. Troeltsch, who at the time of his death two years ago was the deepest philosophical theologian in Germany, was so far from thinking that his reign is now at an end, that he wrote: 'In my opinion the sharper stress of the scientific and philosophical spirit in modern times has made the blend of Neoplatonism and New Testament Christianity the only possible solution of the problem at the present day, and I do not doubt that the synthesis of Neoplatonism and Christianity will once more be dominant in modern thought.'

My object in these prefatory remarks is to convince you that in this *privat-docent* at Rome (for Plotinus was never the Diadochus, the official professor of Platonism at Athens), in this mystic who seems to live in a timeless world, pursuing his quest of the beatific vision in the midst of revolutions and pronunciamientos as calmly as Hegel analysing the determinations of the Absolute while Napoleon's guns were booming round Jena, this champion of a losing cause who never even names the power that was soon to overwhelm him (or does he once glance at Christianity as 'the fraud now so prevalent'?), we are in the presence of one of the great epoch-making personalities, whose part in the history of the world is not yet played out. 'The fire still burns on the altars of Plotinus,' said Eunapius. Yes, it is burning still; it is perhaps 'a candle which will never be put out.'

Our knowledge of the life and character of Plotinus is derived almost exclusively from the biography by his friend and disciple Porphyry. There is a queer naïveté about this tribute, which records supernatural favours shown to his master; but the impression produced is both clear and pleasing. We see the young enthusiast at Alexandria, frequenting the lecture-rooms of this and that philosopher and disappointed with all, till at the age of twenty-eight he discovered Ammonius Saccas and exclaimed, 'This is the man I was looking for.' His discipleship was long. He was nearly forty when he accompanied the expedition of Gordian against Persia, hoping to be able to study the wisdom of the east. Alexandria knew of 'Boutta'; did Plotinus think of travelling as far as India, and studying under some Hindu gymnosophist? We cannot tell. The expedition failed, and Plotinus with difficulty made his way back to Antioch. Thence he went to Rome, which was to be his home for the rest of his life. There he held what the Germans call a Seminar, collecting a number of keen disciples, including a few of the leading men in Rome, one of whom he induced to renounce politics and public honours and embrace the philosophic life. We see him talking with patience in a somewhat disorderly lecture-room, interrupted and heckled by eager youths, but sometimes carried away in a flow of lofty eloquence, during which his fine features seemed transfigured. He wrote with difficulty, having weak eyesight, and never revised his work; his spelling and even pronunciation were faulty. All this must be borne in mind when we groan over the chaotic arrangement and obscure diction of the Enneads.

If it were not for the devoted loyalty and assiduity of his younger friends, especially Porphyry and Amelius, the work of his life would have been lost. There was no ambition in his ultra-modest and selfless nature. He was 'ashamed of being in the body,' concealed his birthday and the circumstances of his early life, and refused to have his portrait painted.

He lived like a saint, ascetically, but without the severe discipline of the Christian monks. His rapt meditations several times brought him, so he believed, to the beatific vision of the mystic, which he describes, or attempts to describe, in language of obvious sincerity. He made no enemies, and was in request as a guardian or trustee, both from his known integrity and business capacity and, we gather, from his affection for young people. After several years of failing health, he died in A.D. 270, at the age of sixty-six.

Only one incident in his uneventful life at Rome need be recorded. He was liked and trusted by the emperor Gallienus and his wife Salonina. Taking advantage of this friendship, he asked the emperor to allow him to found a city, to be called Platonopolis, on a deserted site in Campania. Porphyry expresses annoyance that the emperor's permission was afterwards revoked; but Gallienus probably wished to prevent his friend from doing a foolish thing. The story is interesting because it shows that Plotinus was not content with 'the flight of the alone to the Alone.' He wished after all to set up on earth a copy of the city not made with hands, eternal in the heavens. Perhaps he omitted to inquire whether the site in Campania was malarious, or how many celibate philosophers would be willing to inhabit Platonopolis. Other philosophers have had similar dreams. Locke drew up a code of laws for North Carolina, called the Fundamental Constitution. Berkeley and Coleridge made schemes of ideal commonwealths, which they hoped to see tried. William Penn's experiment in Pennsylvania, modelled partly on Harrington's *Oceana*, was successful.

Such then was Plotinus as a man—a Pagan saint and mystic; not fond of ceremonial worship at the temples—'it is for the gods to come to me,' he said, and shocked his friends by saying it; a moralist who condemned with Christian repugnance one at least of the vices to which Paganism was too tolerant; a citizen detached—too much detached— from the troubles of his country, but surrendered with complete devotion to the career which he thought the noblest; one who could say without self-reproach, 'if any man seeks in the good life anything beyond the good life itself, it is not the good life which he is seeking.' Proclus, the greatest of his successors in the leadership of the Platonic school, pays him this tribute. 'His soul, which he had always kept pure, took flight towards the divine principle, prayed to it and adored it. He had always endeavoured to raise himself above the stormy waves of this brutal life which is nourished on flesh and blood. It is thus that this divine man, whose thoughts were always turned to the Supreme God and the unseen world, merited the privilege of beholding several times the immediate presence of the Godhead, who has neither sensible nor intelligible form, since he is exalted above intelligence and being itself.' This is the beatific vision of the mystics. Plotinus enjoyed it four times during the six years when Porphyry lived with him.

And how can we, in a short time, best convey an impression of his philosophical teaching? He is a writer who has been much misunderstood, not because his thought is really obscure, for I do not think it is obscure, but because few scholars have thought it worth while to bestow upon him one tenth of the trouble which they gladly give to Plato and Aristotle, and because in drawing up the single chapter which was to set Neo-platonism on its right shelf in a collection of fossils, it saved trouble to copy each other instead of grappling with terribly difficult Greek. Within the last fifteen years, this reproach has been largely removed, as the appreciations which I have just quoted prove. Not to speak of my own book, Mr. Thomas Whittaker has written an excellent work on the Neoplatonists, and Mr. Stephen Mackenna's translation[1] only lacks the Sixth Ennead to make it complete. It is thus possible now to assume as proved a view of Plotinus as a thinker which twenty years ago would have had to be defended as a new and original theory.

The three truths which Plotinus is most anxious to establish are (1) the spiritual nature of reality, as against the materialism of the Epicureans and Stoics; (2) the possibility of gaining a real knowledge of ultimate truth, as against the scepticism of the New Academy and the pragmatism of eclectics; and (3) as against the Gnostics, the unity, goodness, and sacredness of the universe. There is no sense in which the charge of 'extreme dualism' can be fastened on Neoplatonism. There are no hard and fast dividing lines anywhere in his chart of reality, no *salto mortale* from one grade of existence to another. He names the rungs on the ladder— the *scala perfectionis*; but he lets us know that it is not really a ladder, but an inclined plane.

There are no distinct traces of Oriental influence on the thought of Plotinus, though at Alexandria, where he spent his youth, all races and all creeds rubbed shoulders. Neoplatonism is the true child of Hellenism, the last chapter in the history of Greek philosophy. The Jew Philo in the first century had shown how Platonism and Hebraism could be amalgamated, and so had St. Paul, the earliest of the great Christian writers, the author of Hebrews, and the Fourth Evangelist; but it is very doubtful whether Plotinus knew anything of Philo, and still more unlikely that he had ever read the New Testament. There is nothing in him that cannot be accounted for without leaving the genuine Greek tradition.

Is he a Platonist or an eclectic? He owes much to Aristotle, something to the Stoics, very little to the New Academy, with which his school always objected to be associated. It was not till much later that the school of Plotinus captured the Academy at Athens, the seat of the official 'successor' of Plato, the Diadochus. But Plotinus believed himself to be merely an interpreter of the divine Plato, from whom he never dissents consciously. Actually, he develops some sides of Plato's teaching, with the help of the long catena of commentaries which had sprung up in the school; and since the fusion of philosophies which at last almost

[1] Now completed.

extinguished all the others had already begun, it is not altogether without reason that he has been supposed by some to have aimed at reconciling Plato and Aristotle, a task which had been consciously attempted in the cognate school of Neopythagoreans. One of these, Numenius, so far anticipated Plotinus that Amelius had to write a treatise to vindicate the originality of his master. Numenius really seems to have tried to incorporate the wisdom of the East in his teaching, and is said to have referred to Christ—respectfully, it would appear. He taught that there is a supreme Godhead, who as regards the world of space and time is a *roi fainéant* (βασιλεὺς ἀργός), and a 'Second God,' who is 'double'—Janus-faced—looking both toward the eternal and toward the temporal worlds. The 'Third God' is the Spirit of the world. The Soul of man is also 'double.' These doctrines certainly resemble the philosophy of the Enneads.

But I must not linger over the obligations of Plotinus to his predecessors. What are the main features of interest in his own system?

I have said that he maintains, in opposition to materialism, scepticism, and Gnostic dualism, that reality is spiritual, that reality is knowable, and that reality is one. In his sytem there are two fundamental trinities. There is the trinity of Divine principles—the Absolute, whom he calls the One, the First, or the Good; Spirit (this is the best English word for νοῦς, which is usually rendered intellect or intelligence); and the Universal Soul. The other is the tripartite division of man into Spirit, Soul, and Body. But I must ask you to remember again that all the names in Plotinus are like the contour lines in modern maps; they indicate not chasms but gradual slopes. This applies to both the trinities which I have named.

In their objective aspect, Body, Soul, and Spirit are respectively the world as perceived by the senses; the world interpreted by the Soul as a spatial and temporal order; and the spiritual world. The organs which perceive the world under these three aspects are the bodily senses, the discursive reason or understanding, and spiritual perception or intuitive knowledge. It is only when we exercise this highest faculty of our nature, 'a power which all possess but few use,' that we are ourselves completely real and in contact with reality. This reality is neither an independently existing external universe, nor a subjective construction created by the mind. It is constituted by the unity in duality of the spiritual faculty and the spiritual world which it beholds in exercising its self-consciousness. Spirit and the spiritual world imply and involve each other; neither has any existence apart from its correlative. If the spiritual world may be called the self-externalization of Spirit, Spirit may with equal propriety be called the self-consciousness of the spiritual world. Plotinus is not an idealist in the modern sense; he does not believe that mind creates its own objects, nor that all reality is thought. The famous maxim, οὐκ ἔξω νοῦ τὰ νοητά, is not an assertion of mentalism; it only means that Spirit does not contemplate the spiritual world as existing independently of itself.

It is to Plotinus that we owe the first clear doctrine of spiritual

existence. Neither Cicero nor Plutarch ever calls the Stoics and Epicureans materialists. Plotinus sees the meaning of 'God is Spirit'; we are
not surprised that one of his disciples declared that the Prologue of the
Fourth Gospel ought to be written in letters of gold.

Matter (ὕλη) is for Plotinus the bare receptacle of forms, the subject
of energy viewed by abstraction as existing apart from the energy which
gives it meaning and existence. It is not 'material'; it is that intangible
all-but nothing which remains when we abstract from an object of
thought all that makes it a possible object of thought.

This difficulty of nomenclature pursues us all through Plotinus.
'Matter' is not material; 'Soul' is often nearer 'Life'; the 'gods' are not
the objects of theistic worship; by assigning 'Spirit' to νοῦς we have left
ourselves with no word for πνεῦμα; and we must beware of importing the
word 'God,' as most translators do, when Plotinus only has 'he,' or 'it'
(of the Absolute). Misunderstood technical terms are responsible for
much confusion in modern books about the Enneads.

A critic may say that Plotinus seems to waver between a true monism,
in which the one real world is set against imperfect constructions of varying
degrees of unreality, and the different idea of a stairway of worlds, in
which the human spirit, obeying its homing instinct, traverses a real
journey 'per tenebras in lucem.' A journey through the unreal, it may
be objected, is an unreal journey. The objection is a serious one, and it
affects other systems as well as Neoplatonism. It is bound up with the
notorious crux, what kind of substantiality we ought to give to evil.
There are two elements in reality as we know it, existence and value.
It is sometimes said, untruly as I hold, that while the natural sciences
confine themselves to the existential aspects of reality, neglecting for their
own purposes all valuation, art, morality and religion give us a kingdom
of ideal values. By the materialism of the last century, the kingdom of
values was described as epiphenomenal. It floated above the real world
as a kind of luminous haze, and was often supposed to be a merely subjective or imaginative picture of the ought-to-be, in no way affecting the
uniform sequence—miscalled causation—of the world of phenomena.
Other theories were those of psychophysical parallelism and neutral
monism, in which the two orders were supposed to keep step without
interfering with each other. How they came to be tied together in a kind
of three-legged race was not explained, and could not be explained.
But the view that science presents us with facts without values is quite
untenable. It is probable that there can be no cognition without valuation, and it is certain that the work of the scientist, which aims at estab-
lishing law, harmony, and uniformity in the natural order, is very far
from being indifferent to values. It is true however to say that the thought
of the last three centuries, dominated by scientific interests, has often
forgotten that other constructions, based on art, ethics, or religion, may
be as legitimate as the scientific construction, which is concerned with
only one value, that of order, and which consequently can only give us
an abstract view of reality. For the other values (and we cannot improve
on the classification of the ultimate values which we find in the later

Neoplatonists and implicitly in Plotinus himself, as Truth, Goodness, and Beauty) claim to be at least as real as the world described by science. We have no right whatever to divide the knowable world into facts which have no value, and values which have no factual existence. That which has no existence has no value; and that which has no value has no existence.

This realization of the intimate and indissoluble connexion of existence and value seems equally fatal to the disguised materialism called epiphenomenalism, and to the opposite philosophy which is sometimes called idealism, but which, to avoid confusion, we will follow Henry Sidgwick in calling mentalism. We must not seek to abolish the duality by negating either side of the opposition.

In Plotinus, as we shall see in the later part of this lecture, we have a courageous attempt to do justice to both sides, to existence and to value. He sees a world characterized by an infinite number of degrees of truth, and by a parallel series of degrees of value. His radical optimism inspires the faith that the fully real is fully knowable, and fully good. This act of faith underlies all Platonism.

There are two difficulties which this philosophy has to encounter. First, is it true that the two series run parallel to each other? Does the increase of our knowledge of reality, whether, as Hegel supposed, through a dialectical process, or by increased knowledge of nature, lead us upward to better and higher spheres of being? Are we justified in saying that the more we know of the world, the more convinced we are that evil is only an appearance?

I have argued elsewhere that whereas the existential scale presents us only with a series of more or less imperfect judgments, ranked by the degree in which they fall short of the standards of scientific truth, namely, inner harmony and universality, our value-judgments, at least in morals and art, require minus signs, registering temperatures below freezing point. There are negative values, which we call the evil and the ugly. If we wish to attribute moral qualities to the governor of the universe, it becomes a problem why there is so much apparent cruelty and injustice in the world.

In the nineteenth century the most popular attempt to bring our judgments of fact and judgments of value together was by throwing our ideals into the future, and by assuming that 'evolution,' which merely means the appearance of more complex forms in the place of simpler, was an automatic machine for generating higher values. That Herbert Spencer and even Darwin held this amiable superstition cannot be denied. Bosanquet says that to throw our ideals into the future is the death of all sane idealism, and this verdict, though harshly expressed, conveys a salutary warning. We cannot solve philosophical problems on the principles of Lloyd Georgian war-finance, by levying unlimited drafts on the future.

The essence of this expedient is to suggest that though judgments of fact and judgments of value—the Is and the Ought-to-be, are at present widely discrepant, there may be a natural tendency for them to converge and ultimately to coalesce. The world is a bad place, but it is getting better. The theory is helped out by the doctrine that God himself is undergoing a parallel course of evolution. He is realizing himself in the creation. Give Him time, and He will fulfil all expectations. According to this popular philosophy, the real at present falls short of the ideal and the ideal is not yet wholly real. Time is the physician who will cure them both, and at last join them together in holy wedlock.

Since this solution never even suggested itself to Plotinus, and would have been summarily rejected by him if it had been presented to him, we need not discuss it any further. It is, I think, manifestly unsatisfactory, both from the scientific and from the religious points of view, and it raises insoluble difficulties for the philosopher.

We must therefore try to forget this modern attempt to solve the difficulty, and consider what alternatives were left for Plotinus. The problem, you remember, is how to bring judgments of existence and judgments of value into a single scheme. One obvious answer is to deny that there is any problem at all. 'Granted that the world is full of evil, why should we expect anything different? There is good in the world, and there is evil. That is how things are.' A favourite theory on these lines was that 'Matter' or 'Flesh' is a substantial reality with evil qualities, and that 'the corruptible body presseth down the soul.' The spiritual journey in that case consists in liberating our personality from the fetters of sense, and escaping into the realm of the pure Ideas. This is metaphysical dualism, and it has been freely attributed to the Platonists. It is not real Platonism, but we have admissions that such doctrines were actually taught by some Platonists in their popular lectures, as good enough for those who could not understand deeper teaching. Platonism has had to pay dearly for this insincerity. Dualism was impossible for Plotinus, who could not allow any substantial reality to an anti-God, a rival to the all-embracing source of being, the One who is also the Good.

The alternative is to retain monism at all costs, and to force our value-judgments to conform to it by holding that evil is only a defect of goodness, its appearance of positive malignity being valid only within the sphere of the moral life. Great violence is thus offered to the moral sense, which is essentially dualistic. It is required no longer to use its minus signs.

This is on the whole the solution to which Plotinus inclines; but he is not comfortable about it. To begin with, he tries, not unsuccessfully, to minimize the importance of physical evil. 'It is unreasonable to find fault with the whole by looking at the parts.' Our world is only a copy of the spiritual world, which it resembles as much as it can. But the conditions of its existence require strife and tension; it is split up into discordant interests. Viewed as a whole, it is very near its archetype. 'All things that are Yonder are also Here.' But when we contemplate it as it affects individuals, it is far from perfect. Nevertheless, it is our fault if we take earthly troubles too seriously. Death only means that 'the actors change their masks,' and no ill-usage can really injure the soul. If we object to seeing our native country conquered, and our friends killed or enslaved,

we should learn to fight better! This is actually the consolation which he
would have offered to Belgium in 1914. In all this the influence of
Stoicism is apparent; and need it be said that Stoicism will carry us a
long way in bearing the inevitable troubles of life like brave men?

But does he not also dally with the dualistic theory of Matter? He
often seems to do so; but when we remember that ὕλη for him is not the
ponderable stuff of the Stoics, but something non-material and all but
non-existent, we must modify this impression. Matter is the principle of
externality, that which Soul has not been able to quicken and transform.
It is the inferior part in every complex. Like St. Paul, he is conscious
that 'the flesh lusteth against the spirit, and the spirit against the flesh,
and these are contrary the one to the other'; but the resisting force is not
the visible and ponderable as such. As a mystic, Plotinus uses the familiar
language about stripping oneself of all that is adventitious to the true
nature of the soul; 'take away everything,' he says to the aspirant who
wishes to see the vision; but this is not metaphysical dualism.

Evil, according to Plotinus, does not touch any of the Divine principles.
Not only the One, and Spirit, but the Universal Soul, are impeccable.
The individual soul also, on its higher side, is impeccable; it is only by
'coming down' into the world of space and time and change (a metaphor
which we must be careful not to take literally) that the soul becomes
liable to sin. The only line of demarcation which we can find anywhere
in this system is that which divides things which have οὐσία—permanent
substantial being—from those which have it not. And this line seems to
cut across the personality of man; for 'the soul is ourselves.' So difficult
did this doctrine of an impeccable soul, intimately bound up with a
lower soul which is not impeccable, appear to the school of Plotinus, that
most of the later Neoplatonists reject the view that the soul 'does not all
descend.' For, asks Iamblichus, 'if the will sins, how can the soul be
sinless?'

Evil, then, belongs only to that part of creation which is not 'divine,'
that is to say, which has no permanent and indefectible being. It is one
side of that tension of Yes and No, in which all things here below subsist.
It is real for souls on their probation, but not real in the fully real world
Yonder.

The half-real world of becoming corresponds to and is in a sense
created by soul, which perceives Matter 'by an illegitimate kind of
thought.' The irrational soul does not see things as they are. The half-
blinded spiritual faculty, the clouded perception, and the indeterminate
object, are all transformed together when the soul is 'awake.' It then
enters the sphere of real being, instead of 'that which we wrongly call
being' here below.

Is then the world here below only illusory? Certainly not. There is a
chain of degrees of reality extending from the One to Matter, on the
verge of non-existence. Plotinus does not pretend to know how or why the
world was created. It was not created in time; it is in a sense as everlasting as its Creator; in fact creation in this philosophy means only
logical or axiological, not temporal priority. There seems to be, he

suggests, a necessity that the First Principle should bring into existence not only every kind of creature, but every degree both of value and of substantiality (I have said that he postulates complete parallelism between these two series). This is what is usually called the emanation theory of Plotinus. He is fond of this metaphor; the higher orders of being 'so to speak overflow' and generate something resembling but less perfect than themselves. Since these creative acts are not in time, he merely means that there is a hierarchy of existences, in which each grade depends on the one above itself, while, until we come to the lowest step, there is a lower which depends on it.

He admits no contradiction in this 'so to speak overflow' from the Absolute. The world is not something added to or subtracted from the Absolute. We shall see that the first determination of the Absolute—the unity in duality of νοῦς and νοητά, is the necessary condition of there being a real world at all; the One is beyond existence. And similarly Spirit (νοῦς) does not lose anything by creating the universal Soul and the world which belongs to it. What we must understand quite clearly is that the higher principles do not live their own life in the lower. Nothing accrues or can accrue to Spirit and the spiritual world from the time-process. The action of the higher principles on the lower is purely one-sided. There are some thinkers who regard it as almost axiomatic that this is impossible. They say that in the spiritual as in the mechanical world there can be no action without reaction. I do not see why they are so sure of this; the argument does not trouble me at all. If it is valid, the whole system of Plotinus falls to the ground. And I ask you to consider whether every philosophy of true Theism would not fall to the ground too. It is clear to me that it would.

As for the world of sense, we have got so far as this, that it is an imperfect construction, based on inadequate 'opinion' (Plotinus will not call it knowledge) of a world which would still be imperfect if we could see it as it is. Modern science of course is well aware that we can see and hear only a small fraction of the vibrations which are known to exist. Our idea of the world is like our notion of a tune played on a piano of which all but a few notes were dumb. There can therefore be no rounded coherent theory of the visible universe. It is not fully real, being a sort of by-product of a higher order; and the organs by which we perceive it are not the organs through which we can behold the world of true Being.

'Nature' (φύσις) is for Plotinus the active faculty of the universal Soul, the expansion and expression of its energy. On the side of Matter, Nature is that which gives Matter whatever substantiality it has. It is, as Schelling says, 'sleeping Spirit'; it is itself unconscious, but casts upon Matter a reflexion of the forms which it has received from above. I am rather fond of one passage in which our author deals with 'Nature.' 'If any one were to demand of Nature why it produces, it would answer, if it were willing to listen and speak: You should not ask questions, but understand, keeping silence as I keep silence, for I am not in the habit of talking.' (I have quoted in my book Walt Whitman's 'the elemental laws never apologize,' and the Greek proverb, ἄπαντα σιγῶν ὁ θεὸς ἐξεργάζεται)

'What ought you to understand? In the first place that what is produced is the work of my silent contemplation; for being myself born of contemplation, I am naturally contemplative. While I contemplate I let fall as it were the lines which mark the forms of bodies.'

All through the system of Plotinus we find the same idea, that the creative principle creates, so to speak, with its back turned. It is when we are aspiring to what is above ourselves that our vision, almost unconsciously, gives form and shape to something in the lower world. 'All life,' he says, 'is νόησις'—contemplative thought. Thus for him creation is a golden chain, by which, as Tennyson says, the creatures are 'bound about the feet of God.' There is, he thinks, a climbing principle, an ἔφεσις, in every order of creation. The world is a Jacob's ladder, which the angels are constantly ascending and descending. But while the ascent is willed, the descent, by which the lower ranks of being came into existence, is unconscious, and we can say very little about it. 'All things pray,' says Proclus, 'except the Supreme.'

I wish I had space to comment on the doctrine of Time in Plotinus. It is difficult, as any discussion of this subject must be, but some of his dicta seem to me to be of permanent value. Time is not merely, in Dr. Schiller's phrase, 'the measure of the impermanence of the imperfect.' It is the measure of a finite activity directed to some end beyond itself. Movement by itself does not need time; time is the potentiality of qualitative change. In modern language, it is the form of the will, and is real in that relation, though not in the perfect unchanging world of eternity. It is needless to say that the picture-book theology of heaven as a fairyland existence in time and space receives no countenance in the Enneads. Ends are realized through time but not in time, which devours its own children. The final satisfaction of human hopes within the temporal series is impossible.

Whether Plotinus was a keen observer of the beauties of nature, we do not know. But he rejects with generous warmth the world-renouncing creeds which he saw around him. 'Do not suppose that a man becomes good by despising the world and all the beauties that are in it. Those who despise what is so nearly akin to the world yonder prove that they know nothing of the world yonder, except in name.'

The Soul is the centre of the Plotinian system, having affinities with every grade in the hierarchy. The human soul is a wanderer among the worlds; it may unite itself to the sphere above, and become spirit, or it may remain entangled in an environment which is below itself and beneath its true dignity. A bad man may lose his soul, but not the soul which he would have called his if he had not been a bad man. For the universal Soul is a Divine being, the Third Person in the Neoplatonic Trinity, in which however the Persons are not coequal. The Soul of the All directs the world from on high, without being involved in it. It is the creator and the providence of the universe; but we must beware of ascribing the modern idea of a 'group-soul' to Plotinus. The universal Soul is in no sense the sum or the resultant of particular souls.

The relation of particular souls to the great Soul is rather obscure;

I will give you Porphyry's explanation, which is quite correct as the doctrine of the school, and rather clearer than anything in Plotinus. 'We must not believe that the plurality of souls comes from the plurality of bodies. Particular souls subsist as well as the universal Soul, independently of bodies, without the unity of the universal Soul absorbing the multiplicity of the particular souls, or the multiplicity of particular souls splitting up the unity of the universal Soul. Particular souls are distinct without being separate; they are united to each other without being confused, and without making the universal Soul a simple aggregate. They are not separated from each other by any barriers, nor are they confused with each other; they are distinct like the different sciences in a single soul.' 'We must preserve the truth of individuality,' says Plotinus, but without losing sight of unity. 'All have a fellow-feeling with each other and with the All; so that when I suffer, the All feels it too.'

The soul neither comes into existence nor perishes; it is in itself the principle of life. When separated from the body, the lower functions of the soul are not extinguished, but are inactive. Opinion, reasoning, and memory are not needed under the conditions of life Yonder. Greek thought would have been horrified at the notion that the soul will be wrapped for ever in what Empedocles called the 'alien garment of flesh.' Flesh and blood cannot inherit the kingdom of God. But Plotinus does not need the hypothesis of an ethereal 'spiritual body.' He is, as I have said, the first philosopher to envisage the conditions of spiritual existence without any residuum of materialism, unless indeed we give that credit to the author of the Fourth Gospel, who wrote, 'God is Spirit, and they that worship him must worship him in spirit and in truth.'

Immortality may mean unending continuance in time, or a state which is absolutely timeless, or a state which transcends time, but for which time has a meaning. The religious faith in immortality, I have said (and I think I am expressing in my own words the view of Plotinus) 'is the faith that all true values are valid always and everywhere; that the order of the universe is just, rational, and beautiful; and that those principles which exalt us above ourselves and open heaven to us are the attributes of the Creator in whom we live and move and have our being.'

How far Plotinus really believed in the transmigration of souls it is hard to say. He is in earnest when he speaks of death as a mere changing of the actors' masks, but scarcely when he indulges in a half-humorous myth about souls being sent to inhabit the bodies of appropriate animals. Nor can he quite make up his mind whether, when the soul 'comes down,' it is 'summoned to do so as by the voice of a herald,' to bring order into created things, thus 'imitating the divine providence,' or whether some pride, or sinful curiosity, prompted it to leave a sphere where it was perfectly happy and innocent. Sallustius and Proclus, later members of the school, teach that every soul must descend once in every cosmic cycle. No possible blame, in their opinion, can be attached to the following of this universal law.

We now come to the world 'Yonder' (ἐκεῖ), which is the heaven of Plotinus and the sphere of solid unchanging reality. From the metaphysical point of view the essential thing to remember is that the spiritual world is a unity in duality constituted by the inseparable correspondence of νοῦς and νοητά. Plotinus takes very great trouble to show that there is no priority; he is neither a mentalist, nor on the other hand is his spiritual world a system of supramundane physics. 'Spirit,' he says, 'in beholding the real beings, beheld itself, and in beholding entered into its proper activity, and this activity is itself.' 'The knowledge of immaterial things as identical with the things known. Thus Spirit and the real world are one.' Reality, for Plotinus, is the first determination of the superessential One; it is absolute identity manifested under the form of essential reciprocity.

The Great Spirit has much the same relation to particular spirits as the universal Soul to individual souls. But Plotinus does not care to describe the Great Spirit as a personal God. The divine is rather the atmosphere breathed by beatified souls. I cannot refrain from quoting the words in which he pictures the happy existence of spirits Yonder. 'A pleasant life is theirs in heaven; they have the truth for mother, nurse, real being, and nutriment. They see all things, not the things that are born and die, but those which have real being; and they see themselves in others. For them all things are transparent, and there is nothing dark or impenetrable, but every one is manifest to every one internally; for light is manifest to light. For every one has all things in himself and sees all things in another; so that all things are everywhere and all is all and each is all, and the glory is infinite. Each of them is great, since Yonder the small also is great. In heaven the sun is all the stars, and again each and all are the sun. One thing in each is prominent above all the rest; but it also shows forth all. There pure movement reigns; for that which produces the movement, not being a stranger to it, does not trouble it. Rest is also perfect there because no principle of agitation mingles with it.'

I hope I have now convinced you that those writers who have dismissed Neoplatonism as the euthanasia of philosophy, as if the clear-headed Greeks at last committeed intellectual suicide by swooning away in a cloud of gas, have proved only one thing—that they have not read their author. But I have no wish to minimize the mystical element in Plotinus, in which the religious philosophy of the Enneads culminates. It is a mysticism built on a basis of rationalism, an ascetic religion which has not renounced humanism; and it is all the more interesting on that account.

The dialectic leads up inevitably to the One beyond Existence. We have been conducted through the sphere of Soul—the One and the Many, to that of Spirit—the One-Many. But behind the sphere of Spirit, in which thought and its object are still distinguishable, there must be the absolute One, the fountain of being. Strictly, this beginning (ἀρχή) is ineffable, we can predicate nothing of it; but in practice Plotinus, though with apologies, invests the Godhead with the attributes of Spirit, only *per eminentiam*. The mystic, even if with Scotus Erigena he says that the Godhead *non immerito Nihilum vocatur*, cannot adhere to this heroic abnegation;

he always tells us a good deal about the One, as Herbert Spencer does about the Unknowable.

But the dialectic is only one of the paths which lead to the One. Plotinus believes that he has had direct experience of the beatific vision. We must remember that it is a fundamental principle of this philosophy that we can only know what is akin to ourselves. The soul can traverse the whole ladder of perfection, because it is or may be in vital touch with every stage of the ascent. Plotinus does not shrink from saying that there is that in us which makes contact with the One possible. His philosophy leads him to this belief, and his personal experience as a mystic confirms it.

There are several passages in which Plotinus refers to this experience. I can only give you two specimens, which will convince you that he is attempting to describe what he has actually seen and known.

'We must not be surprised that that which excites the keenest of longings is without form, even spiritual form; since the soul itself, when inflamed with love for it, puts off all the form which it had, even that which belongs to the spiritual world. For it is not possible to see it or be in harmony with it, while one is occupied with anything else. The soul must remove from itself good and evil and everything else, that it may receive the One alone, as the One is alone. When the soul is so blessed, and is come to it, or rather when it manifests its presence, when the soul turns away from visible things and makes itself as beautiful as possible and becomes like the One (the manner of preparation and adornment is known to those who practise it); and seeing the One suddenly appearing in itself, for there is nothing between, nor are they any longer two but one, for you cannot distinguish between them while the vision lasts; it is that union of which the union of earthly lovers, who blend their being with each other, is a copy. The soul is no longer conscious of the body, and cannot tell whether it is a man or a living being or anything real at all. . . . When in this state the soul would exchange its present condition for nothing, no, not for the very heaven of heavens, for there is nothing better, nothing more blessed than this. . . . All the things that once pleased it, power, wealth, beauty, science, it declares that it despises; it fears no evil, while it is with the One, or even while it sees him; though all else perish around it, it is content, if it can only be with him; so happy is it.'

'We always move round the One, but we do not always fix our gaze on him; we are like a choir of singers who stand round the conductor, but do not always sing in time because their attention is attracted to some external object; when they look at the conductor they sing well and are really with him. Then we attain the end of our existence and our repose; we no longer sing out of tune, but form in very truth a divine chorus round the One. . . . Let him who has not had this experience consider how blessed a thing it is in earthly love to obtain that which we most desire, though the objects of earthly loves are mortal and injurious and loves of shadows, which change and pass; since these are not the things which we truly love, nor are they our good, nor what we seek. But

Yonder is the true object of our love, which it is possible to grasp and live with and truly possess, since no envelope of flesh separates us from it. He who has seen it knows what I say. . . . But the vision is hard to describe. For how can one describe, as other than oneself, that which, when one saw it, seemed to be one with oneself?'

The mystics all speak the same language. But there is something singularly impressive in reading this testimony, vibrating with restrained emotion, not in some ascetic of the cloister, but in one of the great thinkers of all time, a Greek and a loyal disciple of Plato, the last deep organ-voice in that long series of lovers of wisdom, which begins with the cosmic speculations of the Ionians, and ends, as we have seen, in a profoundly religious philosophy. Plotinus is the greatest of all truly religious philosophers. His is a deep spiritual religion resting partly on philosophic thought and partly on intimate personal experience. It stands free of any historical events in past or future. For this reason, he has a message for us to-day. To speak for myself, I have lived with him for nearly thirty years, and I have not sought him in vain, in prosperity or adversity.

O native Britain! O my mother isle,
How should'st thou prove aught else but dear and holy
To me, who from thy lakes and mountain hills,
Thy clouds, thy quiet dales, thy rocks and seas,
Have drunk in all my intellectual life,
All sweet sensations, all ennobling thoughts,
All adoration of the God in nature,
All lovely and all honourable things,
Whatever makes this mortal spirit feel
The joy and greatness of its future being!

S. T. COLERIDGE.

H

CHAPTER IX

SOME MEDIEVAL AND ENGLISH MYSTICS

THE fourteenth century, says Rufus Jones, was marked by an unique flowering of the human spirit. A whole garden full of beautiful souls bloomed as though by a pre-arranged harmony. The Rhine Valley, France, England, Holland and Switzerland all felt the breath of the Holy Spirit. We may think that they followed naturally after the great saints and thinkers of the century before, to whom they undoubtedly owed much. The Schoolmen were too much under the influence of Aristotle, an unmystical philosopher, to give full rein to mystical speculation, though the identification of the Active Reason with the Platonic *Nous* was soon made. Aquinas and his disciples are somewhat distrustful of the mystical doctrine of the spark or apex of the soul which is potentially part of ourselves, and prefer to regard the vision of God, granted mainly in ecstasy, as a supernatural gift. Intuitive knowledge of God, they are inclined to think, does not belong to this life.

It is possible that besides the influence of St. Francis of Assisi, that most Christlike of the saints, in whom the beauty, and even the merry humour, of the spiritual life captivated his followers, the horror of the Black Death, the most terrible affliction that ever befell the civilized world until our two Great Wars, stirred the minds and hearts of the fourteenth century; and the 'Babylonish Captivity' of the Papacy shook men's faith in the authority of the Church. There was an outbreak of free mysticism in the thirteenth century, which the Church dealt with in the usual way. Eighty 'heretics' were burnt at Strasbourg in 1215. But the movement produced one thinker of genius, Meister Eckhart (1270–1327). He was hardly a precursor of the Reformation, still less of Nazism, though Rosenberg declared that in him the Nordic soul first became conscious of itself. But in the philosophy of mysticism he ranks next to Plotinus. 'The highest part of the soul stands above time and knows nothing of time.' 'In eternity there is neither time nor space, neither before nor after; everything is present in one fresh-springing Now.' 'There is a principle in the soul altogether spiritual. I used to call it a spiritual light, or a spark. But now I say that it is free of all names, void of all forms. It is one and simple as God is one and simple.' 'God is nearer to me than I am to myself.' He distinguishes between the Godhead and God. The Godhead is always begetting his Son, the Logos, God revealed in creation. The Father and the Son are united in the bond of Love, personified as the Holy Spirit. Creation is not a temporal process. The archetypal forms, the expressions of God's thought, are the 'natured nature,' and these forms, projected into space and time, are the world of created things. The temporal world is a reflection of an eternal reality. We may find God in the street and in the world no less than in Church or in a cell. God's purpose in contemplation is fruitfulness in good works. The active life is better than contemplation; Martha does better than Mary. But 'those who busy themselves for the sake of something, even their own salvation, are hirelings and not righteous.' This, which might be paralleled from Plotinus, Spinoza, and many Christian mystics, was pronounced heretical. Other notable sayings of Eckhart are: 'God is always ready, but we are unready; he is at home, we are strangers.' 'Every gift of God makes us ready to receive a new gift, greater than itself.' 'All that a man bears for God's sake, God makes light and sweet for him.' 'It is often harder to leave a small thing than a great, and to practise a small work than one which men think great.' 'In prayer when we ask for temporal things we should always add, if it be God's will and for my soul's health. But when we pray for virtue, we need add no qualification.' 'God has left a little point wherein the soul turns back upon itself and knows itself to be a creature.' 'Every man pronounces his own sentence; as he shows himself here, so will be remain for ever.'

No account of mysticism would be complete without some mention of Eckhart, who though long neglected is now justly honoured. The other great German mystics, Tauler the great preacher, Merswin, Ruysbroek, Suso, and the familiar 'Imitation of Christ,' I must pass over, since it is no part of my plan to write a history of mysticism. The most profitable of these writers for modern readers is, in my opinion, the unknown author of the *Theologia Germanica*, which belongs to the school of Eckhart but is more cautious in speculation. We may question the wisdom of the saying that the soul has two eyes, with one of which it sees eternity and with the other the creatures, and that we cannot see with both at once. But he wisely hesitates to call the inner light uncreated[1]; it may be 'a created light, but yet divine, which is called grace.' His warnings against 'the false light,' which 'dreameth itself to be God,' shows that he was aware of the danger of using the language of deification. The life of Christ is 'distasteful and burdensome to nature,' and this is why the false light vainly dreams of union with the eternal God.

We now turn to the great school of English mystics in the fourteenth century, and we may notice first the *Ancren Riwle*, which may have been written by Simon de Ghent, Bishop of Salisbury from 1297 to 1315, or by Bishop Poore, a little earlier. It was addressed to three sisters, anchoresses, who lived at Tarrant Kaines in Dorsetshire. It contains humorous admonitions. They are not to be always chattering with visitors, 'like the cackling anchoresses.' 'More slayeth word than sword.' 'Be glad in your heart if ye suffer insolence from Sturry the cook's knave who washes the dishes.' (So these anchoresses were better off than our post-war ladies!) 'My dear sisters, ye shall have no beast but one cat.' They were to use the following prayer. 'Grant, we beseech thee, almighty God, that him whom we see darkly and under a different form, and on whom we feed sacramentally on earth, we may see face to face and may be thought worthy to enjoy him truly and really as he is in heaven,

---

[1] This, as I have said in an earlier chapter, was one of the charges against him.

through Jesus Christ our Lord.' 'The true anchoresses are birds of heaven that fly aloft and sit on the green boughs singing merrily. A bird sometimes alights on earth to seek food, but never feels secure there and often turns herself about.' There is a close parallel to this pretty comparison in a French poet:

> 'Soyons comme l'oiseau, perché pour un instant
>   Sur des rameaux trop frèles;
> Qui sent ployer la branche, et qui chante pourtant,
>   Sachant qu'il a des ailes.'

More interesting for our purpose are the visions and revelations of *Julian of Norwich*, another recluse. I know no more charming book than hers; it has been edited by Miss Warrack. She tells us that she desired 'a bodily sight' of Christ upon the Cross, that she might be 'one of his lovers and suffer with him.' She prayed for a severe illness, 'if it be thy will that I should have it,' that she might live nearer to God afterwards. The illness came when she was thirty, but 'being in youth I thought it great sorrow to die.' 'Good Lord, may my living no longer be to thy worship.' She recovered, and had many visions, including one nightmare of 'the fiend on my throat.' She distinguishes: 'all the blessed teaching of our Lord was showed by three parts, that is to say by bodily sight, by words formed in mine understanding, and by spiritual sight.' Of the last 'I have told some deal, but I may never fully tell it.' She is one of the happy saints. 'It is the most worship to him of anything that we may do, that we live gladly and merrily, for his love, in our penance.' 'When I saw that God doeth all that is done, I saw no sin, and then I saw that all is well. But when God showed me for sin, he said, All shall be well.' The making all things well is 'a deed which the blessed Trinity shall do at the last day, but how it should be done is unknown of all creatures that are beneath Christ.' When the soul is healed, 'our wounds are seen before God not as wounds but as worships.' Like William Law later, she cannot bear to think of the wrath of God. 'I saw no wrath but on man's part, and that forgiveth he us.' She repeats the mystical doctrines that we must 'noughten' visible things in order to know 'God that is unmade,' and that 'in every soul that shall be saved is a godly will that never assented unto sin.' 'It is high understanding to see and know that God dwelleth in our soul, and a higher understanding to see and know that our soul, which is made, dwelleth in God's substance.' 'Our soul is made Trinity, like the unmade blissful Trinity, and in the making oned to the Maker. This sight was full sweet and marvellous to behold.' 'I understood no higher stature in this life than childhood,' says this cloistered maiden.

It is tempting to add to these quotations, but I hope that all who are attracted by our subject will read this most beautiful gem of medieval literature for themselves.

Since this book is not a history of mysticism, I pass over Richard Rolle of Hampole, whose English writings are of great interest to philologists, and Walter Hylton, the author of the important *Scale* (or ladder) *of Perfection*, to whom I devoted a chapter in my *Studies of English Mystics*.[1] But the most instructive of all the fourteenth century English mystical writings is one which I neglected in that volume, the anonymous *The Cloud of Unknowing*, a work of genius, as Rufus Jones rightly calls it, marked by its high quality of style and originality. The author, who wrote other shorter books, has concealed his identity of set purpose. He may, as Miss Underhill thinks, have been a cloistered monk, but even this is uncertain. It is significant that Aldous Huxley, in his *Ends and Means*, calls attention to this medieval treatise.

The author is not like Julian, who 'knew no letter.' He had studied Dionysius the Areopagite, Richard of St. Victor, Augustine, and probably Bonaventura. He complains in one of his shorter books that many people found him hard to understand, though in his own opinion the *Cloud* was not beyond the intelligence even of 'the lewdest cow.' Modern readers will think that the truth lies between these two opinions.

The Cloud of Unknowing is the divine dark of Dionysius, and until we remember Eckhart's distinction between the Godhead and God as revealed to and immanent in man we shall think that the author has overstressed the importance of the negative road. This is not the most instructive side of the book. What makes it delightful is that the deep spirituality of the author, uncompromising in its demands for a wholehearted surrender of the will and affections to the love of God, is combined with a sound practical wisdom and a very human irritation at the unreality and self-deception of many who fancied themselves called to the life of contemplation. Some of these paraded a vapid spiritual hilarity like 'giggling girls and nice japing jugglers.' 'As for seemly bodily observances, if they be done by stirring of the spirit, then be they well done; else be they hypocrisy.' 'And yet we should not so feed us of the fruit that we should despise the tree.' Others 'sit gaping as they would catch flies. Now truly all this is but deceit, for they have full empty souls of any true devotion. Ofttimes the devil feigneth quaint sounds in their ears, quaint lights and shining in their eyes, and wonderful smells in their noses; and all is but falsehood. Some set their eyes in their heads as if they were sheep beaten in the head, and as they should die anon. Some hang their heads on one side as if a worm were in their ears. Some cry and whine in their throats.' Browning in his 'Spanish Cloister' has imagined the irritation which the little tricks of the inmates often caused to each other.

The following extracts will illustrate the position of the author. 'Time is made for man, and not man for time. God will not in his giving of time go before the stirring of nature. He giveth never two times together, but each one after other.'

'Take heed to the marvellous manner of grace in thy soul. It speedily springs unto God as a spark from the coal.' This sudden flash of spiritual light is noted by almost all the mystics.

[1] Published by Murray in 1906.

'God himself can no man think. He may well be loved, but not thought.' This is not contempt of reason, not the 'il faut s'abétir' of Pascal. It is what St. Bernard means when he says that in love God communicates Himself directly and not by means of symbols.

'There be two manner of lives in Holy Church; the one is active life; the other is contemplative life. Neither of them may be had fully, without some part of the other. A man may not be fully active but if he be in part contemplative; nor yet fully contemplative, as it may be here, but if he be in part active.' He puts Mary above Martha, but, as Richard Rolle says, 'love cannot be lazy.'

The two essential virtues are meekness and charity. 'He who might get these needeth no more for he hath all.' Meekness is a true knowledge of ourselves as we are. He who knows himself truly knows God as far as that is possible in this life.

The Cloud of Unknowing is sometimes pierced by a gleam of ghostly light. 'Of that dare I not speak with my blabbering fleshly tongue.' So St. Paul saw things which it was not lawful for him to utter. And this darkness—'what is he that calleth it nought? Surely it is our outer man, not our inner.'

'The eye of the soul is thy reason, thy conscience is thy visage ghostly.'

'One syllable meant in the deepness of spirit pierceth the ears of Almighty God rather than any long psalter unmindfully mumbled in the teeth.' Prayer should be short but frequent. 'Sin, sin! Out, out!' is a good prayer. 'Do not rudely strain thy body or thy spirit.' 'In all his sorrow a man desireth not to *unbe*; that were devil's madness.' In some of the German mystics we find such phrases as 'ich bin entworden.'

We must beware of what the *Theologia Germanica* calls the false light. 'The devil hath his contemplatives as God hath his.' God's creatures are diverse. Some are weak and need 'sweet feelings and weepings'— we recall poor Margery Kempe—others are strong and need them not. 'Which of these be holier or more dear with God, God wots and I do not.'

'Not what thou art, nor what thou hast been, beholdeth God with his merciful eyes, but that thou wouldest be.' We are what we love, as Augustine says.

In my Bampton Lectures on Christian Mysticism[1] I gave a good deal of space to the Cambridge Platonists of the seventeenth century, a group of philosophical divines who are one of the glories of the Church of England. At first sight their claim to be included among mystics may be disputed, for they are not tired of singing the praises of Reason. 'Sir,' said Whichcote in answer to his critic Tuckney, 'I oppose not rational to spiritual, for spiritual is most rational.' 'Reason is the divine governor of man's life; it is the very voice of God.' 'It ill becomes us to make our intellectual faculties Gibeonites'—hewers of wood and drawers of water to the will and affections. This robust championship of the

[1] Published by Methuen in 1899.

intelligence is very gratifying. That Reason for this group means. spiritual knowledge, Gnosis in the favourable sense, and not the logic-chopping faculty, is plain especially in the discourses of John Smith, the best university sermons that I know. 'Reason is a light flowing from the fountain and Father of lights.' 'Divinity is a divine life, not a divine science, to be understood rather by a spiritual sensation than by any verbal description.' Whichcote's famous Aphorisms, which at one time were to be found in many libraries, are not mystical, but they are full of inspired common sense as well as of deep religious conviction.

The most solid work of this school, Ralph Cudworth's *Intellectual System*, belongs to the Platonic tradition in English philosophy rather than to mysticism. Muirhead has a careful account of it in his book on the Platonic tradition.

The Cambridge school was not popular in the prosaic age which followed. But one of their contemporaries is of permanent importance in the history of religion. It was with good reason that Auguste Comte gave George Fox a place in his Positivist Calendar, which included very few religious leaders. That the Society of Friends, which he founded, is now coming into its own as perhaps the purest form of Christianity, is a belief which is not contradicted by the numerical insignificance of the one institutional body which is content to rely for its authority on the inner light, the indwelling presence of the Spirit of Christ in the hearts of men. The Quakers, to give them the nickname which they have made more than respectable, are not now zealous to make converts. Caroline Stephen, who like several other highly educated persons joined the Society, wrote: 'So long as our principles continue to gain ground, we need not, I think, be anxious about outward and definite membership, and we may even rejoice in the lessening of our isolation. Our fundamental principle of obedience to the light of Christ in the heart is certainly not to be regarded as the distinguishing mark of a sect. The very growth of that obedience must, I believe, lead to the effacing of outlines and boundaries made by human hands. Our framework, beautiful and elastic as it is, belongs to the outward and perishable. To subordinate and if need be to sacrifice whatever is outward and perishable to the innermost, the central and supreme, is the very groundwork of our ideal.' This is the very opposite of the policy of the Roman Church, with its 'compel them to come in.' The one policy has had a resounding and terrible success, the other, if we value power and judge the success or failure of the Gospel by counting heads, has been a conspicuous failure. But this is an utterly false criterion. 'Strait is the gate and narrow is the way that leadeth unto life, and few there be that find it.' Few, no doubt, as compared with the crowd who gather round the broad gate, but very many more than those who have been moved to join this little Society. Some mystics may regard all life as so sacramental that they need no special sacraments; this is perhaps a matter of temperament, and a rather unusual type. Those who are not willing to lose the beauty and dignity of Catholic or Anglican public worship are not to be regarded as less spiritual than those who find more edification in silent meetings in a barn. It is tempting to quote the testimony of two very different authorities, the eloquent Baptist Charles Spurgeon, and the great American psychologist William James. 'George Fox,' says the former, 'left to the Christian Church in the clearest and most unmistakable utterances a testimony for the spirituality of true religion. If you were to read through the lives of all the eminent saints, I believe you would come to the conclusion that of all others George Fox is the most distinct upon the one point, that God is a Spirit, and they that worship him must worship him in spirit and in truth.' William James says: 'The Quaker religion which he founded is something which it is impossible to overpraise. In a day of shams it was a religion of veracity rooted in spiritual inwardness, and a return to something more like the original Gospel truth than men had ever known in England. So far as our Christian sects to-day are evolving into liberality, they are simply reverting in essence to the position which Fox and the early Quakers so long ago assumed.'[1]

There are several reasons why the type of religion of which the Quakers are the most consistent representatives is gaining ground, and is almost certain to gain more ground in the future. In the first place it has nothing to fear from new knowledge, whether scientific or historical. I have shown, what indeed is obvious, that the old scaffolding is no longer able to support the building, and I have argued that it is no longer necessary. It is a peculiarity of theological architecture that the foundations are ingeniously supported by the superstructure. This is considered in my chapter on symbolism. The infallible Church remains erect, but only for totalitarians or Fascists in religion. The infallible book, if we include, as its supporters usually do, the Hebrew scriptures, confuses our understanding of the 'new commandment' given to the world by Christ. Science, as a philosophy of ultimate reality, has been discredited by the most thoughtful of its own votaries. But mysticism, which rests on the apprehension of spiritual values, not on the acceptance of supernatural phenomena or the dismissal of the imponderables into the limbo of 'epiphenomena,' is invulnerable. Next, the uncompromising condemnation of war and violence as an instrument of policy is entirely justified and profoundly Christian. There were naturally two opinions about the conscientious objectors in the two Great Wars; but in this country, at any rate, there will not be much hesitation in condemning almost all war as an unspeakable abomination and a hideous anachronism. 'They that take the sword shall perish by the sword.' Does not the verdict of history confirm these words of Christ? '*Vae victis*,' 'woe to the conquered,' said an ancient conqueror. A modern historian may say with equal emphasis, '*Vae victoribus*,' 'woe to the victors.' Before the rather disastrous concordat under Constantine—it was only sixty years later that a pagan said he would become a Christian if they would make him Bishop of Rome—the condemnation of war by the Church was almost unanimous.

[1] These two quotations are from *George Fox, Some Modern Appreciations*. The Swarthmore Press, 1925.

The Quakers were not the first of the small sects to denounce war; there were many protests remorselessly suppressed by authority. Honesty compels me to say that even Fox was not always consistent. He once wrote a bellicose letter to Oliver Cromwell which would have satisfied the Protector's court poet, Andrew Marvell. But Fox procured for himself six months' imprisonment in a foul dungeon by refusing to accept a commission in the new militia which was being raised in 1650, before the battle of Worcester. The notion of Fox as an army officer is certainly amusing. But was not Horace, a student at the University of Athens, made a colonel or brigadier in the army of Brutus and Cassius, and was not Edward Gibbon an officer of militia?

The conscientious objector is no new phenomenon; in times of war he puts the Government in a difficult position. The early Quakers suffered cruelly; in our time the principle of religious conviction as a ground for refusing to serve in the fighting forces has been grudgingly admitted; in other lands the objector is shot without mercy.

I have had so many disappointments in my hopes for a Christian civilization that I cannot be an optimist. But I do not think it unreasonable to hope that the unparalleled horrors which we have witnessed may bring this atrocious custom to an end. The majority in every country wish only to spend their lives in peace and safety. But they may be swept off their feet by mendacious propaganda. Dictatorships are usually bellicose, because they depend on the army, and soldiers wish for an opportunity to distinguish themselves and receive early promotion. Bureaucracies have little initiative; they are the slaves of the machine which they serve, and the machine may carry them irresistibly towards war, as some Germans, including the Kaiser, confessed in 1914. The middle class is generally pacific, having most to lose by a great war; but we may remember that the French dismissed Louis Philippe and his umbrella because they were 'bored' by peace, and installed Napoleon the Little in his place, to give them glory in Italy, shame in Mexico, and disaster at Sedan. Our own middle class, a few years later, embarked cheerfully in a most unnecessary attack upon Russia. The effect of boredom in politics is greater than is usually supposed. Still, war in the nineteenth century was a very different thing from war in the twentieth. Civilization has had two strokes, and there can be no doubt what the effect of a third stroke would be. We must face the unpleasant truth that to renounce power-politics is to renounce power in politics. If we abjure war and preparations for war we shall not be able to police Europe, and our moral lectures will not be attended to. We may incur severe humiliation and loss. But this is the offence of the Cross. Even if the Devil says to us, 'all these things will I give thee if thou wilt fall down and worship me,' we neither covet the Devil's rewards nor trust his promises. Our God can deliver us, 'and if not, we will not serve thy gods nor worship the golden image which thou hast set up.'

The third thing which has impressed the whole world favourably about the Quakers is the well-administered philanthropic and charitable work that they have done, especially among the victims of the war. They have taken the lead in showing that the love of Christ can overcome the spirit of hatred and the desire for revenge.

The sterling honesty and simple habits of the early Quakers had their natural result in worldly prosperity. Tennyson's gibe at John Bright as a 'broad-brimmed hawker of holy things' was levelled at him as a capitalist no less than as a pacifist. There is a ridiculous story that one of the Gurneys persuaded the Rothschild of the day to attend a Quaker meeting. The Spirit moved no one to speak. As they came out, the old Jew said, 'Now I know why you Quakers do so well in business. I never made so much money in three-quarters of an hour before.' At present, many Quakers favour the left wing in politics. They have no axe of their own to grind in taking the popular side, and they may be trusted to reinforce what idealism exists among the Socialist party.

George Fox (1624–1691), the son of a Puritan weaver, learned the trade of a shoemaker, and also of a grazier. As a boy he passed distressful years in the search for truth, till at the age of nineteen he experienced what the Methodists call sudden conversion. 'When all my hope was gone, so that I had nothing to help me, nor could tell what to do, then, O then, I heard a voice which said, There is one, even Christ Jesus, that can speak to thy condition; and when I heard it my heart did leap for joy. For though I read the Scriptures that spake of Christ and of God, yet I knew him not but by revelation, as he who hath the key did open, and as the Father of life drew me unto his Son by his Spirit.' He became a wandering preacher, and attracted crowds of disciples, especially in the north of England. He was a visionary, subject to trances of unusually long duration, in one of which, like St. Paul on his way to Damascus, he lost his sight. He was once, again like St. Paul, caught up by the Spirit 'into the paradise of God.' He suffered in all eight imprisonments, covering about six years, but his last years, even before the Act of Toleration in 1687, were peaceful. He has often been compared with St. Paul, and the comparison is not dishonouring to the great apostle. In one way they were not like each other. St. Paul's enemies said that though his letters were weighty and powerful, his bodily presence was weak and his speech contemptible. Fox's *Journal* is not the work of an educated man, but his bodily presence was awe-inspiring.

Caroline Stephen says that the Friends are not anxious to proselytise. This is true now, but Fox was an ardent missionary; he twice visited Holland, and even crossed the Atlantic. In spite of savage persecution, the Friends were for a time the most numerous of the dissenting sects.

William Penn gives us a charming portrait of him, 'meek, contented, modest, easy, steady, tender,' 'a man, yea a strong man, a new and heavenly-minded man.' 'The most awful, living, reverent frame I ever felt or beheld was his in prayer.' But he was not always meek or tactful. We cannot imagine St. Paul pursuing King Agrippa's coach, and shouting godly counsels in at the window, which is what Fox did to

Cromwell; and it was hardly prudent, when a magistrate asked him whether he believed in election and reprobation, to answer, 'Yea, and thou art in the reprobation.' Like some of the early Christians on their trial, he was at times provocative.

It is important for the student of mysticism to consider why the Society of Friends fell on comparatively evil days in the next century. It was an anti-mystical period, when 'enthusiasm' was a word of contempt. But the main reason was that the spiritual ardour of the Friends cooled. In 1751 there was a complaint that 'the younger generation do not seem to come up as well as could be desired.' They had begun by despising education, and wishing to cut themselves loose from all traditions. As Burrough, one of the first Quakers, wrote: 'We ceased from the teaching of all men and their words and their worships and their temples, and we met together often and waited upon the Lord in pure silence.' This was a rather disastrous application of the negative road. Besides this mistake, the early Quakers inherited a harshly dualistic theology, and did not at first see how ill it accorded with their own mysticism. In consequence they were bound to hold that the inner light is something wholly alien from human nature, since no son of Adam can have anything good in himself. They spoke of the divine light as supernaturally placed in human nature like a candle in a lantern; they called it a substance entirely separate from man's own being. They modified Calvin's teaching only so far as to teach that every man has one chance of salvation given him. We can do nothing to bring the light into our souls; we must wait till God sends it. By making the light purely supernatural and external, they gained what they wanted, an infallible authority. Of course there is no such infallible oracle; modern Friends have adopted a far sounder philosophy, which sees no difficulty in holding that the Spirit of God speaks in and through our natural faculties, illuminating and transforming our souls. The education is gradual; the Spirit does not flash its full glory at once into our dazzled eyes. Moreover, the light does not shine upon us only; the inspiration of the individual must be checked by due respect for authority and tradition. Petrified tradition, as Edward Carpenter says of civilization, is a disease from which societies seldom recover; but the stored wisdom of the race cannot be spurned without danger.

Of the indwelling Christ Winstanley writes: 'If you expect or look for the resurrection of Jesus Christ, you must know that the Spirit within the flesh is Jesus Christ, and you must see, feel, and know from himself his own resurrection within you.' We believe that Christ rose because we know that He has risen. This is the favourite theme of the epigrammatic verses of Angelus Silesius; we have found the doctrine in St. Paul's epistles.

In 1910 there were 147,000 full members of the Society, the large majority of whom were in the United States. I have written: 'The function of the Society of Friends is to bear witness to the truth of spiritual religion, to maintain the independence and self-sufficingness of this faith, and to prove that it leads to no barren and self-centred detachment from social life and its problems, but rather to a courageous and devoted advocacy of causes in which the spirit of our religion calls for opposition to the current practice of the world.'

Some of the most characteristic mystical writers in English have been poets, and I have dealt with some of them in my chapter on Symbolism. But there is one more name which I should be sorry to omit, for he is one of the glories of Anglican theology and a most charming writer. This is the non-juror William Law, who is best known as the author of that very stern moral exhortation called *A Serious Call*, but who concerns our present subject as the writer of several short and very beautiful mystical treatises, after he fell under the spell of the illuminated cobbler, Jacob Böhme or Behmen. If *The Spirit of Prayer*, *The Spirit of Love*, and *The Way to Divine Knowledge* are not well known to the religious public, the loss is theirs. We cannot afford to let such treasures pass into oblivion.

Like all the mystics, he insists that 'the seed of Christ' is within us. 'What could begin to deny self, if there was not in man something different from self? Unless Christ lay in the soul as its unknown hidden treasure, as a seed of life, a power of salvation, in vain had the holy Jesus lived and died for man. The Word of God is the hidden treasure of every human soul, immured under flesh and blood, till as a daystar it arises in our hearts, and changes the son of an earthly Adam into a son of God. The redeeming work of Christ is to raise the smothered spark of heaven out of its state of death, into a powerful governing life of the whole man. It is your own Cain that murders your own Abel. Do not cross the seas to find a new Luther or a new Calvin, to clothe yourself with their opinions. No, the oracle is at home, that always and only speaks the truth to you. Salvation or damnation is no outward thing that is brought into you from without. Your salvation consists, not in any historic faith, or knowledge of anything absent or distant from you, not in any variety of restraints, rules and methods of practising virtues, not in any formality of opinion about faith and works, repentance, forgiveness of sins, or justification and sanctification, but wholly and solely in the life of God, or Christ of God, quickened and born again in you.' 'There is nothing that is supernatural in the whole system of our redemption, but the supernatural love and wisdom that brought it forth. The Christian religion is the only true religion of nature; it has nothing in it supernatural.' It is a little odd that Law will have nothing to do with the Cambridge Platonists, whose teaching closely resembled his own. But Law was a High Churchman, and the Cambridge group were already nicknamed Latitudinarians.

'Neither reason nor Scripture,' he says, 'will allow us to bring wrath into God himself, as a temper of his mind, who is only infinite, unalterable, overflowing love. Wrath is atoned when sin is extinguished.'

One more quotation may illustrate the beauty and eloquence of his writing. 'This pearl of eternity is the Church, a temple of God within thee, the consecrated place of divine worship, where alone thou canst worship God in spirit and in truth. In spirit, because thy spirit is that alone in thee which can unite and cleave unto God, and receive the working of the divine Spirit upon thee. In truth, because this adoration in spirit is that truth and reality of which all outward forms and rites, though instituted by God, are only the figure for a time; but this worship is eternal. Accustom thyself to the holy service of this inward temple. In the midst of it is the fountain of living water, of which thou mayest drink and live for ever. There the mysteries of thy salvation are celebrated, or rather opened in life and power. There the supper of the Lamb is kept; the bread that came down from heaven, that giveth life to the world, is thy true nourishment; all is done, and known in real experience, in a living sensibility of the work of God on the soul. There the birth, the life, the sufferings, the death, the resurrection and ascension of Christ are not merely remembered but inwardly found and enjoyed as the real states of thy soul which has followed Christ in the regeneration. When once thou art well grounded in this inward worship, thou wilt have learnt to live unto God above time and place. For every day will be Sunday to thee, and wherever thou goest thou wilt have a priest, a church and an altar along with thee.'

It is deplorable that this noble writer should be so little read.

Be not afraid to pray—to pray is right.
Pray if thou canst with hope, but ever pray.
Though hope be weak or sick with long delay.
Pray in the darkness if there be no light.
Far is the time, remote from human sight,
When war and discord on the earth shall cease,
Yet every prayer for universal peace
Avails the blessed time to expedite.
Whate'er is good to wish, ask that of heaven,
Though it be what thou canst not hope to see.
Pray to be perfect, though material leaven
Forbid the spirit so on earth to be,
But if for any wish thou darest not pray
Then pray to God to cast that wish away.

                                    HARTLEY COLERIDGE.

        Ring in the valiant man and free,
          The larger heart, the kindlier hand;
        Ring out the darkness of the land,
        Ring in the Christ that is to be.

                                    TENNYSON.

    In the terrible days we are living in, and the hard times which in one
way or another must follow them, mankind is standing at the cross-roads.
Only two possibilities are open to us: to slide further down into the abyss,
or by a heroic effort save ourselves through Christian renaissance. May the
Lord help us!—S. L. FRANK.

        England, awake, awake, awake!
          Jerusalem thy sister calls.
        Why wilt thou sleep the sleep of death,
          And close her from thy ancient walls?
        Thy hills and valleys felt her feet
          Gently upon their bosoms move.
        Thy gates beheld sweet Zion's ways;
          Then was a time of joy and love.
          And now the time returns again;
          Our souls exalt, and London's towers
        Receive the Lamb of God to dwell
          In England's green and pleasant bowers.

                                    BLAKE.

    The Englishman carries his English weather in his heart wherever he goes,
and it becomes a cool spot in the desert, a steady and sane oracle among all
the deliriums of mankind. Never since the heroic days of Greece has the world
had such a sweet, just, boyish master. It will be a black day for the human
race when scientific blackguards, conspirators, churls and fanatics manage
to supplant him.—SANTAYANA.

CHAPTER X

WATCHMAN, WHAT OF THE NIGHT?

I AM well aware that I might have been wiser not to write this chapter. For what has mysticism to do with past and future, with history and prophecy? It is a vision of timeless reality, which is neither born nor dies, being raised above the changes and chances of this mortal life. We pray God that we who are careful and troubled about many things may repose upon His eternal changelessness.

We have seen how this detachment from worldly affairs has led some contemplatives into an almost callous indifference to natural affection and to love of country. Some of them have felt no sorrow at bereavement. Others, like Plotinus, have said contemptuously that if we object to seeing our country enslaved we should learn to fight better. These things, he would have us believe, do not matter much; 'the actors change their masks,' that is all. Einstein has recently professed the same detachment; it is excusable in a persecuted German Jew. But I cannot think that this attitude is right. Christianity differs from all other philosophies and religions in not offering to make us invulnerable. Ours is the religion of love, and love often hurts. Not justice, which is never done here on earth; not the proud defiance of a Stoic under Nero, nor of a Red Indian at the stake; but the acceptance of suffering which only love can help us to endure. That vicarious suffering—not vicarious punishment—is a holy and divine thing is the lesson of the Incarnation, the offence of the Cross. St. Augustine came to see that Platonism without the Incarnation and the Cross is not enough; it was this that made him a Christian. The mystics of the cloister made their escape from the world. Sometimes they were able to find in the love of God a reflected love of our neighbour. Sometimes their concentration on the inner life became pathological. The best of them realized that the spiritual life is one of withdrawal and return; but in the way of life which they had chosen withdrawal was easier than return. The God Whom Christians worship is the God Who reveals Himself as Love or Goodness, as Truth and as Beauty, and for us while we live here these attributes give a meaning to family affection, to science and the pursuit of knowledge, to art and poetry, and to the chequered records of history. The City of God will never be fully realized on earth; 'its type is laid up in heaven'; but we are to pray that God's will may be done on earth as it is in heaven. This can only be done by those who are led by the Spirit; the world still 'lieth in wickedness'; but we are to endeavour to make all things 'according to the pattern shown us in the Mount'—the Mount of Transfiguration.

There is another consideration which might give us pause. Have any human beings been endowed with the gift of knowing what is going to happen? Successful prophets have been of three kinds. They may prophesy after the event—in sporting language they may back the winner after the race. Historians have no difficulty in showing how blind the Roman government was in persecuting the Christians; how foolish the French aristocracy was in not foreseeing the revolution, and so on. Or they may write the history of the past to suit their own views. We are told that the Deity cannot alter the past, but historians can and do. Or thirdly, powerful men may prophesy what they intend to do, and occasionally they do it.

Apart from these sham prophets, the ironies of history have been colossal. If Tacitus or Trajan had been told that a Christian priest would rule what remained of the Roman Empire from the Vatican, he would have been even more incredulous than indignant. And perhaps the little flock who gathered round their Master in Galilee would have been equally startled and incredulous. In recent history, were not Godwin, Macaulay, and Herbert Spencer convinced that civilized man was becoming more rational and above all more humane? Would they not have refused to believe that wholesale massacres of non-combatants, the uprooting of whole populations after the manner of Assyrians and Babylonians, the reintroduction of torture and religious persecution, would be established once more in Europe in the twentieth century, with very little protest? We remember how Tennyson, giving voice to the political faith of his generation, spoke of freedom slowly broadening down from precedent to precedent. And now we are told by keen observers that we are far on the road to serfdom. Once more, what would Clifford and Tyndall have thought if they had seen scientific discussions of occultism by men like Lodge and Crookes, and if they had read paragraphs on astrology in popular newspapers? It looks as if every climate of opinion prepared the way for a drastic change of weather; as if every institution carried within itself the seeds of its own dissolution. We may also remember that Victorian publicists like Sir Charles Dilke enumerated the Great Powers of the future and omitted to mention Germany. Matthew Arnold and George Meredith knew better.

The prophets have not all been misguided optimists. I once collected, for my own good, a series of dismal prognostications about the fate of this country by Wellington, Wilberforce, and other public men, just before the great outburst of prosperity in the middle period of Victoria's reign.

I am venturing to predict a revival of spiritual and unworldly religion in this country, and no doubt in other parts of western and central Europe. I base this opinion partly on the tendency of human nature to seek for compensations. Now that all the idols of the last century are lying broken at the foot of their pedestals; now that what the Catholics call the last western heresy, the belief in an automatic law of progress, has been so far disproved by events that it has become a manifest absurdity; now that we are losing faith in our political institutions, it is plain that we must either give up hope, as St. Paul accused the pagans of his day of doing, or once more fix our hearts where true joys are to be found, namely, on God and the eternal world. In order to prove my case I must depict the present state of society as I see it. Part of what I say must be controversial, for there are some who are more hopeful than I am about present developments. It is possible that like most old men I can see little that is good in what is new; but much of my diagnosis can hardly be disputed.

The German publicist Sybel made what then seemed a very bold prediction, that universal suffrage would bring to an end popular government. He saw, no doubt, that complete democracy would become a mere auction of the worldly goods of the unrepresented minority, a government by mass bribery. I do not remember whether he followed Plato in believing that what Plato called tyranny and we call dictatorship would be the next stage. It is not easy to imagine that our people would voluntarily submit to a Führer; but if liberty were destroyed there would not be much power of resistance. The new form of corruption is likely to prove far more deadly than the old. None of our national institutions has lost in credit and prestige so much as the House of Commons since the final extension of the franchise and the payment of members.

It is a familiar truth that each generation likes to throw upon the scrapheap the household gods of its parents. To-day the favourite Aunt Sally is Liberalism, which in my young days was professed by all those who wished to be thought intelligent. It is also the mode to speak contemptuously of the middle class, who are the chief custodians of almost all that is worth preserving in our civilization. In some continental countries this class is actually in danger of extinction. Even with us, since it is unorganized and in a minority in almost every constituency, it is threatened with a destruction of its standard of living, which will make it difficult to maintain its tradition of cultivated intellectual life. The loss would be incalculable.

There has never, perhaps, been a time when the sense of impending doom was so widespread. It is a rather new phenomenon, which no doubt has been largely the result of the two Great Wars. The first decade of the present century, though feverish and unhealthy, was not pessimistic. And even after the first Great War there was a revival of confidence, a false dawn of prosperity and a trust that the League of Nations might bring peace and goodwill to a distracted world. That faith, alas, soon became a hope; and now there is nothing left but charity. The financial crisis in 1929, and the rise of militant dictatorship, shattered what remained of optimism. Spengler's strange book, *The Decline of the West*, put into words what very many were thinking.

Have there been any other periods in history when the whole social order seemed to be crumbling? I think there has been only one, the decline and fall of the Roman Empire. The Renaissance and Reformation were domestic affairs of western Europe. The French Revolution attracted great attention because it was the first of its kind; but it only substituted the rule of the middle class for that of an inefficient monarchy. But in the third and later centuries we find, in Christians and pagans alike, a chorus of woe not unlike that which now proclaims the end of an age. The only hope was eschatological; the world was coming to an end, and

I

so much the better. This belief corresponded to the equally baseless dream of a good time coming, which encourages our apocalyptic socialists. The rival religious cults were all religions of redemption, healing and escape. Above all, there was an amazing flight from society to the harshest forms of community life and the solitary austerities of the hermits. The deserts swarmed with monks. Philosophy became religious and mystical. If, as I believe, we are threatened, not with another Dark Age, but with a period of contracting civilization, we are likely to see a revival of community life, and perhaps another flowering time of mystical religion.

Our publicists mostly agree that this is a real *fin de siècle*. Some of them say it is the end of economic man; others that it is the end of the Renaissance; others that it is the end of Church-directed Christianity which began with Constantine the Great. Historians quite rightly try to carve history at the joints. But strictly there are no joints, no ends and no beginnings. It may be that some of our troubles are only the aftermath of the two wars; and if the Russians will allow Europe to settle down, recovery may come sooner than we expect. But there are some very disquieting symptoms.

It is a curious reflection that the growth of societies, and the rivalry between them, may have checked, retarded or even injured biological development. There seems to be a tension between man as an individual and man as a social animal. Extreme results of socialization are of course observable in insect societies, a rather awful warning. The civilized man, whether brain worker or machine minder, is far less independent of his neighbours than the handy savage, who builds his own house. The machine age is not in all ways an age of progress.

Systematic disparagement of the intellect is something new in civilized peoples. That the Germans, of all people, should have fallen victims to such slogans as 'Blood and Soil' is a sinister symptom. And what a depth of vulgarity is disclosed by the contemptuous use of 'highbrow.'

Writers on the present state of our country are almost unanimous in saying that only a 'change of heart'—in other words a renewal of spiritual religion—can save us from disaster. They call attention to the manifest deterioration in moral standards, to the growing laxity in sexual relations, and the spread of dishonesty and thieving. These things are certainly deplorable; but they are the invariable concomitants of a great war, and I see no reason to think that they will necessarily be permanent. In matters of sex, periods of licence and puritanism seem to alternate. The Victorian age was probably the most moral, to use the word in the narrower sense, in the history of our country. A reaction began after the death of Queen Victoria, and the wars have accentuated it. But apart from war-conditions there is evidence that the most squalid kind of immorality, vulgar prostitution, has greatly diminished. Access to contraceptives has no doubt had the effect of turning unlawful indulgence into a different and perhaps less repulsive form. An American investigation reports that 'our men are becoming more moral, our women less so.'

A similar doubt may be felt about what to me is a very unpleasant symptom of barbarization, the unparalleled debasement of painting and sculpture. To those who believe that God reveals Himself as Beauty, the deliberate ugliness of much modernist art must appear nothing less than blasphemous. But perhaps this strange aberration will pass away.

The most grievous setback has undoubtedly been the recrudescence of cruelty in forms which would disgrace even savage tribes. It is the result of the worst form of idolatry, the worship of the State, the Race, or the Class, in place of God. 'Everything is permitted'; we have heard this said in so many words. This repudiation of every check upon human wickedness has been acted upon before now by some of the successful brigands whom posterity has delighted to honour; it has never been quite so shamelessly professed before. But I think we ought to remember that this terrible perversion has not been at all universal, though even we and the Americans have not been entirely immune.[1] To justify the indiscriminate massacre of a hundred thousand non-combatants, men, women and children, in Japan, on the ground that it shortened the war, is to use an argument which might palliate any atrocity. But on the whole, this sinister reversion to something worse than savagery has been confined to four nations, Russia, Germany, Spain and Japan. Of these, Japan is not a Christian nation, and Russia has repudiated Christianity. In Spain the cruelties took place in civil war, which is usually barbarous, and there is a vein of cruelty in the otherwise noble Spanish character. The saddest case is that of Germany, because Germany is one of the most civilized countries in the world. Those who have travelled in that country, who have German friends, who have read German books and enjoyed German music, have been amazed at the revelations of calculated cruelty which have come to light since the end of the fighting. The abominable deification of the State and the Race will account for a great deal, and the ruthless suppression of all adverse criticism in a people accustomed to submit to authority will exonerate a large proportion of the German nation from any share in the guilt. But when all is said and done, there remains a very deep stain on western civilization as represented by one of the great European peoples. When we consider that humanitarianism was named by social historians as the greatest influence upon politics and social morals in the eighteenth and nineteenth centuries, we must sorrowfully allow that subtle poisons have been at work beneath the fair surface of our civilization.

There are therefore good grounds for believing that the nations of Europe, if they are to survive, must pray for a new heart and a new spirit. But in this chapter I am specially concerned to prove that we must face a disappointment of our secular hopes for the continued power and material prosperity of our country, and to express a hope that, as has happened before, 'when he slew them they sought him, and turned them early and inquired after God.' It can hardly be doubted by any candid student of sociology and economics that our period of expansion has come to an end, and that we must face a contracting economy, a reduction in population, and a gradual return to the condition of England before

[1] I hear on very good authority that our Government was not a party to the outrage on Hiroshima.

the industrial revolution. Few will think that this would be an unmixed misfortune, for the town mechanic seems to hate his work. The rustic and the brain-worker, even when they are underpaid, do not strike.

A nation which depends for its bare subsistence on foreign trade can hardly be a working-man's paradise. Countries where workmen give good value for their wages cannot be prevented from competing successfully with those where 'labour' is parasitic upon industry, and where profits are confiscated for so-called social services. Other nations do not seem willing to accept the British working man as an immigrant. In the struggle for existence victory, in my opinion, belongs to nations with a lower standard of living and a higher standard of work. Under-populated countries may no doubt still enjoy for a time the benefits of expansion, including high wages; but for us the principle of diminishing returns has been at work since the beginning of the century.

It is probably also true that the nations bordering on the Atlantic, all of which have a very limited area, have passed their zenith. Just as the discovery of America and the opening of the sea routes to Asia brought to an end the Mediterranean period of history, so the Atlantic countries have no longer the same advantage that they formerly had. And as regards power politics it seems obvious that nations with an almost unlimited area, like Russia and the United States, must be the Great Powers of the future. The Germans saw this, and made a desperate bid to forestall the fate which menaced them, of sinking into a Power of the second rank, by annexing and colonizing Poland and the Ukraine. The balance of power has now been finally upset in favour of the Slav, unless or until 'the course of empire,' which Bishop Berkeley expected to take its way westward, moves at last still further to the east.

That this change in the future prospects of our nation will have a profound effect on the attitude of our people towards what used to be considered success in life can hardly be doubted. Recent legislation has almost destroyed the chief motive for industry, thrift and enterprise. It is no longer possible to 'found a family.' The successful man of business knows that nearly the whole of his earnings will be confiscated by the State. Our young people are more and more inclined to play for safety, and safety generally means some little job in the always increasing army of bureaucracy. Mammon has no more prizes to offer.

Some of our sociologists have painted an unpleasant portrait of the 'acquisitive' Victorian capitalist, as if money-getting were one of our national faults. So much nonsense has been talked about national character that we may be inclined to avoid the subject. But to do ourselves justice, we have never been an avaricious people. Napoleon called us a nation of shopkeepers. We are rather bad shopkeepers. We have neither the industry of the Germans nor the parsimony of the French. We are on the whole a rather easy-going people, fond of good cheer and of life in the open air, proud of our liberties, and willing to pay outward respect, untinged with envy, to our social superiors. We have also, as I have said, a rich vein of idealism, which shows itself in our poets and philosophers, and in our population generally there is a love of home and family life. The opposite impression was caused by circumstances which have ceased to operate—in the brief period when our country was the workshop of the world, and when the rewards of business enterprise were so great as to overweigh natural indolence, not in the majority but in a number of prominent individuals. When therefore I predict a revival of unworldly religion in the near future, I am not postulating a change in the national character, but rather a return to the older ways of living which have given England a high place in the annals of Christendom. Certain temporary conditions which gave a materialistic tinge to our civilization in the Victorian age are no longer operative. Mammon, as we know to our cost, is not the only false god whom nations worship. There are also Moloch and Beelzebub the father of lies. But the elimination of Mammon will give the better elements in our make-up a chance of emerging, if the wage-earners can read the signs of the times.

But what shape will the revival take? Religion, says Whitehead, is not always a good thing; it is sometimes a very bad thing. Several crank religions have been preached in our day. The Catholic Church discourages them successfully; in America they flourish like a green bay tree. It is rash to prophesy. A nation gets the religion which it deserves; a decadent civilization will have a decadent religion.

There are some who, impatient with what they consider the obstinate traditionalism of the Churches, think that a new religion may take the place of Christianity. This seems to me in the highest degree improbable. I should be the last to suggest that the Holy Spirit speaks only to members of the Christian Churches. Such a notion is contradicted by all that we know of the saints and prophets in other religions. But the religion of Christ has proved that it can satisfy the spiritual experience of all men of goodwill. We can no more invent a new religion than we can build a tree.

It may be that the holy fire will be lighted not in the West at all, but in Russia, which has passed through the ordeal of persecution. Hitherto a revival of mystical religion in the East has taken the form of ascetical monasticism. Various causes have prevented eastern Christianity from making its due contribution to theology and Christian philosophy. But now among the Russian émigrés there are men of the highest spiritual and intellectual distinction. The numerous works of Nicolas Berdyaeff are well known to English readers, and the recent book of Frank, *God With Us*, is a gem of the purest water. These writers recognize that the revival must be ascetic, using the word in its proper sense, and they accept the possibility that the persecution of the true faith may not be a transitory phase. The Church, they say, must go back beyond Constantine; it may have to go back to the Catacombs. The Russian Church, stripped bare and despoiled, may start on a career of spiritual conquest unencumbered.

Frank says that Jeremiah's 'new covenant' is the first proclamation of the mystical faith. 'I will put my law in their inward parts, and write it in their hearts.' 'That which is immediately given us in the mystical experience is a reality which we apprehend on the one hand as something primary, as the deepest source and the absolute foundation of our being, and on the other as something absolutely valuable, giving us the supreme joy, satisfaction and delight.' There is no need, he thinks, to try to peep into the future of our souls after death, and indeed this is impossible. 'I know with certainty now that I am eternal.' Christianity is to be found wherever the human heart truly sees itself and in doing so sees God. Truth itself holds for all time and for all men. 'The more we study religion and mysticism, the more clearly do we see the universality of the Christian truth.' 'Every movement of the soul inwards is at the same time its expansion outwards in loving apprehension of the fullness of being; the nearer we are to God, the nearer we are to the whole of his creation.'

My only hesitation in this admirable book is caused by a doubt whether Frank quite realizes that the certainty which he enjoys is not given to us to start with, and is not given to all good people. Faith is an experiment which ends as an experience; but the experiment must be tried first. He who would find the pearl of great price must first sell all he hath to buy it. Moreover, the mystical sense is no criterion of our acceptance with God. There are some who without this encouragement always live 'as in their great taskmaster's eye.' On the other side, there have been visionaries who were not good men.

The chapter called 'Mysticism and the way of the Spirit' in Berdyaeff's book on Freedom is very valuable. Mysticism, he insists, is not a refined psychologism, nor is it an irrational passion of the soul, nor yet simply the music of the soul. Mysticism belongs to the sphere of the spirit and not to that of the soul; it is in a word spiritual not psychological. Windelband says truly, 'while proceeding from the individual, mysticism regards individualism as a sin.' It is an escape from individualism, but not from personality. On the plane of the spirit there is no contradiction here. Nor is it a dreamy condition of the soul. It is essentially realistic and sober in the discerning and discovery of realities. 'The only true mystic is one who sees realities and knows how to distinguish them from phantasies.' 'The foundation of mysticism is an inner kinship or union between the human spirit and the divine. In mystical experience there is no longer any insurmountable dualism between the supernatural and the natural, the divine and the created, for in it the natural becomes supernatural and the creature is deified.' Mysticism is the imminence of the Holy Spirit in the created world. It overrides the barriers which divide Christians. 'Orphism and Plotinus, Hindu mysticism and Sufism, St. John the new Theologian and St. John of the Cross, Eckhart and Jacob Böhme, are all in some measure in agreement.'

Berdyaeff has an interesting paragraph on the difference between Orthodox and Catholic mysticism. The former seeks to acquire the grace of the Holy Spirit; human nature is transformed and deified from within. Man becomes another creature. Catholic mysticism is more Christo-centric. 'Catholic mysticism tends to give a subordinate place to the work of the Holy Spirit.' It is an imitation of Christ in which the sufferings of our Lord are as it were lived through again. Orthodox mysticism knows nothing of the dark night of the soul as a stage in mystical progress. In Catholic mysticism suffering and sacrifice are surrounded by a kind of ecstasy. The gulf between natural and supernatural does not exist for mystical writers in the East. Thomism tends to invest nature with a neutral character fundamentally non-divine. Orthodox mysticism is more akin to German mysticism of the fourteenth century than to the Spanish mystics. But 'Orthodox and Catholic mysticism have an equal right to be called Christian.'

He proceeds to expose the dilemma which pervades all mysticism. In mystical literature we too often find an advocacy of an impersonal and undifferentiated love which means a real hardening of the heart towards all particular affection. 'This comes very near to being not Christian but Hindu.' Christianity is a mysticism of love, and yet individual loves may sometimes come between ourselves and God. 'The difficulty of the spiritual life lies precisely in the necessity of combining detachment from the many and concentration upon the One with the liberation and trans-figuration in the Spirit of all the diverse elements of the world and of humanity.'

I have allowed myself this digression because I think that the West has a good deal to learn from the East, not only from Indian philosophy, which is deficient in what the Russians call creativity, but from the exiles of the persecuted Russian Church, who from their new homes in Western Europe are able for the first time to make us acquainted with a philosophy of religion which is lineally descended from the Greek Fathers. We are, I think, more willing to learn from the Greeks than from the Latins, and, as I have said before, almost every religious revival comes from the fusion of two traditions, as the Christian Church itself was, in Clement's meta-phor, the confluence of two rivers, the Hellenistic and the Jewish.

I have been greatly encouraged by the undoubted tendency of able and independent thinkers to converge upon Christianity of the mystical type as the only hope for civilization. I am far from sharing the inverted snobbishness which disparages the intellect, and would put in its place either emotionalism or pragmatism or one of the new forms of idolatry. Truth is one of the absolute values, and those who seek it must follow the gleam, humbly but confidently, without making concessions to any so-called practical considerations. Blind faith is not faith at all; the sub-mission of the intellect is no part of true mysticism.

If I am right; if we may look for a rebirth of spiritual religion, we must expect that, as in former revivals, it will be very independent of the Churches, and not too kindly regarded by ecclesiastics. I do not think that this is to be regretted. A great deal of the deep despondency which undoubtedly prevails in ecclesiastical circles is due not to the decline in personal religion or in moral conduct, but to the indifference which is now felt to institutional religion, to attendance at church services, and to the pastoral office of the clergy. For this decline there are several causes not connected with personal religion. The spread of education has made the average congregation less willing to sit at the feet of the preacher. New inventions, particularly the motor car and broadcasting, have interfered gravely with church-going, which is no longer a matter of accepted convention. The Anglican Prayer Book, in spite of the abortive and over-timid attempt to revise it, is not really suited to modern tastes. The personnel of the clergy is not what it was fifty years ago. The necessity of subscribing to the creeds, interpreted as meaning literally what they say, has prevented many thoughtful and earnest men from entering holy orders, and it is no disparagement of the disinterestedness of our young men to own that the wretched pecuniary prospects which the ministry now offers has deterred many of the type which formerly produced respected leaders. As an American remarked: 'You cannot expect to get all the cardinal virtues for a thousand dollars a year.' The Free Churches have suffered as much as the Church of England, though it is difficult to believe an Anglican bishop who said that he could staff his diocese with ex-Free Church ministers. The parochial system has broken down in many towns and villages, and those who recall my quotation from William Law, that the mystic carries about with him a church and an altar, will not expect that a revival of mystical religion would do much to improve the professional prospects of the clergy or the corporate Church life of the parishes. These things may be regretted; but they do not necessarily imply that the religion of Christ is decaying. More serious, no doubt, is the complete atheism—it would be incorrect and uncivil to the pagans to call it paganism—in which large sections of our population are allowed to grow up. Since denominational jealousies, and perhaps political prejudices, forbid the teaching of religion in the primary schools, and since parents are too often blind to their responsibilities in the matter, it is difficult to see where a remedy is to be found.

Christianity began as a lay prophetic religion. There was not a single priest among the Apostles, nor does the Epistle to the Ephesians, in enumerating the different kinds of teachers in the primitive community, say 'he gave some, priests.' It is on the laity that the future of Christianity depends, though we must have organization to prevent the 'fruits of the Spirit' from being lost. Inspiration seldom retains its glowing ardour for very long. It either congeals or evaporates, and either process is fatal to it. The Churches exist to preserve some measure of continuity. It is unfortunate that they sometimes strangle the fresh spiritual life which they were founded to protect.

I am preparing to lay down my pen. But I foresee that something may be said which though vulgar ought perhaps to be answered. 'You tell us,' it may be said, 'that there will be a revival of what you call mystical religion. Your chief reason for thinking so is that life in England is going to be so uncomfortable that people will seek for compensation—you actually use this word—in what are called the consolations of religion. This is the characteristic attitude of an old man. You remind us that there was a great outbreak of flight from the world when the Roman Empire was breaking up. So these people simply ran away, and left their country to go to the dogs. They may have been good enough for heaven, but they were of no earthly use. You seem to look forward to something of the same kind. Your mystics save their own souls; society they neither save nor try to save. You leave us in no doubt as to what you think of politics and politicians. If high-minded men will not soil their fingers with such a dirty trade, we shall be governed by crooks; and what will become of the country then? What we want is practical men who will devote themselves to making the masses comfortable; your dreamers are no good.'

This language is most commonly used by a class of men who, though they may be encouraged by ambitious ecclesiastics, have no part nor lot with the religion of Christ, since their standard of values is radically unchristian. They are ready to say with Jacob in the Book of Genesis, 'if the Lord will keep me in the way I am going, and will give me food to eat and raiment to put on, then shall the Lord be my God.' Is the Church to accept the position which the indignant Helen in Homer suggested for Aphrodite, who was perhaps her own worse self? 'Go thou and sit by his side, and let thy feet never bear thee to Olympus; but always sympathize with him and attend upon him, till he make thee his wife—or rather his slave.'

The charge that the 'religious,' in the technical sense, are useless drones might be levelled at scholars and thinkers generally. But a man may be a useful member of society without producing commodities. Was it not Hegel who answered his housekeeper when she wondered why he did not go to church, 'Meine liebe Frau, das Denken ist auch Gottesdienst?' If work is prayer, prayer, meditation, contemplation may also be work. Can we deny that the saints have been great benefactors to mankind? And if the mystics are right, the explorers of the high places of the spiritual world have not wasted their time. As for the taunt that they care only to save their own souls, we may remember how many mystics have spurned the idea of future reward. And after all, our own souls are the bit of garden we are set to cultivate, the bit of line we have to defend. I do not think that there is a large element of calculation in sincere religion. I might have quoted the warnings of Eckhart and other contemplatives, that we ought at once to suspend our communings with God if we have an opportunity of helping our neighbour. The great mystics are quite above criticism on this point.

There is however an element of 'escapism' in all higher religion, and this must be considered a little more seriously. 'O that I had wings like a dove,' says the Psalmist, 'for then would I flee away and be at rest.' 'Thou shalt hide them privily by thine own presence from the provoking of all men; thou shalt keep them secretly in thy tabernacle from the strife of tongues.' 'Let us flee hence to our dear country,' said the Platonists. There have been short periods—they never last long—when men have fancied themselves to be living, if not in the best of all possible worlds, at any rate in a very comfortable abode. Macneile Dixon in his delightful Gifford Lectures thinks that the golden age of Greece and the Elizabethan age were two of them. He forgets that Bacon repeats the gloomy words of Sophocles that the best lot for man is 'not to be born, or being born to die.' Optimism and pessimism often flourish together; the pessimist is sometimes one who has to live with that very irritating person the optimist. He is generally a man who is determined not to be disappointed. In prosperous times men are not conscious of a challenge which they disregard at the peril of those who will come after them. For as Walt Whitman says, 'it is provided in the essence of things that from every fruition of success, no matter what, shall come forth something to make a greater struggle necessary.' But as a rule men have before their eyes something better than their present environment, and they like to dwell in thought on things as they ought to be, as they have been, or as they will be.

For there are various kinds of escapism; the mystics are not the only culprits. We may imagine a golden age in the past, or a golden age in the future. The ancients looked backward, as the Victorians looked forward. Both are retreats into a dream world—this is the essence of romanticism. There is a tendency in human nature to idealize the past; our ancestors 'had more wit and wisdom than we.' And if, as was commonly believed, history moves in cycles, 'Time may run back and fetch the age of gold.' 'The old is better,' is the voice of authority. So we have what are called revivals, revivals of what never existed. '*Quod semper, quod ubique, quod ab omnibus*' is an impressive slogan, even if closer investigation reveals that the first clause means 'in 1563,' the second 'at Trent,' and the third 'by a majority.' In secular history archaism has been disastrous. It produces senseless wars and the preservation of obsolete institutions. There are malignant ghosts which hover over our modern world. Mussolini dreamed of restoring the Roman Empire, though the modern Italians are neither Romans nor imperialists. The Nazis tried to persuade their countrymen that the Germans, a people of mixed ancestry, are pure Nordics of an uniquely noble type, and that they ought to discard an alien Judaistic superstition and return to the paganism in which their forefathers found happiness. Of all ways of escape, archaism is the least fruitful.

Futurism is in part a Jewish legacy. The Hebrews gave history an importance which it never had for the Greeks. At first it was intramundane. The time would come when the chosen people would break its enemies in pieces like a potter's vessel, and rule over the world. When the political prospects of the nation became almost hopeless, apocalyptism succeeded prophecy, and a miraculous 'day of the Lord,' which would redress all wrongs on this earth, was imagined. Christianity inherited a mixed eschatology, partly Platonic and Stoic and partly Hebraic, but supramundane and futuristic. Until the Renaissance there was little interest in a hope for the future of society. *Hora novissima, tempora pessima.* The thoughts about the future life were not at all wholly consolatory. The colours, both seductive and horrible, were heightened, and the scene was, in the popular teaching, quite definitely placed within space and time.

In the seventeenth and eighteenth centuries, which have been called a real age of progress, futurism was secularized, and the idea of human perfectibility became popular. It was a pleasant dream, which was quite erroneously believed to be part of Christianity. Now that the course of events has destroyed it, religion has in consequence been made to share the discredit. The new Chiliasm survives, or did survive till lately, in the visions of 'a good time coming,' indulged in by Rousseau and his followers. The rhapsodies of Godwin and Shelley, and the confidence in the future of Herbert Spencer, are very instructive. As usual during periods of optimism there was an undercurrent of black pessimism, illustrated by Leopardi, and even by John Stuart Mill, who called the world 'an odious scene of violence and cruelty.' Some who would by no means endorse this wholesale condemnation of modern civilization have protested against the romantic futurism of their contemporaries. 'To place our ideals in the future,' Bernard Bosanquet tells us, 'is the death of all sane idealism.' We are reminded of St. Paul's warning, so seldom referred to in modern preaching, 'if in this life only we have hope in Christ, we are of all men most miserable.'

If this confidence in the future, however extravagant may have been some expressions of it, is abandoned, it will mean a very great change in the 'climate of opinion' which has prevailed ever since the beginning of the modern period. Hope has been defined as the anchor of the soul. 'We are saved by hope.' Is not this one of the saving truths which the Gospel brought into a society which 'had no hope and was without God in the world?' Is hope, as Matthew Prior writes, remembering the words which Diogenes Laertius ascribes to Aristotle, 'but the dream of those that wake?'[1] The theory of cycles undoubtedly holds out the prospect of golden ages, flowering times of civilization not less glorious than Periclean Athens or Shakespearean England, in the future. Our scientists tell us that mankind is still an infant, in the stage of the rattle and feeding-bottle. We shall have ample time to try every possible and impossible social experiment, unless indeed, as seems possible, we prefer co-operative suicide. This prospect does not seem too bad; but so strongly has the dream of perfectibility taken hold of us that even so independent a thinker as Arnold Toynbee speaks of the theory of recurrent cycles as extreme pessimism.

Secularized optimism—belief in the unlimited possibilities of human nature—has given birth to various utopias. Characteristically, the earlier utopias were placed in distant parts of the world, the later in more or less distant periods of time. Brazilians or Tahitians were once supposed to live in a happy state of primitive innocence. We need not dwell on these pathetic fancies. The nineteenth century pointed to various asylums in which we could even now take refuge. As Lippmann says, Wordsworth fled from mankind to rejoice in nature. Chateaubriand fled from man to rejoice in savages. Byron fled to an imaginary Greece, William Morris to the middle ages. A few tried an imaginary India. A few an equally imaginary China. Many fled to Bohemia, to Utopia, to the Golden West, and to the Latin Quarter, and some, like James Thomson, to hell, where they were 'gratified to gain that positive eternity of pain instead of this insufferable inane.' Nietzsche, completely disillusioned, cries out 'Where is my home? I seek and have sought and have not found it. O eternal everywhere, O eternal nowhere, O eternal in vain.'

It seems then that the method of escape by futurism is no longer

[1] Stobaeus ascribes this saying to Pindar, Aelian to Plato.

available for us as it was in former times. We do not believe that the present world order is soon coming to an end, nor that we may look forward to steady and almost automatic improvement. And yet we cannot rest content with the world as naïve realism presents it to us. We believe that if our too earthly hopes are doomed to disappointment, God has 'provided some better thing' to take their place.

And so we are driven back upon another way of escape, which is not subject to the neutral time process. The Indians have taught us that we may win deliverance by simply renouncing all worldly interests, and saying, 'eternity, be thou my refuge.' 'Man walketh in a vain shadow,' says the Psalmist, 'and disquieteth himself in vain.' The world in which we seem to live is for them a mere phantasmagoria without meaning or value; let us allow it to pass over us unobserved, and we shall have peace. Complete detachment is the way of salvation. The Indians have never followed this drastic renunciation consistently. Reincarnation seems to give a reality to time which it does not have in this philosophy, and the doctrine of Karma introduces the belief in retributive justice, executed in a rather external fashion, which implies some belief in continued personality. But we are concerned with a theory, namely that we can win salvation by complete flight from the world. From our point of view, this theory is defective because it tries to renounce the conditions of life in this world instead of transforming and consecrating them, and the penalty is that the spiritual world also loses its contents. It is the greatest mistake to attribute this method either to Neoplatonism or to the great Christian mystics. The blank trance, however we may explain it, is not the heaven either of Plotinus or of his Christian successors.

Philosophically, mysticism rests on the doctrine that reality consists in the unity in duality of mind and its objects. It neither, with the subjective idealists, puts matter inside mind, nor, with the materialists, mind inside matter. But it insists that the knowledge of things as they are, the vision of God as partly revealed in His creation, is not given to us to start with. Our knowledge of reality is broken up and distorted. Instead of the One-many, in which distinction remains without separation, we see the One-and-many, a realm of discord and hostility, in which God and the creation are separated and misunderstood. The way to escape—not from the world which God made, but, as Newman wrote in the epitaph which he chose for himself, *ex umbris et imaginibus in veritatem*, is the way of discipline, meditation and contemplation, in a word the way of prayer, if we use the word in its ancient meaning, as 'the ascent of the mind to God.' This is the real way of escape, escape from our lower selves and from the false objects created by our lower selves. All the truth and beauty of the external world are not lost to us; they are restored to us in their true meaning, as reflections of the truth and beauty of the Creator.

I have already dealt with the charge that the mystic does nothing to make the world better. It is simply not true. Our social troubles are the result of a false standard of values. A Christian society would live in peace with itself. What is sometimes called otherworldliness can alone bring health to the world. Religion is not taught but caught from someone who has it. We learn about the spiritual world from those who have been there.

There is one more question which may well be raised. We have noted the remarkable unanimity in the testimony of the mystics, and their complete confidence that the revelation granted to them was genuine. But it may be asked whether this unanimity is any evidence that their experience was more than subjective and psychological, and whether their feeling of certitude should carry conviction to other people. Have not many people held with the utmost assurance convictions which are known to be erroneous and even absurd? As regards the knowledge of God, does not the Roman Church condemn, under the name of ontologism, the belief that there can be immediate and irrefragable apprehension of His presence? Do not some of the best contemplatives warn us seriously against the delusion of the 'false light,' and confirm the line of the old Greek dramatist that 'God always works in silence?' 'He who believes he knows it knows it not,' says the *Sama Veda*; 'he who believes he knows it not, knows it.' It is known to be incomprehensible by those who know it most, and as perfectly known by those who are most ignorant of it.

In attempting to answer this objection, one is rightly chary of speaking of experiences which we have not had ourselves. I know well that I am very far from having earned the divine knowledge which is only imparted to the chosen few who have offered up all that they have to gain it. I can only speak of rare and fitful flashes of light which have seemed to come from some source higher than my own personality. But those who have mounted higher are sure that they have been in contact with ultimate reality, and heard the voice of God Himself, or of the glorified and indwelling Christ. Ought we not to believe them? It is conceivable, of course, that they may be deceived; but if our highest and deepest experiences cannot be trusted, it is useless to seek for truth anywhere.

And when men speak of the impossibility of knowing God, they are surely thinking of the Godhead whom the Platonists say is 'beyond existence,' the Absolute One of whom nothing positive can be said without limiting Him. The God Whom we can worship, Whom we are bidden to love, has certainly not left Himself without witnesses. He has revealed Himself in what modern philosophy calls the ultimate values. He has revealed Himself in pure human affection which is almost more than a symbol or sacrament of the love which the Creator has for His creatures. He has revealed Himself in the Incarnation of our Lord, and in the lives of His most saintly followers. And He has revealed Himself in prayer and meditation. If we do not think of God as so revealed, the love of God is rather difficult to understand.

This, however is not quite what the extreme mystics claim to have experienced. What is it that they have seen, and that you and I have not seen? They cannot put it into words, and sometimes they think it would be 'unlawful' to do so. Some of them have believed that in rare moments of ecstasy they have transcended all distinctions, and passed into a state where even the 'I' and 'Thou' of prayer no longer apply. We may perhaps doubt whether such an experience is what the visionary believes it to be.

We cannot entirely leave behind the conditions which make us human beings. In any case, such strange visitations must not be desired or sought for. The great mystics are emphatic about this, and they are not the foundation of their faith.

We have seen that the psychology of mysticism distinguishes between soul, and spirit. No more need be said on this subject, except that there is no hard and fast line between the two. The scale of values is inevitably graduated, and lines are drawn across it which should be understood to resemble the contour lines on a map. Even the 'soul become spirit' does not rise above symbols of divine truth, and perhaps the mystical vision, if it could be put into words, would reveal nothing new except that God loves us, and has given His Holy Spirit to dwell with us, sanctify us, and transform us, as St. Paul says, 'from glory to glory.' 'The law of the Spirit' of life in Christ Jesus has delivered me from the law of sin and death. This is indeed the 'escape' that we desire. If I am not mistaken, our children and grandchildren will need and prize it more than we do. The darkest hour is just before the dawn.

CHAPTER XI

THE PHILOSOPHY OF MYSTICISM[1]

WILLIAM JAMES's famous book, *The Varieties of Religious Experience*, appeared in 1902. Studies of the psychology of mysticism have poured from the press. In our own country we may name Evelyn Underhill, Mrs. Herman, and von Hügel. In France, Bastide, Murisier, Récéjac, Boutroux, Delacroix, Janet, Poulain, Bremond, Bergson, Bréhier. In America, besides William James, Starbuck, Leuba, Coe, Hocking, Rufus Jones, P. E. More, Pratt, Royce, Bennett. These lists are far from complete. In Germany the subject seems to have aroused less interest; but Otto, not long before his death, published a book dealing with it.

The psychological approach is characteristic of our time. The strong current of anti-rationalism, subjectivism, and relativity which has swept over America and many schools of thought in Europe, has threatened to banish ontology from philosophy, and to leave it with only the theory of knowledge, psychology, and ethics, which are the three parts of Höffding's *Philosophy of Religion*. The importance attached to religious experience has led to a fresh study of the writings of the mystics, which has been supplemented, especially in the United States, by the method of the questionnaire. Medical psychology has been called in, and even the psycho-analysts have offered their contribution.

I should be the last to disparage the value of these researches, which have thrown much light on some of the dark places of the human mind. One may indeed suspect that an undue amount of attention has been given to the abnormal manifestations of a natural and healthy state of the soul. Some of the writers whose names I have mentioned would confine the word mysticism to the pathology of religion, a view which can hardly be held except by those who either give the word a meaning which it does not bear in religious philosophy, or who regard all except the most tepid religious devotion as pathological. Others are willing to treat the testimony of the mystics to their own experiences with great respect, and to allow that their construction of reality may be as worthy of credence as that which forms the basis of naturalism. For instance, William James says, 'The existence of mystical states absolutely overthrows the pretensions of non-mystical states to be the sole dictators of what we believe.' Those who go as far as this have admitted that the mystical experience is one of the facts with which a comprehensive philosophy has to deal. F. H. Bradley's words are well known. 'Nothing can be more real than what we experience in religion. The person who says that man in his religious consciousness is not in touch with reality does not know what he is talking about.'

[1] Lecture delivered at the Evening Meeting of the Institute of Philosophy on March 21, 1938, and published in *Philosophy* in October of that year.

Nevetheless, it cannot be emphasized too strongly that psychology, while it remains within its self-imposed limits, is an abstract study, a branch of natural science. Its subject is the states of human consciousness in and for themselves. The relation of those states to objective reality falls outside the province of the psychologist. Dr. William Brown, who believes in the genuineness of the mystic sense of God, is careful to make this clear. 'If I may speak no longer as a psychologist but as a man,' he writes, 'the experience of life confirms my belief that the possibility of some communion between that (divine) power and the individual is not an illusion.'[1] Some, I suppose, would say that the question of the objectivity of the vision falls outside the scope of philosophy also, since in their opinion all truth is relative, and the quest of the absolute is vain. But those who believe this must remain for ever outside the world in which the mystic moves. For mysticism is essentially ontological; the contemplative cares nothing for states of consciousness. His business is with the ultimately real. He aspires to the vision of God, and believes that this vision is within his reach. If this quest is foredoomed to disappointment, he would be the first to agree with Murisier and Leuba that his whole life has been a delusion. That he may be deceived he knows well. All through his spiritual journey he is on his guard against the 'false light'—against the snares of the Evil One, who can transform himself into an angel of light. But if there is no absolute standard whereby these fraudulent images are condemned as evil, while genuine revelations are accepted as coming from God, he is at the mercy of his own sinful and corrupt nature; his faith is vain, and his earnest, often agonizing prayers are futile.

It is because contemplation—I prefer on the whole to use this word, which is the word used in Catholic theology—is essentially ontological, standing or falling by the Platonic act of faith that 'the completely real is completely knowable,' that there is and must be a philosophy of mysticism. That most of the mystics were not philosophers is true but irrelevant. If the pearl of great price for which they were willing to sacrifice everything is really there, the truth revealed to them is not only one of the facts of which philosophy has to take account; it is the culminating point of philosophy, the goal of knowledge, and the aim of conduct. Their method, as we shall see, involves a certain conviction about the Supreme Reality, a theory of knowledge of a quite distinctive kind, and a scheme of ascent to the goal of earthly existence, which is the vision of God. Although for many contemplatives this quest was embarked on as an act of faith, and proved empirically, it none the less rests on a definite philosophy.

The philosophy of mysticism has indeed been worked out by several thinkers of genius. Plato himself was a mystic, as we might gather from several passages in his dialogues, and most explicitly from the remarkable Seventh Epistle, of the genuineness of which almost all scholars are now convinced. The philosophy of contemplation must always be of the Platonic type. Its greatest thinker is Plotinus; but several Christian

[1] In his contribution to *Religion and Life*, p. 54.

mystics have made valuable contributions—Augustine, for example, Eckhart, and Böhme, and even some Catholic saints who are not ranked as philosophers, like St. Bernard and St. John of the Cross. The scheme, in fact, is unusually definite and uniform in contemplatives divided by place, time, and creed.

There is however in my opinion, a very important difference, affecting the whole philosophy, between European and Asiatic mysticism. I use European and Asiatic as convenient terms; but there have been European thinkers who have belonged to what I have called the Asiatic type, and Indian thinkers, such as the great Sankara, the main subject of Otto's book, who according to him resist the world-renouncing tendency of Indian thought generally. This is the most important point that I shall have to deal with in this lecture, both on account of its decisive significance in forming an estimate of the philosophy of mysticism, and because of the strange misunderstanding which has vitiated most books about the Neoplatonists. I must return to the subject. Here I will only say that by mistranslating Plotinus's 'the One' or 'The First Principle' by the word God, and ignoring the whole rich world of supersensuous reality which is the spiritual home of the Platonist, they have accused these thinkers of deifying an empty abstraction, and hypostatizing the Infinite Not. But this misunderstanding, which is inexcusable in the case of Plotinus, seems to me, judging from very inadequate knowledge of Indian philosophy, to be really characteristic of many of the Hindu thinkers. The sensible world for them is pure illusion; it teaches us nothing; and our refuge from it is in an undifferentiated Absolute with no qualities. Thus, it seems to me, they offer us a journey through the unreal, which can be no real journey, and a rest in the eternal which is too much like the sleep of death. There is much in Eckhart which seems open to the same criticism, though he does not carry these ideas through consistently. But European mysticism generally is free from this error, and I hope to show that the mystical theory of knowledge is inconsistent with it.

Among modern writers who have made contributions to the philosophy of mysticism I may name Edward Caird, Thomas Whittaker, Royce, von Hügel, Urban, K. E. Kirk, Dom Cuthbert Butler, Radhakrishnan and other Indians, Rufus Jones, de Burgh, Urwick, Bergson, and T. H. Hughes. The French Neo-Thomists, such as Gilson and Rousselot, are often helpful.

The word mysticism is so loosely used that I must make it quite clear what I do and do not mean by it. I am willing to accept most of the following definitions. Westcott, without mentioning the word, summarizes exactly what a Platonist believes about the approaches to the vision of God. 'Religion in its completeness is the harmony of philosophy, ethics, and art blended into one by a spiritual Force, by a consecration at once personal and absolute. The direction of philosophy is theoretic, and its end is the true. The direction of ethics is practical, and its end is the good. The direction of art is representative, and its end is the beautiful. Religion includes these several ends, but adds to them that in which they find their consummation, the holy.' These last

K

words will at once suggest Otto's book *Das Heilige*, written long after Westcott. I am not in favour of making 'the holy' a fourth, beside goodness, truth, and beauty. The sense of 'the numinous' may be evoked by the contemplation of any of the three absolute values. Nor am I in favour of postulating a sort of sixth sense which the mystics, it has been suggested, possess for the apprehension of divine truth. Plotinus was saner when he said that we only need a faculty 'which all possess, but few use'; though we must add that all possess it in very different degrees. Leuba says shortly that mysticism is 'an intuitive certainty of contact with the supersensible world.'

I cannot accept any definition which identifies mysticism with excited or hysterical emotionalism, with sublimated eroticism, with visions and revelations, with supernatural (dualistically opposed to natural) activities, nor, on the philosophical side, with irrationalism. I suggest that a generation which treats its experience of ghosts with respect ought not to be rude about the experience of God.

I propose to divide my subject into three sections—ontological, the doctrine of ultimate reality; epistemological, the doctrine of knowledge; and ethical, the chart by which the mystic finds his way up the hill of the Lord.

The common assumption that God is so bound up with the world that it is as necessary to Him as He is to it is incompatible with mysticism. The Supreme, whether we call it God or with Plotinus the One or with Eckhart the Godhead, or with some moderns the Absolute, is transcendent. The notion that God is evolving with His universe, coming into His own, realizing Himself, or emerging, owes its popularity to 'the last Western heresy,' the idea that the macrocosm is moving towards 'one far-off divine event.' There can be no process of the Absolute, no progress, and no change. Exhortations to take time seriously may be in place when we are dealing with history; but to subordinate the Eternal to space and time is a fatal error in metaphysics.

In considering the status of Time and Change in reality, we cannot make ourselves independent of natural science. Our astronomers, when they are confronted with an impasse, may take refuge in Berkeleyan idealism, but this way of escape is illegitimate. We cannot begin with stars and atoms, treated as concrete realities, and end with mental concepts which have no necessary connection with the phenomenal world on which all science is based. Now, however we may define progress, it is quite certain that it is a local, temporary, and sporadic phenomenon in some corners of the universe; to erect it into a cosmic law is not only fantastic but ridiculous. If anything can be pronounced absolutely certain, it is the irrevocable doom of all life on our planet. And if God be involved in the evolution which we rashly assume to be an endless movement in one direction, then God must die.

Writers like Edward Caird seem to regard it as self-evident that the idea of unilateral activity, transeunt causation, is untenable. We are not dealing with physical attraction and repulsion, and I can see no difficulty in it. At any rate, if we reject it, all theism goes with it. Even thinkers so favourably disposed to Christianity as Pringle Pattison never really get beyond pantheism.

It is quite possible that mystical intuition is the source of ontology. In all philosophy we come to a point where we must trust our deepest convictions, which are not arrived at by any process of reasoning, but must be accepted as fundamental facts. Such, I maintain, are the absolute values, Truth, Goodness, and Beauty; and such is the conviction that behind the multiple there must be unity, behind the changing the immutable, behind the temporal the eternal. '*Quod est non fit nec fieri potest,*' says Eckhart. Bradley accepts the dialectic of mysticism when he says, 'The relational form implies a substantial totality beyond relations and above them. . . . . The ideas of goodness and of beauty suggest in different ways the same result. We gain from them the knowledge of a unity which transcends and yet contains every manifold appearance.'

The Platonists, following an important but perhaps isolated statement of Plato himself, place the One, the Absolute, 'beyond existence.' This expression is not used by the Christian mystics, but the difference is really verbal. When Eckhart says, '*Deus est suum Esse,*' he means that God does not *have* Being, but *is* His own Being. When he says, '*Esse est Deus,*' God is predicated of Being, not Being of God. Eckhart, like Plotinus, does not use 'God' of the Godhead: 'God and Godhead are as far apart as heaven and earth.' Of the Godhead nothing positive can be affirmed; and though Eckhart protests that his method is only '*negatio negationis,*' he is certainly in danger of leaving his Supreme Principle void of contents. 'Do not prate about God,' he says. We must also remember, in comparing Eckhart with Plotinus, that '*esse*' in scholastic theology is convertible with '*unum*' and '*bonum,*' and that Plotinus warns us of the danger of trying to get beyond the sphere of Nous, in which the relation of subject and object still exists. In the kingdom of the 'One-Many,' subject and object correspond perfectly, and are inseparable, but they remain subject and object. 'To rise above Nous is to fall outside it.' This is one of the pregnant sayings which interpreters of Plotinus almost wilfully disregard. When we read in Scotus Erigena, '*Deus per excellentiam non immerito Nihilum vocatur,*' we can understand the need of this warning.

There are two paths by which the mystic rises to the contemplation of the Absolute, the path of dialectic and the path of experience. The God of religion is rather the revelation than the revealer. The source of revelation cannot be revealed; the ground of knowledge cannot be known. The Monad is not an atomic individual, but the unity of a group; the One is not one of the units which make up the number two. We have to postulate an absolute Unity behind the duality of the relational form, because we must not reduce either Nous or Noëton to dependence on the other. The philosophy of mysticism is neither subjective idealism nor crude realism.

The latest writer on the philosophy of mysticism, Mr. Hughes, is wrong in saying that Plotinus exhausts the resources of language to assert the personality of the One. The One 'does not think;'[1] he is essentially Will only as being his own cause. But like almost all who speculate about the Absolute or the Unknowable, Plotinus tells us rather too much about him. His successors were driven by their dialectic to postulate some still more ineffable principle beyond the One. 'No monad or triad,' says Dionysius, 'can express the all-transcending hiddenness of the all-transcending superessentially superexisting superdeity.'

In what I have called Asiatic mysticism the denial of all value to the things of sense carries with it a blurring of all distinctions. '*Omnes creaturae sunt unum purum nihil*,' says Eckhart. Thus the supra-real and the infra-real are described by the same word. The Self, which is supposed to be all-inclusive, is really an empty category. Hegelians are fond of putting in the pillory Pope's line, 'As full, as perfect in a hair as heart.' If God is equally present in all things, He is equally absent in all things. This kind of pantheism does not differ very much from atheism, and moral distinctions disappear like all others. Hence the antinomianism of much Indian thought. Sometimes the Asiatic mystic uses language which in spite of its superficial subtlety is really meaningless and absurd. For instance, Jelaleddin writes:

> I am the mast, the rudder, the steersman and the ship;
> I am the coral reef on which it founders.

This is hardly parodied by Andrew Lang's:

> I am the batsman and the bat;
> I am the bowler and the ball,
> The umpire, the pavilion cat,
> The roller, pitch, and stumps and all.

We cannot know the Infinite, for to know is to limit; but we can know the fact of the Infinite, for this is implied in the act of knowing. If the fact of limit only implies the indefinite, the act of limiting implies the infinite. When we have once committed ourselves, by an act of reasonable faith, to the belief that the fully real can be fully known, or, in another phrase of Plato's, that he who is filled with the most real is most really filled, we can hardly stop short of the last step, in which reason comes to rest where all distinctions are reconciled.

Plotinus and the Christian mystics all call the Supreme Principle the Good as well as the One. The Good in this connection is not exactly a moral quality. The Good is the supreme object of all desire. It is the condition of knowledge, that which makes the world intelligible. It is the creator and sustainer of all things. The Good may be defined as unity as the goal of desire. This desire is said to be universal. 'All things pray except the Supreme,' says Proclus. The desire is not only universal but insatiable. 'The soul,' says Plotinus, 'is always attaining and always aspiring.' 'Knowledge itself is desire.' This is why it cannot be content

---

[1] This may be established without my emendation which I consider quite certain (in 3.9.3.) ἀλλ οὐ νοεῖ τὸ πρῶτον ἐπέκεινα ὄντος for οὐ θεοί . . . ὄντες which makes no sense.

even with the attainment of the κόσμος νοητός which is the Platonic heaven. The same craving for the infinite, for the felt presence of God Himself, is characteristic of all mysticism.

The dialectic thus leads logically to the point where it must abdicate in order to enter 'naked,' as they said, into the Holy of Holies. The word 'irrational' is here most inappropriate. The reasoning faculty which the Greeks called *logismos* or *dianoia* is the activity of the understanding only. But νοῦς is the whole personality unified under its own highest part. The faith which began as an experiment, and passed through illuminated understanding, ends as an experience. The intellect is in no way false to itself in recognizing its own limitations.

The path of the dialectic proceeds *pari passu* with inner experience. It might be expected, on the principles of mysticism, that since the human soul is a microcosm, having affinities with every grade of reality, there should be something in the soul which, if only in a flash, can transcend even life in the spiritual world, and find in itself a confirmation of what the dialectic affirms as to the primal source of all reality. This confirmation, according to the mystics, is given now and then in the indescribable experience of trance or ecstasy. That this is a real experience cannot be doubted. It comes in a sudden flash; so Plato describes it in his Seventh Letter, and so Augustine describes it in almost the same words. While it lasts, all the faculties of the mind are suspended; the subject hardly knows whether he is in the body or out of the body. He is convinced, when the vision is over, that he has been favoured with a real communion with the Highest. He cannot describe it, and it never lasts long. There is a curious consensus that about half an hour is what may be expected. The contemplatives have to find room in their scheme for what they believe to be the culmination of the divine favours to them ; the apparent emptiness and formlessness of the vision must be a key to its character; and so they connect it with what the dialectic of their philosophy tells them about 'the One beyond existence.'

It is rash for one who has never experienced anything of the kind to hazard an opinion about it. In one sense the vision of God, as we may call it, occupies a very small place in philosophic mysticism. Plotinus believed himself to have enjoyed the beatific vision four times while Porphyry was his disciple; Porphyry himself had it once; the later Neo-platonists, instead of cheapening it, came to think that it was hardly to be enjoyed in this life. In the philosophic Christian mystics, like Eckhart, it is not stressed. In the ascetic mystics of the cloister the experience seems to have been tasted more often; and instead of being the very rare reward of a long course of ardent devotion and earnest contemplation, there was a tendency to warn aspirants after saintliness that these supernatural favours are often bestowed on beginners as an encouragement, and afterwards withdrawn. Among the lesser mystics we have to allow a heavy discount for hysteria, self-deception, and even unreality. It is safer, I think, to put aside the mass of 'mystical phenomena' which fill the older books, and to study the acknowledged masters of the spiritual life. For them, these experiences are allowed to be extremely rare, and to be the reward of a long and arduous discipline. By far the greater part of recorded divine favours is of interest only to the psychologist, and not always even to him.

And yet we cannot tear out these visions from our scheme. Those who record them—I am speaking only of the leaders—are absolutely sure that they were genuine; they afforded the most exquisite sense of blessedness that can be imagined; and the effects on the character were permanent. The only point that may reasonably be doubted is whether they were rightly explained as a vision of God as He is (this question was hotly debated by the scholastic theologians), or of the 'One beyond existence' of the Platonists. I am myself inclined to think that although progress may be possible within the sphere of the spiritual life, the heaven which the Platonists call ἐκεῖ, 'yonder,' it is hardly conceivable that the human soul should even for a moment escape from the conditions which belong to all finite existence. There must be something of the Absolute in us, say the Platonists; otherwise we could not see the Absolute. But I think we should be wise to accept Plotinus's warning, against ˙ trying to 'wind ourselves too high,' as Keble says.

We must be on our guard against confining contemplation and ecstasy to the religious life. There are, according to our view, three absolute values in which the nature of God is revealed to us. The earnest pursuit of any one of these may give rise to mystical phenomena. What is called nature-mysticism is an important branch of our subject. I will not quote from Wordsworth, the best-known example of this temperament. Almost equally well-known is Tennyson's account of 'a kind of waking trance which I have often had when I have been alone. All at once, individuality seemed to dissolve and fade away into boundless being, and this not a confused state but the clearest of the clear and the surest of the surest, utterly beyond words, where death was an almost laughable impossibility, the loss of personality seeming no extinction but the only true life.' A third admirable example of nature-ecstasy may be found in *The Story of my Heart*, by Richard Jefferies.

Some philosophers have certainly tasted this kind of rapture. Bradley quietly says that 'with certain persons the intellectual effort to understand the universe is a principal way of experiencing the Deity.' And Einstein in an address to an American audience in 1930 says: 'The religious geniuses of all times have been distinguished by this cosmic religious sense. . . . It seems to me that the most important function of art and science is to arouse and keep alive this feeling in those who are receptive.'[1] Poincaré, I believe, went into ecstasy over mathematics.

From the point of view of the philosopher, the weak point in the mystical doctrine of the Absolute is the impossibility of explaining how the One can produce multiplicity out of itself. This is often regarded as fatal to the whole system. Thinkers who belong to this school are well aware of the difficulty. Plotinus argues that the universe would be incomplete unless every possible grade of being, from the highest to the lowest, were represented. But it is not clear how the perfect can be

[1] From T. H. Hughes, *The Philosophic Basis of Mysticism*, p. 186.

completed by the admixture of the imperfect. He uses metaphors—that of a full vessel overflowing, and that of light, which, as he supposes, is diffused without losing anything of its energy. At other times he says, 'It had to be,' which is to give up a problem which can have no solution. The difficulty is not confined to this school of thought. It is wisest to admit that we know neither how nor why there is a universe. The upward path, the return to God, may be traced, and a chart made of the journey. Heracleitus says that the road up and the road down are the same. But the road down, from the Creator to the creatures, is no business of ours, and frankly we know nothing about it.

Mysticism asserts that the world was created, but not in Time. It was not formed by the splitting up of the Absolute into parts, an impossible conception, nor is the time-series the course of God's life. Eckhart is determined to banish the imagery of Time and Space from his conception of the Godhead. God, he admits, 'becomes and disbecomes'; but this is only an accommodation to our ways of thinking in our outward relations. But '*Now* is the minimum of Time. Small though it be, it must go; everything that Time touches must go. *Here* means place. The spot I am standing on is small, but it must go before I can see God.' 'There is no greater obstacle to God than Time.'

Accordingly, the Christian doctrine of the creation of the world in Time is a great stumbling-block to the philosophic mystic. Some had the courage to deny it; others, like St. Thomas Aquinas, say that though all the arguments are against it, we must accept it because it is revealed truth. How such a fact could be revealed is a question which does not trouble him. Creation, but not in Time, means logical posteriority or axiological inferiority; and this is all that mystical philosophy cares to assert.

It is a mystical doctrine, to which Plotinus gives great importance, that all creativity is the result of contemplation. The One, by contemplating itself, produces the world of spiritual reality, the 'intelligible world.' This in turn, by contemplating the One, generates the world of Soul; and Soul, by contemplating the Intelligibles, generates the world of phenomena. Each product is inferior to its archetype, which it resembles as far it can. Every creator then creates, so to speak, with his back turned. This principle has a practical importance in social ethics. The motto of the mystic is 'See that thou make all things according to the pattern showed thee in the mount.'

Before leaving this section of my subject, I will quote the words of J. M. Baldwin's *Thought and Things*.[1] 'In the highest form of contemplation, the strands of the earlier and diverging dualisms are merged and fused. In this experience of a fusion which is not a mixture, but which issues in a meaning of its own sort and kind, an experience whose essential character is just this unity of comprehension, consciousness attains its completest, its most direct, and its final comprehension of what reality is and means.' This, we may say, is the beatific vision of the philosopher, which comes to him, like most discoveries, in a flash. As Augustine says, '*Mens mea pervenit ad id quod est in ictu trepidantis aspectus.*'

[1] From T. H. Hughes, *op. cit.*, p. 83.

If my subject were Neoplatonism as a mystical philosophy, instead of the philosophy of mysticism generally, I should take pleasure in proving how very misleading Edward Caird, followed, as he admits, by von Hügel, is in placing what religion calls salvation in the transient experience of ecstasy, instead of in the rich and bright kingdom of real existence, the intelligible world. But I have vindicated what I believe to be the truth in my book on the philosophy of Plotinus, and I have not much to add to what I said twenty years ago. The intelligible world, which I have called the spiritual world, having decided that 'Spirit' is the least misleading of possible translations of νοῦς, is the heaven of the Platonist. It is the 'place' or state in which individuality survives without separateness; where there are no barriers to complete knowledge of other spirits except those which come from differences of nature; where the divine Goodness, Wisdom, and Beauty are fully present and active; whose perfect fruition is not idle but creative; where, as Plotinus says, 'Spirit possesses all things at all times simultaneously. It *is*; it knows no past nor future; all things in the spiritual world coexist in an eternal Now.' 'Eternity is God manifesting His own nature; it is Being in its calmness, its self-identity, its permanent life.' 'Nothing that *is* can ever perish.'

This full, rich, happy life is what 'the Soul become Spirit,' 'the spirit in love,' yearns after and attains. I insist that the greatest of the mystics makes this life in the intelligible world the centre of his system. But can we deny that many of the mystics, both in Christianity and other religions, have practically adopted another philosophy, traces of which we have already found in Eckhart, a philosophy which begins by denying all value to the world of becoming, which proceeds by peeling the onion, stripping off one after another all that gives colour, variety, interest to life in this world, and ends by grasping zero and calling it infinity?

This is an unsympathetic verdict on the negative way, which has played so important a part in the history of mysticism. It proceeds, I think, from intense concentration of the will upon the goal, which is the vision of God, undimmed by mists and veils. Each experience is rejected in turn as not good enough. It is not realized, as I have said already, that a journey through the unreal is an unreal journey. It is not realized that there are degrees of truth and reality, and that we must take with us whatever on our upward journey we have gained of positive value.

My acquaintance with Indian mysticism is only slight; but it does seem to me that the intelligible world with its rich contents, simply drops out of their scheme. And the intelligible world is not a supernumerary physical world, nor a new heaven and earth to be brought into being hereafter. It is the world which we know, seen as it really is, *sub specie aeternitatis*. 'All that is in heaven is also on earth.' This is one of the pregnant dicta of Plotinus which his commentators have entirely failed to notice.

The theory of reality as constituted by the unity in duality of thought and its object is worked out with great subtlety both by Plotinus and Proclus. It deserves, I think, more attention than either realists or idealists have given to it. But this again belongs rather to a study of Neoplatonism than of mysticism generally, and I will again refer to my book on Plotinus, where it is explained at length. But the theory of knowledge is an essential part of all mystical philosophy, and I must try to give some account of it.

The beatitude, 'Blessed are the pure in heart, for they shall see God,' might be called mystical theology in a nutshell. These writers are fond of saying that like can only be known by like, or in a favourite image, 'We could not see the sun if there were not something sunlike in our eyes.' This law, which is assumed to be self-evident, underlies the whole theory and practice of mysticism. The soul is the wanderer of the metaphysical world. It has its affinities with every grade of being, from the highest to the lowest. It has, as we have seen, a mysterious faculty at the apex of its being which is capable of entering into relations with the Absolute, or, as the Christians said, into immediate relations with God. This was the foundation of the curious theory that in every human soul there is a something which can never consent to sin. This was called by various names, such as the soul-centre, the spark, or the odd word synteresis. Plotinus also had made the highest part of the soul impeccable. It was a debated point among the later members of the school whether the soul 'comes down' (the spatial metaphor should not mislead us) entire, or whether part of it remains 'yonder' in the spiritual world. The majority of the school differed here from Plotinus; for, as Iamblichus asks, 'If the will can sin, how is the soul impeccable?' It enables Plotinus to take a charitable view of sin. 'Vice,' he says, 'is always human, mixed with something contrary to itself.'

If the soul lost contact completely with the spiritual world, it could never rise any higher. The Christian doctrine of grace does not contradict this, for grace, or the Holy Spirit, imparts itself, and becomes, we may say, part of the personality. The spark, according to the bolder mystics, was lighted directly at God's altar, and was actually a divine activity.

Spiritual progress and knowledge of reality proceed in parallel lines. We all make a world after our own likeness. Such as men themselves are, such will God appear to them to be. Thus, although mysticism is built upon a basis of rationalism, at every step we can only see what we deserve to see. The world that we know changes for us, just as a landscape changes as we climb a mountain. It seems to follow that we have no right to dispute what the mystics tell us that they have seen, unless we have been there ourselves and not seen it. When we study the record of the discipline to which the contemplatives subject themselves, we are not likely to claim that we have stood where they have been.

Psychologists have been at work upon these experiences, and have brought in their favourite idea, 'the subconscious,' or 'subliminal self.' There is a subconscious life, a storehouse of powers, instincts, intuitions, inhibitions, good and bad, which now and then come imperfectly into consciousness. But it seems to me very misleading to confound this with the inmost sanctuary of the soul in which the mystic is convinced that the Holy Spirit has His abode. There is nothing respectable about the subconscious as such. It is not as foul as Freud makes out, but it is not the seat of what is best in us.

Christian contemplatives, as early as Clement of Alexandria about A.D. 200, have divided the course into three sections, purification, enlightenment, and unitive love. Clement puts faith in the first place, faith being, to use a recent definition, that of Frederic Myers, the resolution to stand or fall by the noblest hypothesis. This reasonable venture is combined with a determined effort to cleanse the soul of all that may impede its upward progress. But it is worth while to insist that both Plotinus and some of the Christian mystics require the aspirant first of all to practise the 'civic virtues,' those which society requires of us. The discharge of this debt must precede even the cleansing, chiselling, and polishing of our own statue which Plotinus tells us that we must work at.

The second state, enlightenment, means that we have come to realize the existence of new values, to which we were at first blind. These values become facts which our philosophy must find room for. Then, as Clement says, 'Knowledge, as it passes into love, unites the knower with the known. He who has reached this stage may be called equal with the angels.'

It is not suggested that the need of purification and enlightenment can ever be outgrown. But there is a real change in the personality. Plotinus calls it the soul becoming νοῦς; St. Paul calls it the change from the psychic to the pneumatic man. The Christian writers, following St. Paul, prefer πνεῦμα to νοῦς; but the words are practically identical.

This raises the important question whether the philosophy of mysticism leaves room for the idea of personality in God and man. 'Mysticism,' says Keyserling, 'always ends in an impersonal immortality.' In considering this problem, we must remember that neither ancient philosophy nor Christian theology had any word for personality, nor felt the want of any word. 'Hypostasis' and '*persona*' by no means corresponded in meaning, and when these words were applied to the 'Persons' of the Trinity, neither of them meant anything like what we mean by personality. When modern theologians make personality the centre of their system they are at best translating Christian philosophy into an alien dialect. They are using a new category which was neither used nor missed by ancient thought. For instance, Pringle Pattison says, 'Each self is an unique existence, which is perfectly impervious to other selves—impervious in a fashion of which the impenetrability of matter is a faint analogue.' Scientifically, the illustration is as unfortunate as the Neoplatonic notion that light loses nothing in radiation; but how utterly contrary to traditional philosophy is this strange doctrine of impervious selves, '*solida pollentia simplicitate!*' Mysticism denies it *in toto*. Lewis Nettleship unconsciously paraphrases Plotinus when he says, 'Suppose that all human beings felt habitually to each other as they now do occasionally to those they love best. So far as we can conceive of such a state, it would be one in which there would be no more individuals at all, but an universal being in and for another; where being took the form of consciousness, it would be the consciousness of another which was also oneself—a

common consciousness.' As Plotinus says of the life yonder, 'each is all
and all is each, and the glory is infinite.'

The Christian mystics use extravagant language about the necessity
of abolishing the 'I' and 'mine.' These are barriers between the soul and
reality, which must be levelled. If this looks like abolishing personality,
the answer is that the abstract ego, a figment, is quite different from the
full and rich experience to which we hope to attain, a unification and
concentration which is at the same time infinite expansion. The centre
remains, but the circumference is boundless. '*Christus in omnibus totus*'
is the Christian form of what the Neoplatonists say about the undivided
nous.

The idea of an abstract ego seems to imply three assumptions—
that there is a sharp line separating subject and object; that the subject,
thus sundered from the object, remains identical through time; and that
this impervious entity is in some mysterious way both myself and my
property. The mystics would deny all three. 'It is not *my* soul,' says
Eckhart, 'which is transformed after the likeness of God.'

In Aldous Huxley's book, *Ends and Means*, there is an interesting
discussion of this subject. Fully agreeing with the words of Keyserling
which I have just quoted, he says, 'Those who take the trouble to train
themselves in the arduous technique of mysticism always end, if they go
far enough in their work of recollection and meditation, by losing their
intuitions of a personal God, and having direct experience of a reality
that is impersonal.' He goes on to argue that the worship of a personal
God is a lower kind of religion, which generally ends in attributing to
the Deity very human passions, and which encourages the mawkish
sentimentality and emotionality which were encouraged in the Counter-
Reformation, and from which, he thinks, Catholic Christianity has never
completely recovered. 'It has also led to that enormous over-valuation
of the individual ego, which is so characteristic of Western popular
philosophy.'

I think there is much truth in this. But when an educated Christian
insists that God is personal, he means mainly that prayer is not a soliloquy.
Meredith's saying, 'He who rises from his knees a better man, his prayer
has been granted,' does not quite satisfy us. It is also true that only the
permanent can change. Impersonal is a negative word. Plotinus insists
that distinctiveness is real, though separateness is transcended.

The true mystical doctrine is that each man's self is determined by his
prevailing interests. Where our treasure is, there will our heart, our self,
be also. What we love, that we are. Most of us live on the psychic, the
intermediate plane; we may rise above this, or fall below it. Our personality is what we are able to realize of our opportunities, which are
potentially infinite. The ego or self is not given us to start with; we do
not yet know ourselves. The mystics speak of a strong attraction which
the higher exerts upon the lower. We are drawn upwards by love and
desire for what is above us. The Greeks speak quite confidently of the
universal desire to *know*; it would be well if modern ethics made more
of this. Platonism speaks of the attraction of the *beautiful*; this again should

not have been ignored. The desire for the vision of God, the *morally* perfect Being, has been emphasized by all Christian contemplatives. But the prayer of Crashaw's St. Teresa, 'Leave nothing of myself in me,' is understood by all of them. 'Personality on'y exists because we are not pure spirits,' says Lotze. It is a question of defining a word. We might say with equal truth that pure spirits alone are fully personal, and that personality in its ideal perfection exists only in God.

I pass to another problem. 'Mysticism,' says Nettleship, 'is the belief that everything in being what it is is symbolic of something more.' 'Every truth,' says Penington the Quaker, 'is shadow except the last. But every truth is substance in its own place, though it be but a shadow in another place. And the shadow is a true shadow, as the substance is a true substance.' This has been called nature-mysticism; it is as prominent in some mystics as it is absent in others. The philosophical question is whether, as Plato thought, the visible world may lead us up to the perception of the divine Forms, or whether, as some mystics have held, they are mere hindrances, 'the corruptible body pressing down the soul.' The truth seems to be that all life is sacramental, but in various degrees. The mystic does not need 'mere forms,' and often rejects cultus and ritual for this reason; but to the devout worshipper these are not mere forms.

It has been said that dogmatic theology is only the intellectual presentation of mystical symbols. I do not altogether like this; for the subject-matter of dogmatic theology is very largely the pictorial imagery which is the natural language of devotion among the '*simpliciores*.' To represent eternal truth under the forms of space and time, the universal as the particular, the action of God in the world as miracle, is natural and normal in popular religion. But this movement is in the opposite direction from mysticism, which always views these pictorial presentations of divine truth with impatience, and often tries to dispense with them. The well-known couplets of Angelus Silesius have all this motive. 'Were Christ born a thousand times in Bethlehem, and not in thee, thou art lost eternally.' 'Where the body lies,' says Böhme, 'there is heaven and hell. God is there, and the devil, each in his own kingdom. The soul needs only to enter by the deep door in the centre.' 'This pearl of eternity,' says William Law, 'is the temple of God within thee, where alone thou canst worship God in spirit and in truth. This adoration in spirit is that truth and reality of which outward forms are only the figure for a time.' 'Heaven is not a thing without us,' says Whichcote, 'nor is happiness anything distinct from a true conjunction of the mind with God.' It is needless to multiply quotations; this language is common to all the mystics. The best of them insist that a symbol must have a real resemblance to the thing symbolized. Fanciful and 'loose types of things through all degrees,' as Wordsworth calls them, are no part of true mysticism.

Necromancy, astrology, alchemy, palmistry, and spiritualism are the reproach of mysticism, and have nothing to do with the philosophy which is our subject. It may be, as the later developments of Neoplatonism suggest, that this philosophy is inadequately protected against these perversions; but we need not stop to deal with either these or with the morbid hallucinations which fill Catholic histories of the mystics.

'It is an accursed evil to a man,' Darwin once wrote, 'to become so absorbed in any subject as I am in mine.' That great man realized what a sacrifice he was making, and we honour him for it. The contemplatives of the cloister were even more absorbed in their inner conflicts than Darwin was in natural history, and of course they suffered for it severely, sometimes even to the peril of their reason; we ought to be able to make allowances for the effects on the mind of extreme specialization, carried on under the unnatural conditions of monasticism.

This extreme concentration has had an unfortunate effect on the ethics of mysticism. I am excused from discussing this subject both by limitations of space and by my title, which confined me to the philosophy of mysticism. I cannot therefore consider the relation of mysticism to asceticism. The Platonic mystic lives in strict training; if he does not, he is a dilettante. But he does not maltreat his body, which on the contrary he tries to keep fit. The Indian fakir, the pillar-saint, the flagellant, are an aberrant type, practically extinct in the West. We may leave them to the student of morbid psychology.

It may be said that the desire to torment the body follows logically from the dualistic philosophy which connects evil with matter. Metaphysical dualism is inconsistent with mystical philosophy, the tendency of which is to deny any substantiality to evil. It is no solution of the problem to say that evil is only *privatio boni*; the ethical scale of values contains minus quantities, which must somehow be acknowledged. The doctrine that 'matter,' which in Neoplatonism is immaterial, the phantasmal substratum of all that exists, is somehow responsible for evil is not very different from saying that evil has no positive being. But in practice 'the flesh' was often substituted for 'matter,' and a kind of subordinate dualism, never countenanced by the leaders of the school, attached itself to the popular preaching of Platonism. This notion, which took deep root in the East, quite apart from mysticism, undoubtedly encouraged the aberrations which I have mentioned. But it is no part of our subject.

Mysticism as a philosophy will not satisfy anti-intellectualists or pragmatists or sceptics or agnostics or materialists or those who take Time so seriously as to put God inside it. It is a philosophy of absolutism, which offers an experimental proof of itself. The proof is terribly hard, because it requires the dedication of the whole life to an end which is not visible when we begin to climb. Our world must change again and again, and we with and in it. The pearl of great price is there, and within our reach; but we must give all that we have and are to win it. As the Stoic Manilius says:

Quid caelo dabimus? Quantum est, quo veneat omne?
Impendendus homo est, Deus esse ut possit in ipso.

BIBLIOGRAPHY OF MODERN BOOKS

I have not burdened the text of this book with footnotes and references. The asterisks in this list convey my grateful thanks for special help.

ALEXANDER, S. *Time, Space and Deity.*

ALLEN, A. V. G. *Continuity of Christian Thought.*

*ANGUS, S. *Mystery Religions and Christianity.*

*BERDYAEFF, N. *Works.*

BEVAN, E. *Symbolism.*

BOSANQUET, B. *Works.*

*BRABANT, F. H. *Time and Eternity.*

BRADLEY, F. H. *Appearance and Reality.*

BROWN, W. *Personality and Religion.*

BURNET, J. *Greek Philosophy.*

BUTLER, CUTHBERT. *Western Mysticism.*

CHANDLER, A. *Works.*

DEISSMANN, A. *St. Paul.*

DELACROIX. *Études.*

*FRANK, S. L. *God With Us.*

GAUSS, S. *Plato's Conception of Philosophy.*

GRAHAM, J. M. *The Faith of a Quaker.*

GRUBB, E. *Authority and the Light Within.*

GUNN, J. A. *The Problem of Time.*

*HERMAN, MRS. *Meaning and Value of Mysticism.*

HOCKING, W. E. *Religious Thought of the West.*

*HÜGEL, F. VON. *Works.*

*HUGHES, T. H. *Philosophical Basis of Mysticism.*

HUXLEY, A. *The Perennial Philosophy.*

JAMES, W. *Varieties of Religious Experience.*

*JONES, RUFUS. *Works.*

KENNEDY, H. A. A. *St. Paul and the Mystery Religions.*

*KEYSERLING, COUNT. *Unsterblichkeit.*

KIRK, BISHOP. *The Vision of God.*

MARCHANT, J. *Anthology of God.*

MOBERLY, R. C. *Atonement and Personality.*

Oxford Book of Mystical Verse.

*PRATT, J. B. *The Religious Consciousness.*

PRINGLE PATTISON, A. S. *Works.*

RADHAKRISHNAN, S. *Works.*

*ROHDE, E. *Psyche.*

SHEEN, F. J. *God and the Intelligence.*

STEWART, J. A. *The Myths of Plato.*

TAYLOR, A. E. *Works.*

UNDERHILL, E. *Mysticism.*

URBAN, W. *The Intelligible World.*

*URWICK, E. J. *The Message of Plato.*

WATKIN, E. T. *Philosophy of Mysticism.*

WHATELY, A. R. *The Inner Light.*

INDEX